The Normalization of War
in Israeli Discourse, 1967–2008

The Normalization of War
in Israeli Discourse, 1967–2008

Dalia Gavriely-Nuri

LEXINGTON BOOKS
Lanham • Boulder • New York • Toronto • Plymouth, UK

Published by Lexington Books
A wholly owned subsidiary of The Rowman & Littlefield Publishing Group, Inc.
4501 Forbes Boulevard, Suite 200, Lanham, Maryland 20706
www.rowman.com

10 Thornbury Road, Plymouth PL6 7PP, United Kingdom

British Library Cataloguing in Publication Information Available

Library of Congress Cataloging-in-Publication Data
Library of Congress Cataloging-in-Publication Data Available

ISBN 978-0-7391-7260-5 (cloth)—ISBN 978-0-7391-7261-2 (electronic)
ISBN 978-1-4985-1097-4 (pbk)

To Arie

Contents

Acknowledgments

This book was published with the support of **The Harry S. Truman Research Institute for the Advancement of Peace**, The Hebrew University of Jerusalem.

I acknowledge with gratitude Netta Richter Levin's contribution to the translation and editing of this book.

In memory of my friend, Professor Miriam Shlesinger, who passed away in November 2012.

Preface

In January 1991, just a few days before the outbreak of the Gulf War, Professor Tania Reinhart, the lecturer in a course I was taking at Tel Aviv University—a course on metaphors—received an e-mail from Professor George Lakoff at UC Berkeley:

> An open letter to the Internet from George Lakoff (1991), Professor of Linguistics
> To Friends and Colleagues on the Net:
> January 15 is getting very close. As things now stand, President Bush seems to have convinced most of the country that war in the Gulf is morally justified, and that it makes sense to think of "winning" such a war. [. . .] I have found that the justification is based very largely on a metaphorical system of thought in general use for understanding foreign policy. I have analyzed the system, checked it to see what the metaphors hide, and have checked to the best of my ability to see whether the metaphors fit the situation in the Gulf, even if one accepts them. *So far as I can see, the justification for war, point by point, is anything but clear.*

E-mail had just come onto the scene in those days, and the idea of wide distribution of letters via the computer network was both innovative and curious. Even more innovative for me was the idea that George Lakoff was trying to prevent a war, no less. The very fact that a linguist was assuming this role left a strong impression.

Twelve years later, in the winter of 2003, in response to the Second Gulf War, Lakoff wrote again:

> My 1990 paper did not stop Gulf War I. This paper will not stop Gulf War II. So why bother? I think it is crucially important to understand the cognitive dimensions of politics, especially when most of our conceptual framing is

unconscious and we may not be aware of our own metaphorical thought. I have been referred to as a "cognitive activist" and I think the label fits me well. As a professor, I do analyses of linguistic and conceptual issues in politics, and I do them as accurately as I can. But that analytic act is a political act: *Awareness matters. Being able to articulate what is going on can change what is going on—at least in the long run.*

* * *

In the summer of 2006, at the beginning of the Second Lebanon War, millions of Israelis in northern Israel found themselves hiding out in bomb shelters, as the Katyusha rockets continued to descend out of Lebanon. At the same time, hundreds of thousands of Lebanese civilians had become refugees overnight. The scenes of havoc and destruction on both sides of the border were horrendous. And yet, 82 percent of the Israelis were watching the media coverage supported the war. Only a few hundred people showed up for the anti-war demonstration in Tel Aviv—a demonstration that went virtually unnoticed by the media.

How might we account for the fact that most Israelis supported another war in Lebanon, when the Lebanese mud from the previous round was only beginning to dry off? (The last accord of the First Lebanon War [1982] was signed only six years earlier, in 2000, when the IDF withdrew from Lebanon.) Morek and Pincus (2000: 1) have put this query in the form of two relevant (and arguably naïve) questions:

> What can persuade millions of men, and increasingly also women, to overcome the extremely powerful survival instinct and go to battle, risking death or at least maiming, often seemingly gladly? [. . .]
> Why do the nations not rise unanimously in protest and revolt against their leaders who impose such suffering on them?

I started writing this book in the summer of 2006, during the Second Lebanon War, in an attempt to suggest some answers to these basic questions. During the thirty-five days of the war, I followed every story, every item on radio, the television, and the press, and listened carefully to the discourse of Israel's political and military leaders, journalists and citizens.

Two days after the war ended, I arrived at UC Berkeley as a visiting scholar. Soon after that, when I met George Lakoff, I shared with him the dramatic role of his 1991 letter—which had served as the inspiration for this book—and of his memorable pronouncement: *"Awareness matters. Being able to articulate what is going on can change what is going on—at least in the long run."*

* * *

At this point, it may be appropriate to provide a brief description of "identity of the author." I am a liberal, secular, leftist Jewish Israeli, living near Tel Aviv. I am also a scholar engaged in critical discourse analysis. As Hodges and Nilep (2007: 4) remind us:

> Critical scholarship does not pretend to operate from an Archimedean point outside the social world it studies. Critical scholarship recognizes that such a view from nowhere does not exist, and that analysts are also participants in the world under study. Our subject positions as scholars must therefore be taken into account. In addition, critical scholarship is motivated not only to study society for what it is, but for what it might become. In this way, critical scholarship desires to expose existing wrongs in society in an effort to shape a better world. Critical approaches, therefore, take a keen interest in understanding the working of power in an effort to counter abuse of power.

The text that follows is a summary of several years of research centering on Israeli war discourse. The studies presented in the respective chapters were written from my vantage point in the areas of Cultural Studies and Critical Discourse Studies—but they also reflect my close involvement in the object of my research, as an Israeli citizen living in the shadow of an ongoing national conflict. This double perspective is not easily resolved: I am a scholar committed to disinterested academic research, but I am also the mother of Shira, a soldier in the Israel Defense Forces, and of Dan (age thirteen). From the moment Dan was born, the countdown began—the countdown of a mother whose hopes and anxieties all center on the persistent question: Will there be peace by the time Dan has to enlist? My writing must be critical but it is not without an identity. It is typical of war and peace researchers, but it is also unique to those of us who are Israeli. What I face is not only an academic obstacle. This point of departure is precisely what allows me to adopt a multidimensional observation and realize that peace and war are no mere abstractions.

The point of departure of this book lies in the vital role of language and of discourse in creating a "culture of peace" as well as a "culture of war." The Israeli war discourse contributes to a reality of recurrent involvement in wars. In other words, the basic assumption of this book is that discourse and language reflect outlooks and ways of thinking, but they also construct reality and shape our behavior. An analysis of the Israeli war discourse attests to the need for a change in the discourse and in the Hebrew language when it comes to creating a culture of peace.

The book reflects a central discursive concept: the Normalization of War. This discourse in turn exposes a deep and recurrent flaw in Israeli war discourse, since it leads us to see war as an integral part of life.

WHAT IS WAR-NORMALIZING DISCOURSE (WND)?

Throughout the Gulf War (1991), due to recurrent missile attacks on Israel, gas masks were distributed by the authorities to the Israeli citizens, who were required to carry them twenty-four hours a day. During a concert in Jerusalem, a siren was heard. People in the concert hall took out their gas masks and silently put them over their faces. Solo violinist, Isaac Stern also put on his mask and kept on playing. This picture has become part of the national album. It symbolizes the impossible embedded tension of War-Normalizing Discourse (WND) in Israel.

WND is a set of linguistic, discursive and cultural devices aimed at blurring the anomalous character of war by transforming it into an event perceived as a "natural" or "normal" part of ordinary life. Since Israel's establishment, it has taken part in eight wars, more than almost any other western democracy in the post-World War II era.[1] The WND described here evolved over these years (although we can trace its roots to the early days of Zionism in the late nineteenth century) in response to the recurrence of wars. The tendency to "normalize" war is found not only in the verbal discourse but also in various cultural practices. Indeed, the exceptional scene at that concert in Jerusalem aptly illustrates the surreal encounter between war and normal life in Israeli reality.

WND serves two distinct needs: first, it is used by political and military leaders in initiating new wars, helping them create a consensus around new military operations. Second, it may be adopted by the country at large, and function as a psychological mechanism that allows citizens to get through a routine of recurrent wars. The fact that WND is the servant of two masters— leaders and civilians alike—enhances its durability and renders it particularly stable, to the point where any attempt to oppose it or to criticize it is almost bound to fail; in short, what we have here is a "win-win discourse." WND has survived a long line of political leaders since 1948, and I will argue that after such a long period of use, it has become an organic part of the Israeli public war discourse. In fact, it has become an integral part of *Israeli identity*. What is more important: like the sorcerer's apprentice, it has gradually taken on a life of its own, no longer serving the needs of either the hegemony or the civilians, but promoting and sustaining an independent agenda or, more specifically, a *culture of war*.

In the coming chapters I will analyze WND: its aims, its components, its *functions*, the agencies that take part in its construction, its various manifestations in Israeli culture and the motivations and factors which have shaped it.

THE STRUCTURE OF THE BOOK

This book begins with a theoretical chapter, focusing on WND's components and basic assumptions. The first chapter also aims to contextualize WND in the global arena, and points out parallel discursive phenomena in non-Hebrew war discourses. The second chapter introduces a Cultural Approach to Critical Discourse Analysis (CCDA), an approach developed for the sake of the analysis, and includes methodological principles of analysis.

The analytical chapters (3–7) demonstrate various manifestations of WND in Israeli discourse and may also be read separately (modular reading). Chapter 8 demonstrates how canonic and non-canonic Hebrew literature adopted the unwritten rules of WND and anti-WND between 1967 and 1973. The concluding chapter demonstrates the role of WND in concrete situations of peace and war. It also points to normalizing discourses in the context of other social phenomena, such as the normalization of poverty and disabilities.

* * *

The Normalization of War is a deep flaw in Israeli war discourse. The removal of this flaw is important both theoretically and empirically. Above all, I hope that by focusing attention upon the Normalization of War, I may make a practical contribution to the promotion of education for peace and the advancement of the cause of peace in our region.

Focusing on Israeli war discourse, the main purpose of this book is thus to introduce WND as an analytical tool aimed at exploring war discourses and providing a comparative perspective. As always, the application of analytical tools to a specific discourse is far from clear-cut. Nevertheless, or maybe precisely because of this difficulty, it is important to revisit the field of critical analysis of war discourses and to reorganize it. Such a mapping will contribute to a systematic critical analysis of war discourses from a cross-cultural and an interdisciplinary perspective, exposing the circulation of the same *discursive strategies* that enable the initiation of new wars around the globe.

This book is not an attack against Israel. Rather it is a warning signal, admonishing us to heed the power of discourse and culture to shape a national "common sense" that supports and sustains a *culture of war*.

Dalia Gavriely-Nuri
Tel Aviv, August 2012

NOTE

1. This is undoubtedly true if we consider not only the "quantitative" but also the "qualitative" aspect of these wars: Israel was under an immediate existential threat during three wars (1948, 1967, and 1973).

Chapter One

War-Normalizing Discourse (WND)

COMPONENTS OF WAR-NORMALIZING DISCOURSE (WND)

At the heart of this book are two key questions:

1. Does the Israeli war discourse play a part in the recurrence of wars?
2. If so, can we identify mechanisms or strategies that are typical of this discourse?

The first question presents the basic assumption of this book: that the Israeli war discourse plays an instrumental role in the ongoing participation of Israel in wars. The second question presents the book's basic hypothesis: that a *mega cultural-discursive code* enables and supports the use of military power in general and participation in wars in particular. We may call this code *War-Normalizing Discourse* (WND).

WND aims to portray war as a "normal" part of life. It masks, reduces, and even cancels out the negative and anomalous effects of war on citizens' everyday life. In this book, "war" shall be defined in a broad sense, as including not only warfare and warriors, but also the surrounding military practices such as the development or acquisition of weaponry.

Before introducing the *discursive strategies*[1] used in WND, it is important to focus on some general facts and presuppositions in order to contextualize WND within the Israeli culture.

War is an abstract concept that fosters the construction of discourse. Even for Israeli citizens, the majority of whom have served in the army, the concepts "war," "battle," and "battlefield" remain vague. The Yom Kippur War (1973) was the first time that the Israeli public was exposed to media coverage of a war in actual live pictures (Israeli television started broadcasting in

1

1969). In fact, until the Second Lebanon War (2006), which was covered by the media through intensive visual images, most Israeli wars entered public consciousness through words.

It is also important to remember that although Israel has taken part in eight wars since its establishment in 1948,[2] the majority of Israelis have continued to lead a "normal" life in terms of the common Western criteria of "normal" life, and have carried on with their usual routines (going to work, engaging in leisure activities, etc.) throughout that period.

In the context of Israeli culture, we may perceive WND as a cultural creation intended to aid the normalization of life during periods of war. It forms part of the cumulative common endeavor pursued by political leaders, journalists, military commanders, writers and citizens, which is aimed at allowing normal life to continue its course.

Within the general framework of WND, this book defines four specific analytical tools to facilitate the analysis of Israeli war discourse. I will refer to these as *the functions of normalization* (the "*functions*"): *Euphemization, Naturalization, Legitimization*, and *Symbolic Annihilation*. Let us first understand their theoretical origins.

In his book, *Ideology and Modern Culture* (1990), Thompson distinguished five general *modes of operation*—devices for constructing and conveying meaning in the social world—by means of which ideology infiltrates the discourse: *legitimization, dissimulation, unification, fragmentation*, and *reification*. He then derived a total of thirteen typical *strategies of symbolic construction*. Three of these strategies are relevant for our analysis: *Euphemization*, which represents a practice in "terms which elicit a positive valuation" (p. 62); *Naturalization*, which allows "a state of affairs which is a social and historical creation [. . .] [to] be treated as a natural event or as the inevitable outcome of natural characteristics" (p. 66); and *Legitimization*, which represents a practice as "legitimate, that is, just and worthy of support" (p. 61).

Inspired by these strategies, I define the first three *functions* of WND:

1. *Euphemization*: Giving the concept of war a positive appearance, character, or valuation. For example, in euphemistic discourse, war is depicted as a special opportunity to demonstrate bravery and comradeship in a way that is not possible in everyday life. War may also be perceived as an event that gives purpose to life itself. Fulfilling the *function* of euphemization, the discourse gives the impression that the participation in war can later be exchangeable in civilian life for material rewards, social status, or self-esteem.

2. *Naturalization*: Representing war, which is a human creation and a kind of natural force, as a natural event or as the inevitable outcome of

the laws of nature. Naturalization reduces the importance of human choice and decision making in the context of war and warfare.

3. *Legitimization*: Representing war as being just, legitimate, rational and worthy of support, and as representing a moral act. Legitimization blurs certain aspects of war such as the disproportionate use of power and money and, of course, erroneous decision making.

The fourth *function* is *Symbolic Annihilation,* a term inspired by Gerbner (1972) and Tuchman (1978). The latter wrote:

> Consider the symbolic representation of women in the mass media. Relatively few women are portrayed there, although women are fifty-one percent of the population [. . .] others are trivialized: they are symbolized as child-like adornments who need to be protected [. . .] in sum, they are subject to *symbolic annihilation.* [emphasis added] (p. 8)

Following this, I define *symbolic annihilation* of war as a total exclusion of war, or some of its components, from the discourse by omitting or blurring its basic characteristics, such as death and destruction of the environment, or the moral, emotional, and economic damage that it may cause.

As an analytical tool, WND will be defined as a discourse that fulfills at least one of the four *functions*. In practice, it often achieves two, three or even four *functions* simultaneously. For example, when wounded soldiers were shown in Israeli television during the Second Lebanon War, they were usually depicted as sleeping angels rather than as suffering people. In addition, the coverage emphasized the soldiers' endurance and the medical staff's flawless teamwork, and excluded harsh pictures, such as bleeding organs and the mess and confusion surrounding the care of the injured. This type of coverage fulfills two *functions*: euphemization of the wounded soldier and the medical staff on the one hand, and symbolic annihilation of the harsh aspects of the situation on the other. The analysis in the following chapters will examine the encounter between the four *functions* and specific events in the Israeli war discourse.

WND Matrix

Following Fairclough (2009: 174), who defined *strategy* as the combination of *goals* and *means*, it is possible to depict the components and processes of WND as an imaginary *multiplication table* of *war-normalizing strategies*. This table combines horizontal *functions* ("goals") and vertical *discursive elements* ("means"). *War-normalizing strategies* are defined as *discursive elements*, which contribute to WND by fulfilling one of the four *functions*.

"Discursive elements" include various "means," such as: names, narratives, metaphors as well as frames, analogies, and presuppositions. For example, the encounter between metaphor (*discursive element*) and euphemization (*function*) creates a *euphemizing metaphor*; the encounter between framing (*discursive element*) and legitimization (*function*) creates a *legitimizing framing*. "Discursive elements" are derived from a broad definition of "discourse" which includes verbal practices (e.g., political speeches), visual practices (e.g., photographs) and cultural practices or cultural sites (e.g., military marching). Table 1.1 presents the components and the process of WND.

Table 1.1.   The Multiplication Table of WND

Functions/ Discursive elements	Euphemization	Naturalization	Legitimization	Symbolic annihilation
Names				
Frames				
Analogies				

The use of the *multiplication table* of WND leads us to what may be called the *WND Matrix*, presented in table 1.2.

Table 1.2.   WND Matrix

Macro Strategies	Micro Strategies
Normalizing Names	Euphemizing names
	Naturalizing names
	Legitimizing names
	Annihilating names
Normalizing Frames	Euphemizing frames
	Naturalizing frames
	Legitimizing frames
	Annihilating frames
Normalizing Analogies	Euphemizing analogies
	Naturalizing analogies
	Legitimizing analogies
	Annihilating analogies

Obviously, the four *functions* presented in tables 1.1 and 1.2 are merely examples and by no means a conclusive list. However, for the purpose of analyzing war discourse, they represent a useful and authoritative method. The concepts of *Abstraction* and *Generalization* (Peled-Elhanan, 2010: 391), *Universalism* (McCartney, 2004: 401), and many other concepts suggested by Thompson (1990) may also facilitate future discussions on war discourses.

It is also important to note that distinctions between the different *discursive elements* (and consequently, between *war-normalizing strategies*) are not always clear-cut. For example, the same verbal phenomenon may be classified as either "narrative," "frame/framing," or even "metaphor." Artificial analytic tools often prove too rigid for certain discursive phenomena. Moreover, researchers often use different definitions to describe the same phenomena, depending on their discipline or school. I hope the analytical tools suggested in this chapter will help establish greater uniformity in the terminology of this field, and a more systematic approach to the analysis of war discourses.

Now that we understand WND as a general theoretical framework, let us move on to locate it in specific cultural contexts.

WND'S GLOBAL MARKET

This section will focus on various national war discourses in order to identify *the global market of WND,* that is, the various reflections and appearances of WND in discourses around the world. The section aims to address two questions in particular:

1. How has the concept of "war" been shaped and constructed in different cultures and discourses during the past two decades?
2. What do *Critical Discourse Analysts* do when they research "war discourses"?

Bourdieu (1977/2003) drew a distinction between *symbolic capital* (i.e., prestige, honor, attention) and *cultural capital* (i.e., competencies, skills, qualifications) as key sources of power and, more specifically, as tools for exercising symbolic violence. Following Bourdieu, I propose another variant in the field of power and symbolic violence: *discursive capital.* The aim of discursive capital, available and accessible to members of specific discursive communities, is primarily to achieve social dominance and promote political interests.

For example, the *discursive capital* available to Israeli politicians when initiating a new war includes the metaphors "a few against many" and "the whole world is against us," which imply that a new threat is imminent. These metaphors are well established in Israeli culture and are deeply rooted in Israeli history. They are *cultural codes* in the sense that they form part of the network of shared values, norms, and beliefs that construct a cultural community's "credo," due to their constant recurrence in set combinations (I will try to define *cultural codes* more carefully later). At the same time, they also form part of the Israeli *discursive capital:* They are among the ready-made resources that Israeli leaders can easily use to promote their political agenda, in this case, justification of a new war.

Like economic capital, *discursive capital* may be exchanged in an imaginary *global discursive market*, that is, in a global market that is open to all political leaders for "trading" *discursive capital*. In the case of initiating a new war, discursive capital promoting the use of military power may be traded. Therefore exposing some of the "goods" that make up the rich stock of Israeli discursive capital may be of interest to non-Hebrew speakers as well.

It is surprising to learn that some popular "goods" that are traded daily on the *global discursive market* were originally coined in Hebrew, and only later spread to other parts of the world. For example, it seems that former Israeli Prime Minister Ariel Sharon holds the "copyright" for what we may call the *Rhetoric of Evil* (Ivie, 2004), which was later adopted by George W. Bush Jr. and became a kind of Western *cultural code*.[3] On September 11, 2001, Ariel Sharon made a speech in the Knesset and declared it a day of mourning:

> [. . .] as we bow our heads and share in the sorrow of the American people [. . .] The fight against terrorism is an international struggle of the free world against the forces of darkness that seek to destroy our liberty and our way of life. I believe that together, we can defeat these *forces of evil*. [emphasis added]

That same day, Sharon appeared on CNN offering his condolences using the same terms and metaphors. Two days later, Bush used the word "evil" no less than five times in his first statement referring to the terrorist attacks (Kellner, 2007), and on January 29, 2002, he used the term *axis of evil* in his State of the Union Address. The existence of a *global discursive market of war rhetoric* that includes cultural and cross-cultural codes explains how the analysis of different national war discourses can help the decoding process.

WND appears to be a useful analytical tool for providing a comparative perspective on war discourses. I argue that significant parts of the critical studies that focus on the concept of "war," especially CDA, use one or more of the *functions* and *discursive elements* of WND.

Who Needs to "Normalize" War?

As implied above, WND is not an original Israeli invention designed to answer the unique needs of Israeli society. Since World War II, any democratic parliament wishing to initiate a war has had to overcome not only legal barriers, but conceptual and cultural ones as well. In other words, the need to legitimize war arises not only from the limitations imposed by international law, but also from cultural-cognitive and psychological factors embedded in the historical experience of the twentieth century.

Shaw (2002: 343–44) argues that in the course of the twentieth century, warfare has been thoroughly delegitimized. He reviews a number of twentieth-century historical events, which led to the perception of war as immoral. For example, the trenches of Flanders during World War I created the paradigm of "senseless slaughter." According to Shaw, this paradigm remained influential throughout the twentieth century, and he depicted the Western democracies in World War II as "heavier-hearted" (Ibid) when resorting to war.

During most of the second half of the twentieth century, the threat of nuclear extermination created an overwhelming perception that great wars should be prevented at nearly any cost. Moreover, the Vietnam War reinforced anti-war sentiment because it had shown how even a war not involving the use of nuclear weapons might nevertheless involve senseless slaughter. However, Shaw had also identified a turning point: Margaret Thatcher, he argued, had pioneered a different approach in the Falklands, and at the end of the Cold War the United States had begun to successfully legitimize its participation in hot wars as well. President George W. Bush "kicked the Vietnam syndrome" (Ibid.) in 1991 with the War in Iraq. Thus, the ground was well prepared for President George W. Bush Jr. to declare the war on terror—the international military campaign launched with the 2001 invasion of Afghanistan in response to the September 11 terrorist attacks.

In light of these events, I argue that the four *functions* of WND as a global mechanism for the "normalization" of war—and especially the *function* of legitimization—aim to sustain the revival of the concept of war, and diminish the cultural-cognitive dissonance described above. "The renaissance of warfare is one of the most striking features of the early twenty-first century. [. . .] war, it seems, is not the prerogative of international criminals, but the first resort of the righteous" (Shaw, 2002: 343). My claim is that *the global WND* helps normalize this "abnormality." The following chapters will contain an analysis focusing on the Israeli case. First, however, I will demonstrate how certain manifestations of WND may easily be found in the *global discursive market* discussed earlier.

Cross-Cultural Analysis of WND

I shall start with a short survey of some studies that demonstrate a connection between the concept of "war" and three *functions*: euphemization, naturalization, and symbolic annihilation. The main part of this chapter will be dedicated to the *function* of legitimization because of the dominance of this *function* in the current studies of war discourses. Focusing on this *function*, I will exemplify various *micro-strategies* of WND (e.g., war-legitimizing metaphors, war-legitimizing narratives). In this context, I offer the term *the global market of the just war discourse* to show the exchange of *micro-strategies* between various war discourses. The WND Matrix helps reveal some common elements, as well as the common logic of war discourses in general and of war legitimization in particular. Hopefully, the logic of the Matrix will help reveal some elements hitherto unaccounted for in war discourses and will help this field of research become more balanced and complete. As in the Periodic Table, some parts of the Matrix are yet to be explored.

Euphemization

In 1946, George Orwell wrote:

> [. . .] in our time, political speech and writing are largely the defense of the indefensible. Things like the continuance of British rule in India, the Russian purges and deportations, the dropping of the atom bombs on Japan, can indeed be defended, but only by arguments which are too brutal for most people to face, and which do not square with the professed aims of the political parties. Thus, political language has to consist largely of euphemism, question-begging and sheer cloudy vagueness. (Orwell, 1946: 111)

With these words, Orwell identified the specific linguistic device of *euphemism*, and in fact implied the broader phenomenon of *euphemization* in political discourse. Bourdieu (1977/2003: 196) defined euphemization as an "elementary form of the labor of objectification which eventually leads to the juridical definition of acceptable behaviour" (see also Chambers, 2003; Chilton, 1987).

The awareness of euphemization as a broad *discursive strategy* that requires classification has increased during the last two decades in CDA studies. Chilton and Schäffner (2002: 14) talked about "euphemizing strategies"; Chouliaraki (2007: 3) defined "strategies of aestheticization" in the context of war and warfare as "strategies that represent the war as a spectacular operation rather than as a political fact." In his article "Dehumanizing People and Euphemizing War," Bosmajian (1984) argued against the euphemization of weapons and of the pain, suffering, and death that their use would cause. He also contended against the abuse of euphemisms as a linguistic device that purifies "the brutality and inhumanity of our policies and practices."

Other studies have pointed out mutual connections between the initiation of wars and the euphemization of national identity. For example, McCartney (2004) argued against the way in which the idea of "American exceptionalism" and the ethos of "American mission" were used to serve the aggressive U.S. foreign policy from 9/11 to the Iraq War. He wrote:

> In practice, American nationalism influences U.S. foreign policy by layering altruism on top of basic, self-interested power-seeking behavior while allow-

ing Americans to believe that their good intentions lack a selfish dimension
and are truly, in some objective way, good for others (McCartney, 2004: 406).

McCartney then showed how this superior and euphemized self-image led to
the initiation of the Iraq War. In the terminology of this book, McCartney
pointed to what may be called "self-euphemization in the service of WND."

The analysis of the *function* of euphemization in the context of war and
warfare is often conducted in connection with the analysis of another *function*, usually legitimization. Some studies have explored the phenomenon of
framing war as a "moral" act in order to euphemize, and at the same time
legitimize, its initiation. Fairclough (2007) has shown that the increasing
association of moral claims with combative action, and the justification of
war in the name of the "liberation" of the Iraqi people, were two key features
in Blair's 2002–2003 speeches. From an alternative perspective, Chouliaraki
(2007) has argued that the legitimacy of war does not only rely on the old-fashioned ethos of propaganda, but also capitalizes on the huge influence of
media entertainment. She has claimed that "the most effective work of legitimization takes place through leisure and seemingly 'innocent' entertainment" (Chouliaraki, 2007: 4). In this context, Machin and Leeuwen (2007)
have shown that PC games and Hollywood cinema serve as powerful tools
for legitimizing US-led military solutions to local conflicts around the globe.
It seems that these tools also serve the *function* of euphemization.

Naturalization

Two general questions concerning the *function* of naturalization arise in the
context of our discussion:

1. What human practices are subjected to naturalization?
2. What are the aims of naturalization?

Regarding the first question, philosophers have pointed to the encounter
between "naturalization," "culture," "history," and "politics," exposing the
way in which culture and history are presented as a part of nature rather than
as the result of human choice. In his discussion on *myths*, Barthes (1977)
argued that the main function of myths is to naturalize the culture: to make
dominant cultural and historical values, attitudes, and beliefs seem entirely
"natural" and "normal," as "the way things are" (Barthes, 1977: 45–46,
quoted in Chandler, 2008). Hall (1996) described "the naturalization effect"
as "treating what are the products of a specific historical development as if
universally valid, and arising not through historical processes but, as it were,
from Nature itself" (Hall, 1996: 33; see also Hall, 1997: 171). Dunmire
(2009: 198) discussed the ways in which naturalization legitimizes policy,

and by so doing implied that a political agenda could also be subjected to a "naturalization" process.

As for the *aims* of naturalization, some researchers connect the *functions* of naturalization and legitimization. "Naturalization [. . .] denies morality and replaces moral and cultural orders with the 'natural order' when 'natural' actually means justified or true" (Van Leeuwen, 2007: 99, quoted in Peled-Elhanan, 2010: 384). In such cases, "morality and nature become entangled" (Ibid.). Bellamy (2004) takes us back to our main issue: the naturalization and legitimization of war. He writes:

> Another important element of the tradition of "just war" is natural law, which, among other things, insists that sovereigns have a right to use force to uphold the good of the human community, particularly in cases when unjust injuries are inflicted on others. However, although this "humanitarian exception" (rooted in natural law) to positive law's ban on the use of force is morally appealing, the Iraq case demonstrates the dangers of "abuse." "Abuse" refers to cases where moral arguments are used to justify a war that is not primarily motivated by the moral concerns espoused, but by the short-term interests of those instigating violence. (Bellamy 2004: 132)

We will return to these aspects of the *function* legitimization later.

Symbolic Annihilation

The *function* of symbolic annihilation is taken from media studies (Gerbner, 1972; Tuchman, 1978) and usually refers to people rather than objects. There are no studies directly connecting this term with the concept of war. In critical studies of war, the term "exclusion" is quite common, and is sometimes used in a similar way to "symbolic annihilation." Both are used to expose how the harsh effects of war are "excluded" from the discourse. For example, Peled-Elhanan (2010) examined reports about massacres in Israeli secondary school history books published between 1998 and 2009. She used the phrase "exclusion of elements" (p. 390) to show "how the reports (in the history books) on massacres omit the reasons for the killing, exclude both the immediate and the long-run consequences for the victims and any verbal or visual proof of their suffering, as well as details that may raise unnecessary questions regarding the legitimacy of Israel's actions and goals" (Ibid.).

While Elhanan-Peled (2010) connected exclusion or, in our terminology, symbolic annihilation, with legitimization, other studies associated symbolic annihilation with euphemization, representing them as two sides of the same coin. For example, Mellor (2009) analyzed the mechanism of mediating war on the front-page articles of four pan-Arab newspapers, printed during the war in 2003. She argued that the news texts mitigated the Iraqi suffering either by excluding ordinary Iraqis from the reports or by overemphasizing the role of the Iraqi resistance: "the portrayal of the war as an aesthetic event [does not] help in reflecting the Iraqis' suffering" (Mellor, 2009: 426).

Similarly, Chouliaraki (2004) demonstrated that in BBC footage in April 2003, the catastrophic spectacle of the Baghdad bombardment was narrated and filmed in such a way as to be contemplated from a distance and without human presence. "This combination is instrumental in aestheticizing the horror of war" (Chouliaraki, 2004: 141). In the same context, she also used the phrase "scene of suffering without a sufferer" (Ibid.). In another study, Chouliaraki (2006) followed Boltanski's (1999) book *Distant Suffering* and argued that the bombardment of Baghdad in 2003 during the Iraq War was filmed in long-shot and presented in a quasi-literary narrative that capitalized on the aesthetics of horror.

Elhanan-Peled (2010), Mellor (2009), and Chouliaraki (2004, 2006) demonstrated the verbal and visual uses of the *symbolic annihilation* of war.

Legitimization

As was previously noted, both the initiation of a new war in a democracy and the use of military power in general, present a clear challenge to the political discourse, which is obligated to legitimize such actions. Therefore, various *discursive strategies* aimed at fulfilling the legitimization *function* have evolved, and a large number of critical studies for the purpose of exposing them followed. The invasion of Iraq in 1991 and 2003, and the War in Afghanistan in 2001 provided further reinforcement to this direction of research. Most studies have focused on the American war discourse, especially the discourse of the two Bush administrations. Other studies dealt with different war discourses such as the British and Spanish.

The study of the legitimization of wars "addresses the ways in which political and media discourse construe war as a legally and morally acceptable project" (Chouliaraki 2007: 3). Some researchers have offered a systematic analysis of *justification strategies* (De Cillia et al., 1999: 160; Wodak et al., 2009/1999: 189), *legitimization strategies* (Machin and Van Leeuwen, 2007; Van Leeuwen, 2007), and *legitimization techniques* (Van Dijk, 1998: 253). Following Van Dijk, Dunmire (2009: 198) defined *legitimization techniques* as socio-political acts that assert "good reasons, grounds, and acceptable motivations for past or present actions that could be criticized by others." Rojo and Van Dijk (1997: 560) distinguished three different levels of discursive legitimization: the pragmatic act of justification of controversial actions and policies; the semantic representation of one's view of the events as true and reliable; and the socio-political authorization of the legitimizing discourse itself.

Before analyzing the manifestations of the *function* of legitimization in various national war discourses and the *micro-strategies* that serve this *func-*

tion, let us try and precisely delineate the borders of this *function*. "Legitim-ization," as referred to here, is narrower than "justice," yet broader than "law." It includes either the *jus ad bellum*, i.e., the criteria that are to be consulted before engaging in war; or the *jus in bello*, i.e., how combatants are to act or should act once the war has begun. For example, while metaphors like "a smoking gun" aim to justify *the initiation* of a new war, metaphors like "smart bomb" and "surgical strike" (which will be discussed later) aim to justify *the use* of disproportionate military power.

The legitimizing discourse includes some issues that often overlap:

Logic: Rationalizing or giving the raison d'être of the war by clarifying what the war is about, why it is being waged and for what purpose, and who the opponents are. This goal has been especially important since 9/11.

Morality: Making the war seem as moral as possible. For example, by showing that all diplomatic efforts have failed, and that there are no other solutions ("last resort").

Worthiness: Explaining the advantage of initiating a war in comparison to avoiding any kind of military actions. The "worthiness" may consist in saving lives, or may be diplomatic or even economic worthiness.

In the following sections, I will try to chart the *global market of the just war rhetoric* by applying a theoretical classification to its *micro-strategies*. In this way, I intend to demonstrate how the *WND Matrix* may serve as a useful and consistent tool for the comparative analysis of the legitimization *function*.

One clarification is required here: The attempt to map the *global market of the just war rhetoric* leads to a classification problem. As previously mentioned, researchers may use parallel names for the same *micro-strategies of legitimization*, depending on their specific discipline. Some researchers from the discipline of communication studies use the term "framing" to refer to what linguists call "metaphor," while other researchers use the term "nar-rative" for the same phenomenon. For example, Amer (2009) used the con-cept "framing" for what can also be called "naming," while Hulsse and Spencer (2008) used "metaphor" for what can also be called "framing." As always, the application of analytic tools to a specific discourse is far from clear-cut. Nevertheless, or maybe precisely because of this difficulty, it is important to start reorganizing the field of *WND micro-strategies*. Such a classification will contribute to a systematic critical comparative analysis of war discourses from a cross-cultural and interdisciplinary perspective, expos-ing the circulation of the same discursive manipulations that enable the initi-ation of new wars around the globe. The findings are summarized in table 1.3, which appears at the end of this chapter.

Legitimizing narratives: Narratives are a basic tool for legitimization. Hayden White (1980) insisted that writing about a historical event is never a transparent or neutral reflection of reality. In his words: "Could we ever [go about] narrativizing without moralizing?" Within the context of the war-legitimizing discourse, Van Leeuwen (2007) used the term "mythopoiesis" to define "legitimization conveyed through narratives whose outcome rewards legitimate actions and punishes non-legitimate actions."

Right after the initiation of the Iraq War, Lakoff (1991) wrote about the narrative behind the initiation of this war, which he called "The fairy tale of the Just War":

> The most common discourse form in the West where there is combat to settle moral accounts is the classic fairy tale. When people are replaced by states in such a fairy tale, what results is the most common scenario for a just war.

He went on to explain the role of the heroes:

> The fairy tale has an asymmetry built into it. The hero is moral and courageous, while the villain is amoral and vicious. The hero is rational, but though the villain may be cunning and calculating, he cannot be reasoned with. Heroes thus cannot negotiate with villains; they must defeat them. The enemy-as-demon metaphor arises as a consequence of the fact that we understand what a just war is in terms of this fairy tale.

Twenty years later, Dunmire (2009) defined the "9/11 changed everything" narrative. She argued that this narrative reflects a post-Cold War desire to maintain the U.S. global supremacy by preserving its military pre-eminence (Dunmire, 2009: 196). The events of 9/11, then, are to be viewed not as the material and temporal cause behind the Bush Doctrine but as a *legitimizing device* (Van Dijk, 1998) whereby the Administration construed the doctrine as the "natural" response to the 9/11 attacks. This is a good example of the connection between the two *functions*: legitimization and naturalization.

Legitimizing myths: Here, the term "myth" refers to an idealized naïve story, which describes reality without raising too many questions (Ohana & Wistrich 1987:12).[4] In many cases, a myth can serve all four *functions* of WND. Barthes (1972) pointed out the triangular connection between myth, naturalization, and legitimization:

> Myth [. . .] purifies [things] [. . .] it makes them innocent, it gives them a natural and eternal justification, it gives them clarity [. . .]. In passing from history to nature, myth acts economically: it abolishes the complexity of human acts, it gives them the simplicity of essences, it does away with all dialectics, with any going back beyond what is immediately visible, it organizes a world which is without contradictions because it is without depth, a world

wide open and wallowing in the evident, it establishes a blissful clarity: things appear to mean something by themselves. (Barthes, 1972: 142–43)

The Israeli *just war rhetoric* includes a fixed cultural arsenal of ready-made legitimizing and delegitimizing myths that political leaders can easily use to their advantage whenever they initiate a new war. Many of these myths relate to the identity of the Israeli or Jewish people and their opponents throughout history (Almog, 2000; Bar-Tal, 2000; Don-Yehiya, 1993; Gertz, 2000; Frank & Rowland, 2002; Leibman & Don Yehia, 1983).

For example, the aforementioned *mythic metaphor* (Gavriely-Nuri, 2010a) "the whole world is against us" alludes to an enduring state of siege and the existence of a fixed coalition determined to destroy Israel and the Jewish people. This myth is complemented by another mythic metaphor: "In every generation they rise against us to destroy us," which originally appeared in the Passover story (Haggadah), a text read annually during Passover's traditional feast. The historical and cultural foundations for these legitimizing and delegitimizing myths are inculcated through the Israeli education system. Israeli children are familiarized with these myths in school and through the media and literature. They can easily identify a long chain of mythological "lunatics" (or inherently "evil" leaders) who sought to destroy the Jewish people, starting with the Pharaoh (Egypt) and Antiochus (Ancient Greece), and extending to Hitler, Saddam Hussein, Nasrallah, and Ahmadinejad. These two myths are essential components of the construction of the in-group/out-group discourse (Rojo & Van Dijk, 1997: 539), helping to preserve an enduring barrier between Israelis and "the rest of the world," a basic dichotomy that serves the Israeli war rhetoric.

Legitimizing Frames: A "frame" is a *micro-discursive strategy* that guides people toward "seeing" and interpreting an event in a particular way (Entman, 1993, 2003, 2004). The American and international response to the attacks on the World Trade Center in 2001 was led by the Bush administration (as well as by other leaders whom it inspired), which framed the situation as a *war on terror* or a *global war on terrorism* (e.g., Graham et al., 2004; Griffin, 2004). This framing did more than simplify a complex reality in order to make it more mentally manageable (Kruglanski et al., 2008); most researchers perceive the framing *war on terror* also as a war-legitimizing framing which aims to facilitate the use of military power (e.g., Graham et al., 2004).

In contrast to this common perception, Hulsse and Spencer (2008) have demonstrated the disadvantage of this framing as a legitimizing *micro-strategy* and have offered an alternative. They have explored the metaphors attached to Al-Qaeda in the *BildZeitung*, Germany's largest tabloid newspaper, in the aftermath of the terrorist attacks in New York and Washington (2001), Madrid (2004), and London (2005), and have identified a process of *refram-*

ing: at the beginning, the *BildZeitung* used the framing *war on terror*, which constructed Al-Qaeda as an army, a state-like actor; later, the press framed Al-Qaeda as a "criminal organization." Hulsse and Spencer (2008) discussed the advantage of the new framing:

> No longer is Al-Qaeda a "like unit," basically enjoying the same sovereignty as we do. Now, as a criminal actor, it is being subjected to our laws. This makes Al-Qaeda an actor that is inferior rather than equal to us; it constitutes a clear hierarchy between them and us. Furthermore, it constitutes Al-Qaeda as an illegitimate actor, an outlaw. Hence, the metaphorical shift from war to crime not only entails a devaluation of Al-Qaeda but also its delegitimization. (Hulsse and Spencer, 2008: 585)

Later, I will return to the point of *delegitimizing micro-strategies*.

Beyond an analysis of the *war on terror*, Lazar and Lazar (2004, 2007) have demonstrated that 9/11 is not the sole or even primary context for understanding post-9/11 discourses. Rather, they argued that these discourses must be situated within the broader "New World Order" discourse, which has been evolving since the end of the Cold War (Lazar & Lazar, 2004: 224). In a similar context, Erjavec and Volcic (2007: 125) have used the concept "New global discursive order." The framings "New World Order" and "New global discursive order" are powerful *micro-strategies* of legitimization. They contextualize any military response to the events of 9/11 not as part of a local conflict but rather as an attempt to make the whole world a better place to live in. Within such a framing, the invasion of Iraq can easily be accepted and justified.

To complete the picture, here is one more framing for the 9/11 events. Chouliaraki (2007) has claimed that in the absence of a legal basis for military intervention in Iraq, the pro-war coalition elites sought legitimacy by promoting a moral argument, which she called "the humanitarian argument," rather than logic or worthiness (Chouliaraki, 2007: 4). She added:

> [. . .] legitimacy requires the ongoing, adaptable and strategic use of political discourse in the service of military projects; the hard power of war needs to be framed by the soft values of humanitarian care for the Iraqi people and of global security for the world population. (Ibid.)

Indeed, none of the above researchers used the term "legitimizing framing." However, had they applied the terminology of this book, the *discursive strategies* they pointed to could easily be classified as such, thus promoting a cross-cultural analysis of WND.

Let us now briefly look at other legitimizing *micro-strategies*.

Legitimizing Names: Legitimizing naming is the act of giving a name to a military practice (e.g., war, operations, or weaponry) for the purpose of surrounding the use of military power with a rational or moral aura. On October 7, 2001, the War in Afghanistan began in response to the 9/11 attacks, with the US Armed Forces' Operation Enduring Freedom. A few years later, the Iraq War, or *Operation Iraqi Freedom*, was a military campaign that began on March 20, 2003 with the invasion of Iraq (see: Chambers, 2003). Needless to say that freedom is a basic American ethos, and the appearance of this ethos in the name of an operation legitimates the action under the three meanings that were discussed above: it is logical, it is moral, and it is worthy of support. Chapter 3 will focus on naming and present many examples of this *discursive strategy*.

Legitimizing Presuppositions: "A presupposition is something the speaker assumes to be the case prior to making an utterance" (Yule, 1996: 29, quoted in Mazid, 2007: 354). The ultimate goal of most presuppositions is to make the speaker's beliefs and sets of values seem as the only natural, correct and legitimate ones. The implied conclusion is, of course, that they may not be questioned by the listener. Mazid offered a thematic categorization of the major presuppositions identified in the speech delivered by George W. Bush nine days after the 9/11 attacks. Many of them pertain to the construction of the American self-image and "the manufacturing of an enemy" (Mazid, 2007: 366). These constructions are aided by presuppositions such as a "normal course interrupted," a "peaceful life attacked," and "possibilities and hopes killed" (Mazid, 2007: 365). Generally speaking, Mazid demonstrated how Bush's presuppositions constructed an opposition between the United States as the land of freedom, progress, democracy, pluralism, and the source of humanitarian aid, and "those who attacked America [who] are enemies of freedom" and " their attacks are acts of war" (Mazid, 2007: 369).

Legitimizing Analogies: Livnat (2011) has demonstrated the legitimizing force of analogies in the Israeli press in the case of an IDF military operation carried out during 2002. During the course of the operation, an Israeli elite commando unit captured the armed ship *Karine A* that was making its way from the Persian Gulf toward the Israeli coast. The Israeli press covering the event repeatedly used one single analogy—that the operation was "like the operations in the movies"—and compared the operation to Hollywood action films (Livnat, 2011: 12). Livnat argued that the use of this analogy was part of the negotiation over the facts of the event and its significance. In the terminology of this book it may be said that the analogy was a *discursive strategy* aimed at legitimizing the conflict and clarifying who the opponents were. As in the case of the American *axis of evil* the analogy of an action film implies that there is a conflict between a clearly "good" side, and a clearly "bad" one. In Livnat's words:

> [. . .] the effectiveness of the analogy is derived from the fact that Hollywood thrillers have a number of characteristics that are usually absent from a politi-

cal event which is part of a long-lasting dispute: The viewer of the movie is usually given a clear picture of who the "good guys" and "bad guys" are [. . .] [and] is usually given a clear concept as to the goals of each side. The movie usually enables the viewer to easily understand and assess the outcome attained through a specific action [. . .]. This analogy thus serves to clarify the meaning of the political events in simple terms of good and bad, success and achievement. (p. 13)

Legitimizing Implicatures: Van Dijk (2005) analyzed the "political implicatures" in the speeches delivered by Prime Minister José María Aznar in the Spanish Parliament in 2003, in which he legitimated his support for the US and its impending war against Iraq. Political implicatures are defined as "specific political inferences that participants in the communicative situation, for instance, MPs in a parliamentary debate, may make on the basis of (their understanding of) this speech and its context" (Van Dijk, 2005: 66). Van Dijk identified in Aznar's speeches political implicatures that were used to justify the new war by first re-defining the situation and then creating a positive self-presentation and a negative presentation of the other. The re-definition of a given situation involves portraying it in a way that makes the proposed policy understandable, reasonable, and legitimate (p. 72). Defining the situation as a "crisis" or a "threat" helps justify military intervention. The creation of a negative presentation of the other entails the derogation of the "enemy," which is crucial for clarifying that the speaker is complying with the basic accepted codes of behavior in political democracies (p. 77).

Apart from the political implicatures, Van Dijk also pointed out "semantic implications" (p. 69). He argued that most of the semantic implications in this case concerned Iraq and Spain's policy. That is, the implications of Aznar's actual statements could be inferred not only from the topics he talked about but also from "the general knowledge we have about Spain, terrorism, international policy, Iraq and so on" (Ibid.).

Legitimizing Recontextualization: Recontextualization "involves a movement of discourse(s) [. . .] across practices, from one type of a practice [. . .] or context to another" (Erjavec and Volcic, 2007: 127). Erjavec and Volcic (2007) explored how young Serbian intellectuals re-contextualized George W. Bush's *war on terrorism* discourse in order to retroactively legitimize Serbian violence against Muslims in Bosnia and Kosovo during the 1990s. They analyzed interviews with Serbian intellectuals and found that the main characteristic of all the interviews was the use of G. W. Bush's *war on terrorism* discourse, which they reformulated according to their own political-historical context, so as to create a *Serbian war on terrorism*.

Legitimizing Metaphors: In this section, I will give a brief demonstration of war-legitimizing metaphors. For that purpose, I shall focus on one specific example, namely, the metaphor of war as medicine (For a detailed discussion of metaphors, see chapter 5). Musolff (2007, 2010) explored Hitler's anti-

Semitic imagery in *Mein Kampf*, and especially the conceptualization of the German nation as a (human) body that had to be cured from a deadly disease caused by the Jewish parasites. De Leonardis (2008), on the other hand, investigated the political discourse in Italy and argued that the use of metaphors drawn from the field of medicine has become very common during the last few years. His research included examples such as the terms "prescriptions," "drastic treatments" and "shock therapies" appearing in the political discourse in relation to war and public policy, or the reference to public enterprises or bodies as "patients that need to be cured" (De Leonardis, 2008: 33). In regards to the global war discourse, he wrote:

> In the 1991 Gulf War and in the 1999 Kosovo War, politicians, generals and journalists consistently and obsessively made use of medical metaphors such as "surgical bombings" [. . .] or "surgical war" [. . .]. One may well point out that there is a real "epidemic" of such metaphors, and that a medicalization of political discourse is definitely taking place. (De Leonardis, 2008: 33–34)

When the enemy is depicted as a disease or infection, then the war against it acquires the positive value of a remedy, and the army's task is seemingly to provide a cure by purifying or sterilizing the infected area.

Delegitimizing: In the same way in which *war-legitimizing* micro-strategies were clearly identified by using the *WND Matrix*, *delegitimizing* micro-strategies, aimed to delegitimize opponents and their struggle or war, may also be clearly identified using the same method. Previously, we mentioned how Hülsse & Spencer (2008) have demonstrated *micro-strategies* aimed to delegitimize Al-Qaeda. Much rarer are studies like the one performed by Mellor (2009), which explored the delegitimization of the USA. Mellor analyzed the front-page articles from four pan-Arab newspapers and showed how a delegitimizing metaphor supported "the politics of pity to trigger sympathy for the Iraqis" (Mellor, 2009: 411). The Palestinian newspaper *Al Quds Al Arabi*, for instance, constantly used the metaphor of the USA as a butcher who commits massacres, thus enforcing the victimization of helpless Iraqis (Ibid.).

Amer (2009) provided a rare complementary perspective when he explored the delegitimization of the "Second Palestinian Intifada"—in his eyes a legitimate national liberation struggle—in the *New York Times*. His research analyzed Thomas Friedman's columns, which appeared in the op-ed page of the *New York Times*. Using the terminology of this book, Amer exemplified several *micro-strategies* of delegitimization, like framing and naming. For example, he explained why Friedman called the war "Arafat's war":

> Here Arafat and the Palestinians are cast in the negative agent role of the "attacker" and the "transgressor," and therefore are held responsible and

blameworthy for the events. By implication, this attribution of negative agency and responsibility to the Palestinian side is likely to position Israel in the semantic patient role of the "victim," which is facing Arafat's transgression and war. (Amer, 2009: 11)

Interestingly enough, Amer's analysis reminds us of Lakoff's analysis of the Bush administration in 1991, only in a reversed reflection. While Lakoff exposed the legitimizing *micro-strategies* used by Bush to legitimize the invasion of Iraq, Amer pointed out the delegitimizing *micro-strategies* that were used by Friedman to delegitimize the Palestinian struggle.

A Matrix of de-euphemization, that is, one that presents strategies which aim to de-euphemize opponents, may also be added to our Matrix of war-delegitimization. I shall leave this mission for future research.

Table 1.3 schematically maps some examples of legitimizing *micro-strategies* from the *global market of the just war rhetoric* discussed above.

Table 1.3. The Global Market of War-Legitimization

Micro-strategy	Researcher	Specific content	What for?	Which war?	Which discourse?
Legitimizing narrative	Dunmire (2009)	"9/11 changes everything"	To justify the dimension of the military response	The War in Afghanistan (2001) and The Iraq War (2003)	American
Legitimizing myth	Gavriely-Nuri (2010a)	"The whole world is against us"	To create a constant threat	Different wars (1948-2008)	Israeli
Legitimizing frame	Griffin (2004)	"War on terror"	To intensify the dimension of the threat	The War in Afghanistan (2001) and The Iraq War (2003)	American
Legitimizing name	Chambers (2003)	"Operation Iraqi Freedom"	To clarify the goal of the war	The Iraq War (2003)	American
Legitimizing presupposition	Mazid (2007)	"Those who attacked America are enemies of freedom"	To clarify identity opponents	The Iraq War (2003)	American
Legitimizing analogy	Livnat (2011)	"The military operation was like those in the movies"	To clarify the opponents' identity ("good" vs. "bad")	Military operation (*Karine A Affair*) (2002)	Israeli
Legitimizing (semantic) implication	Van Dijk (2005)	"A crisis that confronts the international community"	To connect "us" (the Spanish) to the crisis	The Iraq War (2003)	Spanish
Legitimizing recontextualization	Erjavec & Volcic (2007)	"The Serbian war on terrorism"	To depict "us" (the Serbians) as victims	The Bosnian war	Serbian
Legitimizing metaphor	Musolff (2007, 2010)	WAR IS MEDICINE	To legitimate annihilation of the opponents (Jews)	World War II	Hitler's *Mein Kampf*
Delegitimizing name	Amer (2009)	"Arafat's War"	To define the aggressor	The Second Intifada (2000)	American
Delegitimizing metaphor	Melor (2009)	THE U.S. IS A BUTCHER	To expose the results of the war	The Iraq War (2003)	Palestinian

THE HISTORICAL ROOTS OF ISRAELI WND

In the former section, I discussed various aspects and examples of the *Global Market* of WND. To complete the introduction, in this section I shall go back to the Israeli WND and briefly present its historical roots. More specifically, in this section I shall examine the *function* of euphemization as reflected in the canonical Hebrew literature since the beginning of Zionism at the end of the nineteenth century. This literary-historical point of view will complete the cross-cultural perspective and also serve as an introduction to the analytical chapters that follow.

A panoramic view of the term "war" in Hebrew literature reveals a pendulum motion between two dominant models that have developed in parallel. The first is characterized by the glorification of fighters, of fighting, and of military force. The second emphasizes the tragedy, pain, suffering, and destruction brought about by war.

A widespread claim in research is that "the Jewish people never excelled at singing songs of war" (Keren, 1991: 83). Most of the war songs that appear in the Bible were composed by the prophets in times of danger. They remain negligible in comparison with those same prophets' visions of peace (Ibid.). In fact, until World War I, Hebrew literature wrote very little about the experience of battle, with a few exceptions. For example, in Abraham Mapu's novel,[5] *Guilt of Samaria*, (1865) the author attempts to re-create the biblical and post-biblical world and describe a Jewish military state (Miron, 1992: 23).

However, the beginning of the Zionist settlement marked a turning point. During this period, a process of "creating a new picture of the past" (Bitan, 1996: 186) was taking place, and myths of "bravery under fire" provided a central means to this end. "The yearning for honor, bravery, power and a different Jewish personality was part of the debate surrounding the quality of the new Jewish identity. Active Judaism was supposed to be both a means and a guarantee for parting with the exilic Jewish past" (Ibid., 185).

A first major expression of the tension between the two models of war can be seen in the 1930s, when a group of artists, led by the poet Avraham Shlonsky,[6] began to display an attitude of pacifism similar in spirit to that displayed in post-World War I Europe. In 1932, an anthology edited by Shlonsky was published under the title *Thou Shalt Not Kill! A Small Compilation of Poems against the War*. The book was a collection of poems opposing the war, written during World War I. "In as much as Zionism is irretrievably bound with nationalism and militarism," Shlonsky wrote, "it is inherently flawed" (35). Two years later, Nathan Alterman,[7] arguably the most renowned Israeli poet of the twentieth century, wrote the poem *Don't Give Them Rifles*. Two of Alterman's most important works: *Joy of the Poor* (1941) and *Plague Poems* (1944), were written in the context of a world war and were harbingers of change: "Alterman returned here to war poetry that is like a glorious monument of marble or bronze" (Miron, 1992: 41).

The oscillation between these two models increased after each of Israel's wars. The literature written on the subject of the 1948 War also oscillated between two opposing poles: on the one hand, the writers were clearly impressed with the power revealed in the battles and with the fighters' combative ability. On the other, the tragic loss of young lives was emphasized time and again, and difficult questions arose in the public, concerning the justification of war and the continued use of force. The attitude of *Dor Ba'aretz* ("Generation in the Land"), a group of Israeli writers who wrote during the 1940s and 1950s about the experience of war, often focused on descriptions of personal, direct, and stressful battle experiences. Their poems and stories are characterized by a great sensitivity to the tragic aspects of war. These evidently were not poems of praise and glory.

A clearly contrasting example is Alterman's poetry in *The Seventh Column*.[8] Miron terms it "propaganda poetry," since it is written in an optimistic spirit, with an assured justification of battle and of victory, and a drastic trivialization of the price paid by those who were killed (Miron, 2003: 51). "*The Silver Platter*[9] is just about the only *Column* in which the poet [Alterman] refers to the rebirth of the State of Israel from the aspect of its human and moral price" (Miron, 2003: 66). Additional flaws found by Miron in the poetry of "older generation" poets like Alterman include submergence of the topic of war in "a deluge of superlatives," and in a rhetoric that sets young fighters apart and represents them "as encircled by haloes" (Miron, 2003: 52).

The 1956 War (the Sinai Operation) also preserves the oscillation between these two war models. The conquest of the Sinai Peninsula was associated with the biblical Mount Sinai. Hadari points to a fundamental change that occurred, in her opinion, in relation to previous literary traditions:

> The transformation [after the 1956 War] is sharp and sudden. Poems, songs, newspaper articles, reportages, and speeches in the daily press and in periodicals, along with philosophy and thought, devoted themselves to the portrait of the young soldier as a knight charged with a messianic mission. The writers turn to biblical sources, interpreting them through topical transference from God to the soldier. (Hadari, 2002: 84)

At the same time, other voices began to appear. Being the first *war of choice* fought by Israel, the 1956 War raised doubts regarding the justification of continuing to rely on and believe in the "life by the sword" ethos (Gertz, 1996: 35). The doubts concerning the necessity of this war moved some of the writers at that time to question the glorification of the war heroes. This situation led to the creation of A. B. Yehoshua's first allegories, among them

The Last Commander (1962), which is centered on a group of fighters who prefer sleep to war.

In chapter 8, we shall complete this short literary-historical survey with the post-1967 WND.

NOTES

1. De Cillia, Reisigl and Wodak (1999:160) define "strategies" as "plans of actions with varying degrees of elaborateness, the realization of which can range from automatic to conscious, and which are located at different levels of our mental organization."

2. Israel participated in wars in the years 1948, 1956, 1967, 1969–1970, 1982, 2006, and 2008, and was attacked in the Gulf War of 1991. Five of these wars were initiated by Israel. In addition to "official" wars, Israel experienced two intifadas (1987–1993 and 2000–2004) and repetitive long periods of bombing suffered by border settlements (e.g., a couple of years of bombing settlements close to the Gaza Strip, especially after the "withdrawal" in 2005), which were not counted as "formal" wars.

3. According to some views, the "Rhetoric of Evil" echoes Reagan's "Evil Empire" discourse. However, my claim is based on Ivid's (2004).

4. For definitions of "myth," see also Honko, 1984.

5. The novels of Abraham Mapu provided inspiration for the emergence of the Zionist movement at the end of the nineteenth century.

6. Avraham Shlonsky (1900–1973) is one of the most significant Hebrew poets in the twentieth century.

7. 1910–1970.

8. Alterman's weekly column in the Labor daily *Davar*.

9. Alterman's most well-known poem, a canonical text read on Israel's Remembrance Day.

Chapter Two

A Cultural Approach to Critical Discourse Analysis (CCDA)[1]

This chapter describes the Cultural Approach to Critical Discourse Analysis (CCDA), which is the approach adopted in this book. CCDA aims to expose the various ways in which *cultural codes* are embedded in discourse, and contribute to the recurrence of abuses of power. I shall attempt to represent CCDA not only as a theoretical framework, but also as a practical tool for decoding the cultural baggage contained within discourses. It is my view that the connection between culture and discourse is relatively underdeveloped in many CDA studies—perhaps because of the complexity and ambiguity surrounding the concept of "culture," or simply because most CDA researchers are linguists rather than cultural researchers.

I shall first contextualize CCDA within the field of CDA. I shall then move on to describe some basic theoretical and methodological principles of CCDA, attempting in particular to define the process of *decoding cultural codes*. In the last section, I shall discuss the potential role of CCDA in the promotion of a universal "culture of peace."

Critical Discourse Analysis (CDA) traditionally aims to produce insights into the ways in which a discourse may reproduce social and political inequality, and abuses of power and domination (cf. Chilton, 2004; Fairclough, 1995). Accordingly, a core theoretical and empirical question in CDA is "how human minds can be tricked, deceived or manipulated through the use of language" (Chilton, 2005: 41). Van Dijk argues that CDA researchers should not only be interested in describing the interesting properties of political rhetoric, but also in explaining them. "In order to explain them, we need to relate them to such socio-cognitive representations as attitudes, norms, values and ideologies" (van Dijk, 2007: 62). These two statements are in fact the point of departure for the application of CCDA.

Within the plethora of approaches to CDA, Ruth Wodak and collaborators have developed during the last decade another important approach (De Cilia et al., 1999; Wodak et al., 2009/1999), which is called *the Discourse-Historical Approach* (DHA).[2] Like DHA, CCDA also aims to strengthen CDA as a multi-disciplinary approach by emphasizing the analysis of yet another dimension of the discourse—the cultural one.

Although many critical researchers have analyzed specific national cultures (e.g., De Leonardis, 2008; Achugar, 2007), the theoretical research on culture as a key player in discourse analysis only began to emerge in the last few years (e.g., Carpentier and Spinoy, 2008; Kövecses, 2006; Scollo, 2011; Pardo, 2010). In a recent study, Scollo (2011) offered a comprehensive and useful comparison of culturally inclusive approaches to discourse analysis and communication. Her research focused especially on the approaches criticizing what she referred to as "Western-biased theories." I argue that CCDA offers a way to enrich the ongoing discussion concerning the encounter between culture and discourse in general, and the triangle discourse/culture/critical analysis in particular. It does so, not only by focusing on specific national cultures (in this case the Israeli culture), but mainly by considering culture itself as a discursive mechanism. To begin our discussion of CCDA, I shall suggest a definition of "culture," which will provide the background for later sections.

CULTURE AS A "DATABASE"

Swidler (1986: 273) argues that "culture influences action not by providing the ultimate values towards which action is oriented, but by shaping a repertoire or 'tool kit' of habits, skills, and styles from which people construct 'strategies of action.'" Similarly, Peleg (2003: 44) refers to "culture" as an admission ticket to an exclusive club whose members have similar codes of thinking, behaving and expressing themselves. In contrast to those images of a fixed tool kit, or of a membership to an exclusive club, I suggest that we adopt a metaphor from the contemporary field of high-tech. *Culture* may be considered as a "database" which only members of a specific community can access and navigate, and only they can therefore find specific "links" to certain issues. The content of these "links" is comprised of *cultural codes*—compact packages of shared values, norms, ethos and social beliefs.

The advantage of such a conceptualization lies in the dynamic character of the search process. As a metaphor, the concept of a "database" cuts across the social hierarchy, thereby allowing many voices to participate in the discourse, relatively free of structural filters. Therefore this metaphor implies that culture is, in fact, an adaptable repertoire of *cultural codes* at the disposal of the members of a given cultural community.

For example, navigating *the Israeli cultural database* surrounding the term "captivity" will lead, among other things, to two *cultural codes*:

1. The ethos of *fighting until the last bullet*, and the preference of this ethos to the option of falling captive.
2. The mythical story of the Israeli soldier Uri Ilan from 1954, who committed suicide when he was captured by the Syrians, so as not to reveal any secrets under torture. Ilan left a note between his toes saying "I did not betray" which made him a myth in Israeli culture.

Between the years 2006–2011, the Israeli soldier Gilad Shalit was being held captive by the Hamas in the Gaza strip. The Israeli discourse on Shalit and especially the question of his "price" (i.e., how many Hamas prisoners Israel should release in a POWs' "transaction") was based, among other things, on these *cultural codes*.

CCDA: GENERAL PRINCIPLES

The following principles inform CCDA's focus on the cultural aspects of a "text" (verbal and non-verbal alike):

- No text is independent of its cultural contexts.
- CCDA employs tools and methodologies taken from the discipline of cultural studies, such as the heuristic of *decoding cultural codes.*
- Decoding *cultural codes* demands not only intimate familiarity with a community's language, culture and history. It also demands a special awareness that frequently "social and historical creation [. . .] [is] treated as a natural event" (Thompson 1990: 66).
- CCDA seeks to explore the global dictionary of power and manipulation by focusing on the *cultural and cross-cultural codes* activated by *discursive strategies.*
- Cross-cultural or multi-cultural perspectives facilitate the identification of unique elements belonging to specific cultural codes and thus contribute to the process of decoding them.
- CCDA analyzes *verbal and non-verbal* practices (e.g., visual practices as well as cultural sites) alike, because it does not focus on the study of linguistic structures as such.
- CCDA analyzes *factual and fictional* discourses alike, assuming that a fictional short story may also act as a repository of cultural codes, and has the same potential of being implicated in the reproduction of power abuse as a political speech, for example.

- CCDA demonstrates that as far as the rhetoric of power is concerned, there is no difference between small and large cultural communities.

CCDA: PRINCIPLES OF ANALYSIS

The essence and mission of CDA remains "the systematic and explicit analysis of the various structures and strategies of different levels of text and talk" (Van Dijk, 2008, cited in Baker, et al., 2008: 280). CCDA meets this commitment, and further expands the analysis to include a wide variety of non-linguistic "data" as was outlined above. The CCDA of a certain discourse is operationalized through three analytic stages. I shall first outline these operational stages, and then discuss each in more detail:

1. CCDA focuses on one or more specific *discursive strategies*. Considering that a strategy is a combination of goals and means (Fairclough, 2009/2001: 174), CCDA is interested in discursive "means" (e.g., metaphors, narratives, frames) that promote specific "goals" (i.e., political agenda or specific policy).
2. CCDA exposes and decodes the cultural codes that are activated by these discursive strategies.
3. CCDA shows how the encounter between discursive strategies and cultural codes encourages the reproduction of power abuses.

Mazid (2007) gives a good illustration of how this process works in practice: she focuses on the major presuppositions, that is, *discursive strategies* (stage 1) in the speech delivered by G. W. Bush nine days after the 9/11 attacks in order to justify a new war. Many of these presuppositions are based on specific American *cultural codes* (stage 2), for example, the ethos of "America as the land of freedom" (Mazid, 2007: 369). She shows how the encounter between these presuppositions and cultural codes was used in the theoretical "manufacturing of an enemy" (Mazid, 2007: 366) and for the practical goal of justifying the initiation of a new American war (stage 3).

Discursive Strategies

A broad definition of *discourse* and *discursive strategies* may best serve CCDA's goals. As previously mentioned, *Discourse* is taken to include not only verbal practices (e.g., political speeches), but also visual modes (e.g., photographs and video clips) and cultural sites. *Cultural sites* are "those locations where the collective representations—the dominant symbols, beliefs and assumptions—of society are conveyed" (Lomski-Feder & Ben-Ari, 1999: 12). For example: national ceremonies such as military marches, and as we see later, the awarding of military decorations.

A basic principle of Foucauldian thought maintains that discourse defines and produces the objects of our knowledge. The Foucauldian concept of discourse is not a purely linguistic concept, but rather a concept that encompasses both language and practice. Since "all social practices entail meaning, and meanings shape and influence what we do, all practices have discursive aspects" (Hall, 1992: 291). This conceptualization attempts to overcome the traditional distinction between what one says (language) and what one does (practice). Indeed, some CDA researchers analyze visual language (e.g., Chouliaraki, 2006; Machin, 2007; Machin & van Leeuwen, 2007), but it seems that in most CDA studies *discourse* is still taken to be language (Chilton, 2005: 20). An integrative analysis of linguistic, visual, and cultural sites will be more effective in exposing *cultural codes* embedded in the discourse.

Cultural Codes

I define a *cultural code* as a compact package of shared values, norms, ethos and social beliefs. The "package" may appear as, inter alia, a historical event which is well known to members of the community; a geographical site with special significance for the members of the community; or a national hero (or heroine) to which the community members ascribe a certain *added value*. Understanding the *added value* of cultural codes is tantamount to decoding them. Due to their constant repetition in various contexts and combinations, the cultural codes construct and reflect a community's "common sense."

"Cultural codes don't fall from the sky" (Keller, 2004: 3); they are derived, among other things, from the community's common experience. Rather than constant structures, cultural codes are created in a dynamic and ongoing social construction, which continuously influences their cultural status. At the same time, these cultural codes affect society. Cultural codes are mechanisms of both selection and interpretation: first, they sift out from the endless flow of reality the occurrences to be considered as "important"; and then, they direct their social interpretation. In so doing, they link contemporary occurrences with past experience, and lead and direct the social reality.

As was mentioned before, cultural codes are usually inaccessible for members of other cultural communities (Hall, 1980, 1993; Simons & Hyatt, 1999). Therefore, decoding them requires, among other things, familiarity with the history and the basic social beliefs of a certain cultural community (regarding the Israeli social beliefs see Bar-Tal, 2000; Gertz, 2000; Katriel, 1991, 1999; Liebman & Don-Yehiya; Zerubavel, 1995). However, this decoding process requires more than just a thorough familiarity with the history, culture and everyday life of a given community. The decoding process also requires a specific awareness of these codes, which most members of cultural communities may be blind to because of the tendency to take them for granted. Thus, a cross-cultural perspective, as offered for example by Shi-xu (2005), may contribute to the process of identification and even to the decoding of cultural codes by pointing out their "artificiality": what sometimes seems completely "natural" to community members, may in fact be a product of social and cultural construction.

To illustrate, let us focus on a literary example. In a short story from 1971, the well-known Israeli play-writer, Hanoch Levin, wrote:

> One night, Pshishpsh climbed the water pipe attached to one of the houses all the way to the third floor, where he saw an open window [. . .] as his eyes got accustomed to the darkness in the room, he saw a large bed, with a woman lying upon it. Apart from the woman, [. . .] the room was completely empty, there was not one piece of furniture and even the walls were bare [. . .]. [Pshishpsh thought to himself:] if this woman is wealthy enough that she is able to allocate a whole room for one bed, she must have other rooms, a room for every piece of furniture, a room for a chair, a room for a table, a room for a closet, a room for a radio, a series of small, cosy rooms for clothes, [. . .] a room for a plate, a room for a fork, a room for a sugar cube. (Levin, [1971], 1987: 73. Translated by the author)

Pshishpsh's perception of the connection between space and objects is full of irony and criticism against the basic *cultural code* of affluent society, which may be summarized in the motto "the more—the better." Pshishpsh adopts a kind of a counter-cultural code, we may even say an idiosyncratic cultural code, which maintains that "less is more"—the fewer objects one has in a room, the wealthier one is. This example demonstrates that *no text is independent of its cultural contexts*. The example also clarifies the role that cultural codes play in the process of understanding and interpreting reality.

Thus, we can sum three basic principles regarding *cultural codes*:

1. Cultural codes operate like the skeleton of the human body—though they are not manifest, they provide the foundations for the entire culture.
2. Cultural codes operate like an undeclared social compass, directing the community's members as to how to rationalize and legitimize policy and decision making.
3. Cultural codes are invisible not only to non-members of a community, but also to members of a community who may be blind to them because they perceive them as "natural," or as "common sense."

CCDA AND A "CULTURE OF PEACE"

Apart from "local" *cultural codes,* we can identify *cross-cultural codes,* which can be "exchanged" within an imagined *global discursive market.* As we previously noted, it seems that former Israeli Prime Minister Ariel Sharon holds the "copyright" for what we may call the *Rhetoric of Evil* (Ivie, 2004), which was later adopted by G. W. Bush Jr. and became a Western *cultural code* to a certain degree.

If we accept the idea of a *global discursive market* of cultural and cross-cultural codes, we can then see the contribution of CCDA not only to the uncovering of oppressive discourses but also to the promotion of a "culture of peace."

The concept *culture of peace*, which was formulated at the *International Congress on Peace in the Minds of Men* held in Cote d'Ivoire in 1989, can help point out the common universal roots of different national cultural discourses that promote peace. In 1998,[3] UNESCO has adopted the following definition of a *culture of peace*:

> It consists of values, attitudes and behaviors that reflect and inspire social interaction and sharing based on the principles of *freedom, justice and democracy, all human rights, tolerance and solidarity*, that reject violence and endeavor to prevent conflicts. [emphasis added]

CCDA should not focus solely on specific national discourses in order to expose *discursive strategies* and *cultural codes* that support abuses of power. Rather, it should encourage cross-cultural and comparative research in order to promote universal values, attitudes and behaviors based on the principles of freedom, justice and democracy, all human rights, tolerance and solidarity.

For instance, Cameron (2007) investigated emergent patterns of metaphor in a reconciliation talk between an IRA bomber and a victim and offered the following conclusions:

> Metaphor plays a role in the re-humanization of individuals away from the limited stereotypes as "enemy" and offers affordances for empathic understanding of the Other [. . .]. Metaphors in the talk expressed pain, violence and many other feelings, emotions, reflexes and reactions, with striking metaphors contributing to the "affective climate" of the meetings. (Cameron, 2007: 219)

By pointing out the *discursive strategy* "reconciliation metaphors" within a specific cultural and political context, Cameron demonstrates not only that "metaphors can kill," to paraphrase Lakoff's words, but also how they may contribute to humanization and reconciliation. Thus, not only can CCDA be applied for the exposure of *oppressive discursive strategies* and *cultural codes*, but it may also provide a complimentary point of view of discursive tools that practically promote a *culture of peace*.

The concept *culture of peace* may be perceived as a mega "positive" *cultural code*. In contrast, the focus of this book will turn towards a mega "negative" cultural code: *The War-Normalizing Discourse (WND)*. In the following chapters, variances of this code in the Israeli discourse will be analyzed and some of their consequences revealed.

NOTES

1. An earlier version of chapter 2 appeared in *Journal of Critical Discourse Studies*, 9(1), 77–85: Gavriely-Nuri, Dalia (2012). *Cultural Approach to Critical Discourse Analysis* is available online at www.tandfonline.com/doi/abs/10.1080/17405904.2011.636484.
It is published by permission of the publisher. Copyright © 2012 Taylor & Francis Group.
2. De Cillia, Reisigl, and Wodak (1999:156) define the *Discourse-Historical Approach* as an attempt "to integrate all available information on the historical background and the original sources in which discursive 'events' are embedded [. . .] and explores the ways in which particular types and genres of discourse are subject to diachronic change." About the *Discourse-Historical Approach*, see also Reisigl & Wodak (2001); Wodak & Weiss, (2005).
3. *Resolution Adopted by the General Assembly, United Nations* (a/res/52/13).

Chapter Three

War-Normalizing Naming

From Operation Peace for the Galilee to
Operation Cast Lead[1]

On the morning of 6 August 1945, the United States Army Air Force dropped the nuclear bomb Little Boy on the city of Hiroshima. The detonation of a similar nuclear weapon, Fat Man, over Nagasaki followed three days later. These two bombs caused the deaths of over 200,000 Japanese civilians. Thirty-seven years later, in 1982, the IDF invaded southern Lebanon in what had initially been called Operation Peace for the Galilee. It ended three years later, after 675 Israeli soldiers and 17,825 Lebanese and Syrian civilians and soldiers had lost their lives.

These apparently straightforward and, in a way, naïve-sounding names— Little Boy, Fat Man, and Peace for the Galilee (*Shlom Ha'Galil*, later known as the First Lebanon War), all had the same basic effect: directing public opinion away from some of the most difficult features and disturbing questions concerning the use of military power.

This chapter explores the subject of *war-normalizing naming*. War-normalizing naming is the act of naming military practices (e.g., operations and weaponry) so as to create the impression that the use of military power is a common, everyday and even banal practice. War-normalizing naming, as a discursive strategy, is part of the broader *WND*.

The present case study analyses a corpus consisting of 239 names of Israeli military operations conducted since 1948, as well as the names of weaponry (tanks, crafts, missiles, etc.) used by the IDF. The analysis of this corpus will attempt to address the following three questions:

1. How does war-normalizing naming function?
2. How does a nation's cultural apparatus sustain war-normalizing naming?
3. What are the negative aspects of military practices that the war-normalizing naming aims to "normalize"? (Consider the following possibilities: difficult consequences, evasion of legal responsibility, moral issues.)

This chapter will take our understanding of WND one step further, by providing the theoretical and analytical tools required in order to explore the cross-cultural components of the military naming process. For example, Operation Iraqi Freedom (2003) forms part of the American military lexicon; Operation Truthful Promise (2006) is the name given by Hezbollah to its kidnapping of two Israeli soldiers. These examples imply that the phenomenon of military naming, and thus the War-Normalizing Discourse, is by no means an exclusively Israeli invention. Therefore, the chapter also points towards the possibility of further research in the international arena.

This in-depth analysis of military naming opens the analytical section of this book, because the act of naming is particularly intuitive. Names help us frame our expectations and our understandings. An analysis of military naming also illustrates, simply and effectively, how the four *functions* of WND interrelate. The coming chapters will gradually proceed toward increasingly sophisticated discursive devices.

The current chapter begins with definitions of war-normalizing naming. The subsequent analysis is conducted in two parts: the first will examine the corpus of military names; and the second will go on to provide an in-depth study of two particularly interesting names—Operation Peace for the Galilee (1982) and Operation Cast Lead (*Oferet Yetzuka* 2008). In addition, this chapter will include a discussion of the concept of "military operation" in Israeli public discourse. The chapter concludes with a demonstration of the war-normalizing naming in non-Israeli discourses.

WHAT IS WAR-NORMALIZING NAMING?

Military names function like calling cards; they convey a certain image of military practices to the public and, in so doing, act as an important link between the military and civil society. Solomon Fisher's statement—"[We] constitute our world in the very act of naming" (1985: 152)—can be complemented by Bourdieu's cogent comment: "When you show—you hide" (Bourdieu, 1980). The claim of this chapter is, therefore, that military naming is a simple and useful *discursive strategy,* which helps situate military practices within our conceptual world. It blurs or even neutralizes negative attitudes toward those practices by masking their costs, particularly if they are human.

Market studies have shown that a product's name is the most effective mode of product-consumer communication (Murphy, 1978: 100; Sullivan, 1998). Consider Recital, Sonata, and Nocturno—the commercial names given to three medications for treating depression and insomnia: citalopram, aaleplon, and sopiclone (respectively). They represent what can be called *medication-normalizing naming*, that is, a common commercial practice for blurring the association of a medication with some condition of ill health. Wrapping these medications with names evoking concert halls undoubtedly helps "block" or "annihilate" consumer awareness of—or interest in—any side effects and other inconvenient truths concerning the drugs. The systematic use of the *semantic field* of *Music* for marketing prescription drugs implies the technique's utility, which may also be used in other domains—such as the military naming, a point I will return to later.

Inspired by John B. Thompson's theory as presented in his 1990 book, *Ideology and Modern Culture* (see chapter 1), I define four *functions* of WND, which may be applied to define and analyze war-normalizing naming: euphemization, naturalization, legitimation, and symbolic annihilation.

To illustrate the analytic benefits of these *functions*, let us begin with one war-normalizing name: Operation Rainbow through the Clouds *(Mivtza Keshet Be'anan)*. This name was given to a controversial short-term Israeli incursion (2004) into the Gaza Strip aimed to locate the tunnels dug to connect the Strip with Egypt primarily for the purpose of smuggling weapons into Gaza. The operation's name recalls the rainbow's ephemeral beauty *(euphemization)* and compares the operation with the natural cycle of rain followed by sun *(naturalization)*. The word "rainbow" is particularly resonant: Being a clear reference to the biblical story of Noah's Ark, it *legitimates* the operation by alluding to the defensive character of the action—protection of the Israelis from annihilation just as Noah protected the world's animals. This name also fulfills the *function* of *symbolic annihilation* by shifting the public's thoughts towards the diaphanous heavens and away from earthly death and destruction, accompanying military actions.

ANALYSIS OF A CORPUS OF MILITARY NAMES

In chapter 1, we defined *WND* as covering not only battles and battlefields but also weaponry, preparations for war, and so forth. That being the case, the corpus analyzed in this chapter consists of two parts: The first includes names of IDF operations conducted between 1948 and 2008 (76 names in total); the second includes names of IDF weapons, used by the IDF between the years 1948–2008. Some of these weapons were developed by Israel's military industries and some by foreign firms (163 names in total).

A comprehensive open-access database listing Israeli military operations and weapons has been compiled by Wikipedia's Israeli website.[2] The list's limitation is clear: neither secret operations nor weaponry still considered confidential are included in it. However, since the present research does not aim to detail the process of military naming from a historical or technological perspective but rather from a cultural and political one, the naming of secret operations is less relevant. Whatever contributions their names may make will be marginal in terms of the logic or outcomes of this study.

It is important to note that the term "operation" is used rather broadly within the Israeli military discourse. It may denote activities of a very short (a couple of hours) to a very long (years) duration, activities initiated during wars, or isolated actions (I shall return to this point later). Moreover, in Hebrew, the difference between a "battle" and an "operation" is sometimes vague. Within the context of the present research, I will use the term "operation" as it appears in IDF historiography.

Dominant Semantic Fields and their Functions

In the first part of the analysis, I identified the *dominant semantic fields* of the names in order to create a number of defined core groups. For the purpose of the research, I used a simple definition of "semantic field"—namely, a group of words relating to the same subject or concept, for example: food, clothing, or emotions:

> On a very general and intuitive level, we can say that the words in a semantic field, though not synonymous, are all used to talk about the same general phenomenon, and there is a meaning inclusion relation between the items in the field and the field category itself [. . .]. The notion of a semantic field can be extended intuitively to any set of terms with a close relation in meaning, all of which can be subsumed under the same general label. (Akmajian et al., 2001: 239–240)

Identification of a group of words belonging to the same semantic field relies on the ability of the native speaker "to say that the word 'island,' for example, belongs to the field of Geography and the word 'hope' belongs to the semantic field of human feelings/emotions" (Sovran, 2000: 34).

Within this analysis, a semantic field is classified as *dominant* if it appears at least seven times in the IDF operations corpus and at least five times in the weaponry corpus. However, it is important to remember that semantic fields are rarely identified or classified in a clear-cut fashion. In order to achieve the utmost precision, I correlated the names and fields using a Hebrew language thesaurus (Avneyon, 2000), a guide to Israeli and Jewish names (Arazi 1982) and several Bible concordances, aided by my knowledge as a Hebrew native-speaker and consumer of Israeli culture. As might be expected, many names may be classified into more than one semantic field. In those cases, the names were included in all the corresponding fields simultaneously.

Familiarity with Israeli culture allowed me to identify two dominant semantic fields: *names and concepts from Nature,* and *names and concepts from the Bible,* as shown in table 3.1.

Table 3.1. Dominant Semantic Fields in Names of Israeli Military Operations, 1948–2008

Names and Concepts From:	Number	%
Nature	22	27%
The Bible	31	38%
Others	29	35%

Table 3.2 includes the full classification of the 76 names of military operations; table 3.3 provides some examples from among the 163 names given to weaponry.

Table 3.2. List of Names of Israeli Military Operations, 1948–2008

Nature	The Bible	Other
Aviv Neurim (spring of youth)	*Amora* (biblical city of Gomorrah)	*Abirei Lev* (knights of the heart)
Barak (lightning)	*Asaph* (name of a Levite)	*An-Far* (abbreviation of Anti-Faruk, King of Egypt)
Bin-Nun (nun is a fish; hence, a fish's offspring)	*Balak* (biblical king of Moab)	*Betek* (a cut, also defloration [of virginity])
Brosh (cypress tree)	*Barak* (biblical military leader)	*Chishul* (strengthening)
Chasida (stork)	*Ben-Ami* (literally: son of my people)	*Derech Nechusha* (resolute path)
Dekel (palm tree)	*Bin-Nun* (Moses' successor)	*Din Vechesbon* (accountability)
Erez (cedar tree)	*Chametz* (leavened bread, to be disposed of during Passover)	*Egrof* (fist)
Geshem Rishon (first rain)		*Gis* (brother-in-law)
Gishmei Kaitz (Summer rains)	*Chiram* (king of Tyre)	*Hashmed* (destruction)
Hahar (the mountain)	*Chomat Magen* (defensive shield)	*Hatchala* (beginning, making a new start)
Hava'at Bikurim (offering of first fruits, an ancient custom)	*Chorev* (Horeb, name of a mountain)	*Kilshon* (pitchfork)
Invey Za'am (grapes of wrath)	*Dani* (Dan, one of the twelve tribes of Israel)	*Kitur* (siege)
Keshet Be'anan (rainbow through the clouds)	*Erez* (cedar is a metaphor for strength in the Bible)	*Matate* (broom)
Litani (name of a river)		*Mavet Lapolesh* (death to invader)
Makat Barak (lightning strike)	*Gideon* (biblical judge)	*Medina* (state)
Shamaim Kchulim (blue sky)	*Harel* (altar, also angel)	*Moked* (focus, focal point)
		Namal (port)
		Opera

Sheleg (snow)
Shirat Hatzaftzafa (singing of the poplar tree)
Suzana (rose, Shoshana in Hebrew)
Tarnegol (rooster)
Ya'el (ibex)
Yuval (river, stream)

Hava'at Bikurim (ancient custom of offering first fruits)
Kedem (east, also antiquity)
Keshet-Be'a'nan (a sign of God's promise to Noah and humanity)
Lot (Abraham's nephew)
Maccabi (Maccabean)
Mateh (rod, stick, and also a tribe)
Nachshon (biblical character, also: initiator, pioneer)
Pleshet (Philistine land)
Tevat-Noach (Noah's ark)
Yitzhak (Isaac, Abraham's son)
Ya'el (biblical heroine)
Yevusi (Jebusite)
Yiftach (biblical judge)
Yoav (King David's military commander)
Yonatan (Jonathan. Saul's son)
Yoram (biblical king)
Za'am Ha'el (wrath of God)

Uvda (fact)
Oz (courage)
Regel-Etz (wooden leg)
Sabena (name of an airline, involved in terrorist attacks by Palestinians and heroic rescue by Israel)
Sachar Holem (just reward, fair payment)
Shinuy Kivun (change of direction)
Shoter (policeman)
Tinok (baby)
Yekev (Wineyard)
Yemei-Tsuva (Days of Penitence. In the Jewish tradition: days of self-reflection)
Ytzuv (stabilization)

Table 3.3.   Examples of Names of Weapons in IDF Use, 1948–2008

| Weapons Manufactured in Israel | | Imported Weapons | |
Nature	Bible	Nature	Bible
Barak (lightning)	Barak (lightning)	Ayyt (eagle)	Romach (spear)
Dvora (bee)	Dlila (Delilah,	Baz (falcon)	
Kfir (young lion)	Samson's wife)	Dolphin	
Nachshol (breaker)	Dvora (Deborah, a biblical prophetess	Gal (wave)	
Namer (leopard)	and judge)	Karnaf (rhinoceros)	
Sa'ar (storm)	Gavriel (the angel	Netz (hawk)	
Nesher (eagle)	Gabriel)	Peten (desert cobra)	
Puma (puma)	Merkava (carriage or	Ra'am (thunder)	
Shaldag (kingfisher)	chariot)	Re'em (oryx)	
Shavit (comet)	Nimrod (name of a biblical hunter)	Sayfan (gladiolus)	
Shipon (rye)		Sufa (storm)	
		Tzefa (viper)	

In the second part of the analysis, I focused on how each of the *dominant semantic fields* activates the four *functions* of WND. Each name was analyzed separately. Next, all the names in each distinct semantic field were reviewed in order to identify the *functions* activated by the respective fields.

Nature

Naturalization: The use of names from the semantic field of *nature* conceptually turns military practices into common phenomena, as if they were an ordinary part of the normal chain of natural events. The name Operation First Rain (*Geshem Rishon*) for example, gives the impression that this operation is part of the regular cycle of the seasons. Operation Lightning Strike (*Makat Barak*) was used to refer to the fervor and speed displayed by Special Forces units when performing what was later considered a controversial series of "targeted killings" in the Gaza Strip.

Euphemization: Nature, as a semantic field, also provides endless references to beautiful, fascinating, and appealing phenomena. Names from this field include these examples: the Comet (*Shavit*), as well as the Rainbow (*Keshet*), and the Poplar's Song (*Shirat Hatzaftzafa*). When such names are applied to operations and weaponry, they bring to mind aesthetic and visually forceful events. Other names may evoke nature's power. Thus, we find armored vehicles called Puma (a quick, strong and lithe animal)[3] and heavily armored Jeeps called Storm (*Sufa*). We also find names such as Operation Snow (*Mivtza Sheleg*) which bring to mind the force of a snowstorm, and the cleanliness and purity of the color white. However, *sheleg* itself denotes more than the Hebrew word for snow, it is also the acronym of Operation Peace for the Galilee, the original name of the First Lebanon War; the name *Operation Snow* thus applies *naturalization* and *euphemization*.

Legitimization: In associating military practices with "nature," a name may suggest the event's inevitability—its uncontrollable progression according to the laws of nature. The *Lion (Lavi)* multi-billion-dollar jet fighter development project, initiated in the 1980s, falls into this category. The aircraft's name, *Lion*, implies that the struggle for survival in the Middle East is unavoidable, just like the one in nature. According to this analogy, which compares Israel to a lion, military superiority is a prerequisite for achieving and maintaining Israel's stature as "king of beasts." In this specific case, the reference is to aerial superiority. Clearly, such an analogy legitimizes any level of investment.[4]

Symbolic annihilation: Nature, in its pristine form is, as mentioned, uncontrollable. Hence, the application of names taken from this semantic field symbolically annihilates the volitional element of military practices, that is, the conscious decision making behind them. Therefore, this act averts allusions to human choice or responsibility in relation with the initiation of wars or their long-term consequences.

The Bible

Before beginning our discussion, it is important to stress that the efficient assignment of biblical names to military activities rests on widespread cultural resources going beyond rudimentary familiarity with the Old Testament (Shapira, 2005). Although Israel is not a theocracy, the majority of Jewish-Israelis, religious and secular alike, study the Bible for at least ten years, as a compulsory school subject. This semantic field clearly exploits deeply entrenched knowledge and connotations, ingrained by the state through the education system.

Biblical names are widely employed for *euphemization* due to the wealth of commonly known names associated with positive values and attributes and may also serve as allusions to a divine purpose. For example, Operation Yoav reminds one of the heroism of Yoav, King David's chief commander; the name Carriage or Chariot (*Merkava*), given to the IDF's main battle tank, alludes to the splendor of the Holy Chariot; Gabriel (*Gavriel*), the name of the Lord's archangel, adds a sense of radiance and mission to an Israeli missile.

Biblical names are also major carriers of *legitimization*. To illustrate, consider Operation Wrath of God (*Zaam Ha'el*), a covert operation directed at the killing of persons alleged to have been directly or indirectly involved in the massacre of Israeli athletes at the 1972 Munich Olympics.[5] Indeed, the phrase Wrath of God is absent from the Bible although each word (in Hebrew: *Zaam* and *Ha'el*) appears separately.

What is most remarkable about names originating in this semantic field in our context is the way in which the naming process combines *legitimization* with *naturalization*. Biblical names sustain the belief in the Jewish people's historic-religious right to the Land of Israel by implying that the current use of military power protects this "natural" right. The names of biblical heroes (*Yael, Barak, Bin Nun*, the previously mentioned *Yoav* and others), like those of biblical enemies (*Pleshet* [Philistine], *Yevusi* [Jebusite], or *Chiram* [King of Tyre]) strengthen this association.

Symbolic annihilation: Whereas turning to names from nature invites a sense of the unavoidable, biblical names such as the aforementioned Wrath of God, give a sense of divine purpose to operations, weaponry and soldiers who, as such names suggest, carry out their duty like missionaries committed to execute God's will. Such names therefore annihilate those aspects of military activities that may still be associated with human decision making and human choice.

FROM OPERATION PEACE FOR THE GALILEE TO
OPERATION CAST LEAD

Naming, and war-normalizing naming in particular, has *functions* that go beyond the four previously mentioned: euphemization, naturalization, legitimization, and symbolic annihilation. Therefore, to fully comprehend the process of naming, we are required to bear in mind the other linguistic structures and cultural connotations embodied in military names. In this section, I conduct an in-depth analysis of the two Israeli names which I found most interesting due to their complexity: Operation Peace for the Galilee and Operation Cast Lead.

Operation Peace for the Galilee

As mentioned, Operation Peace for the Galilee was the original official name given to the operation which begun with the IDF invasion of southern Lebanon in 1982 (see also Ish-Shalom, 2010). Although the active fighting lasted for three years, the Israeli forces finally left Lebanon only in the year 2000. The name itself embodied the operation's official objective: to bring peace to the Galilee—a region in northern Israel—which was threatened by PLO insurgent attacks. The official Knesset website states:[6]

> The invasion into Lebanese territory was intended for the destruction of the PLO's infrastructure in South Lebanon; the organization's bases were a source for Katyusha attacks towards Northern Israel and they housed terrorists that would infiltrate into Israel.

By referring to a region, Galilee, the name gives the impression that the fighting will take on the character of a local conflict. It implies that the war is not between Israel and Lebanon or between Israel and Syria, but a small-scale military action aimed at improving the welfare of a specific area, or at resolving a quarrel between two neighbors. However, this superficial interpretation is called into question the moment we begin critical analysis. First, the name Peace for the Galilee is an imprecise translation. The literal translation of the original name in Hebrew is Peace *of* Galilee (*Shalom Ha'galil*) rather than Peace *for the* Galilee (*Shalom La'galil*). In other words, the Hebrew version is calmer and more restrained in its implications of violence than is the English one: While the Hebrew name describes a desirable situation, the English name stresses the actions required for achieving this objective: "bringing" peace to Galilee (i.e., war).

Furthermore, the combination of the antithetical terms "peace" and "war" reverses the normative charge of the word "war."[7] This is not an Israeli invention (Kellner, 2007). In his essay *Politics and the English Language* (1946), George Orwell refers to some similar reversals with respect to the

terms "peace" and "pacification" as they arose in post-World War II discourse: "Defenseless villages are bombarded from the air, the inhabitants
driven out into the countryside, the cattle machine-gunned, the huts set on
fire with incendiary bullets: *This is called pacification*" [emphasis added].[8]

Inversion of traditional meanings was part of *Newspeak*, the language
Orwell developed later in his dystopian novel *1984* (1949). In the appendix
of this book, Orwell included an essay about *Newspeak*:

> NEWSPEAK was the official language of Oceania and had been devised to
> meet the ideological needs of Ingsoc, or English Socialism [. . .]. The purpose
> of Newspeak was not only to provide a medium of expression for the world-
> view and mental habits proper to the devotees of Ingsoc, *but to make all other
> modes of thought impossible*. [emphasis added][9]

Taking our cue from Orwell, we cannot contest the combination of "peace"
with "war." No one would argue that bringing peace is not a fair and legitimate national or military objective. The name Peace for the Galilee therefore
fulfills at least two of the four *functions* of WND, especially legitimization
and symbolic annihilation.

Operation Cast Lead

Operation Cast Lead (*Mivtza Oferet Yetzuka*) is the name given to a three-
week-long confrontation in the Gaza Strip that took place during the winter
of 2008–2009. On 27 December 2008, Israel launched a wave of air-strikes
against targets within the Gaza Strip in order to halt the rockets which had
been fired into southern Israel for many years. In response, Hamas intensified
its rocket attacks and their range.

Like the two wars in Lebanon (1982 and 2006), Operation Cast Lead
raised two central issues within the ongoing public debate. The first was the
operation's justification and legitimization, especially given the bad experience of the Second Lebanon War (2006) that had been waged only two years
earlier. The second issue referred to the justification of the operation's tac-
tics, especially the massive bombing of Gaza's civilian population and infrastructure. Was this truly an appropriate and proportional reaction to the harm
caused to Israel? In contrast to the First Lebanon War but similar to the
Second Lebanon War, large parts of Israel's civilian population became directly involved in the war. For the first time since 1948, major cities like
Ashdod (Israel's fifth-largest city in terms of population, situated only 30 km
south of Tel Aviv) were under attack. Hundreds of thousands of Israeli residents spent time in shelters or temporarily left their homes to escape the
ongoing rocket fire (an average of thirty-nine rockets was fired daily).

The war-normalizing name Operation Cast Lead reflected these challenges. The operation's name carries several connotations to Jewish culture

with the key overall connotation being the holiday of Hanukkah. It is important to note that most of these connotations are lost in the English name, thus a detailed discussion of the Hebrew name may be useful for the non-Hebrew speaker.

Hanukkah, also known as Festival of Lights, is an eight-day holiday commemorating the rededication of the Second Temple in Jerusalem at the time of the Maccabean Revolt against the Greeks (second century B.C.E.). Its main symbol is the menorah, which burned for eight days despite the one-day supply of oil; hence, it is a holiday devoted to the beauty of light. The holiday therefore combines the cultural memories of a religious miracle, the joy of Jewish activism and the national victory.

A fuller understanding of the name "Cast Lead" requires familiarity with the spinning top (*sevivon*), one of the traditional children's games played during Hanukkah. The spinning top symbolizes the miracles granted to the Jewish people during the rebellion. Several dedicated songs are traditionally sung every evening of the Hanukkah, one of the best known ones is "In Honor of Hanukkah" (*Lichvod HaChanuca*). Its lyrics were written by Hayim Nahman Bialik (1873–1934), a pioneer of modern Hebrew poetry, and include this verse: "Teacher bought a big top for me, Solid (*cast*) *lead*, the finest known"—which brings us back to the military operation. The name *cast lead* thus reminds us not only of the Lord's intervention on behalf of the Jews, but also of the innocence of a toy. In this sense, the Israeli name brings to mind the aforementioned Little Boy, the benign-sounding name given to the American atomic bomb dropped on Hiroshima.

In WND terminology, the name Operation Cast Lead *justified* national initiatives by creating a historical link between the brave victorious Maccabees and the IDF soldiers. Its reference to cast lead arouses faith in the IDF's power and, perhaps, in the nation's endurance. The name *euphemized* the military operation and the soldiers and *symbolically annihilated* some difficult questions regarding the war, its conduct, and its goals. We will return to these points in the coming section.

THE TERM "MILITARY OPERATION" IN HEBREW

The last three wars initiated by Israel, Operation Peace for the Galilee (the First Lebanon War), Operation Just Reward (or "Fair Payment" a literal translation of the Hebrew *Mivtza Sachar Holem*; the original name of the Second Lebanon War) and Operation Cast Lead raise one basic question: Why call a military action an "operation" if it is in fact (although not formally) a "war"? The answer rests on the precise meaning of the term "military operation" in the Israeli public discourse.

Generally speaking, in comparison to the term "war," the term "military operation" refers to a short term and confined military action. Within the context of our conceptual framework, the use of the term "operation" in place of "war" furthers WND, especially symbolic annihilation and legitimation. It diminishes the cognitive and emotional impact, by "de-dramatizing" the initiation of a new "war." Sometimes, the vagueness inherent in the word "operation" within the Israeli public discourse veers the discourse away from its volitional and preparatory aspects—those associated with policy and decision making. The term gives the impression of an ad-hoc counteraction rather than of a calculated process of long-term planning. Unlike the case of a war, political leaders may announce the launch of a new operation within a short space of time.

Put simply, the term "operation" dulls public awareness regarding an action's place in foreign policy and reduces potential criticism against the exploitation of military power. Worthy of note in this regard is the meaning of the term in the Israeli civil arena, where *mivtza* (operation) means the sale of goods for reduced prices for a short period of time, a "sale." If we assume that the direction of the term's movement was from the civilian to the military lexicon, then the brevity of the period of the "sale" blurs further the public perception of what a military operation really entails. With this in mind, we can now return to the examination of the three "operations" in question.

Operation Peace for the Galilee was declared at its onset as a limited military operation: the Israeli forces were meant to penetrate into Lebanon and stop up to 40 km from the northern ceasefire line with Lebanon, which was the farthest distance from which the firing of Katyusha rockets could threaten Israel. Yet, the original intentions regarding the operation's true scope and duration continue to be points of contention to this very day. In contrast, Operation Just Reward should have been named a "war" from its very beginning since it aimed to achieve far-reaching goals and its duration was essentially unlimited in time. Evidence for this conclusion is found in the major speech delivered by Prime Minister Ehud Olmert on 17 July 2006, the sixth day of the war:

> And in Lebanon, we will insist on compliance with the terms stipulated long ago by the international community, as unequivocally expressed only yesterday in the resolution by the 8 leading countries of the world:
> The return of the hostages, Ehud (Udi) Goldwasser and Eldad Regev;
> A complete cease fire;
> Deployment of the Lebanese army in all of Southern Lebanon;
> Expulsion of Hezbollah from the area [. . .].[10]

Only on 21 March 2007, seven months after the end of the war, and following a campaign of public criticism (especially by bereaved families), Israel's

Ministerial Committee for Symbols and Ceremonies has decided to rename the conflict according to its popular and more accurate name: the Second Lebanon War.

This discussion about the precise meaning of the term "military operation" does not serve merely for semantic or academic purposes. The following example is intended to dispel any doubts regarding the importance of a name or title: In the case of the Second Lebanon War, the Israeli government approved the plan of the "operation" as presented by top military echelons after a discussion which only lasted three hours (Zisser, 2009: 301). Had the action been called a "war" rather than an "operation," it seems unlikely that the debate would have ended so quickly, or that the public would have accepted the decision with such equanimity.

Rapaport (2007: 36–39) also pointed out some of the implications of the name "operation" on the government's process of decision making:

> During its meeting on the night of 12 July [2006], which began shortly after a hurried debate on security, led by Olmert, the Israeli government fulfilled its traditional role as a rubber stamp. [. . .] Few if any understood the collective responsibility resting on their shoulders as a government sending the IDF on a broad mission, even if the word "war" was not specifically mentioned. [. . .] The ministers had unanimously sent the IDF to war without understanding what they had done.

The Winograd Commission[11] likewise referred to the tragic outcomes of the vague definition of the Second Lebanon War:

> We are investigating the conduct of the war that Israel concluded with a victory that can be considered ambiguous, contrary to the judgments of those who managed it on behalf of the military. A central factor contributing to this outcome was the fact that up to, and even after, the fighting, there was no explicit determination, accepted throughout the IDF command that this was indeed a state of war, which is governed by a different set of rules from those guiding the conduct of ongoing yet intensive security actions, or of military operation. This lack of internalization among the military and political ranks regarding the nature of the situation they were contending with was responsible for the series of decisions made by commanding officers that together contributed to the war's illusive outcome. This ambiguity continued despite the position taken by many at the very early stages of the conflict that the IDF was indeed engaged in a war. Their allegations did not, however, provide the foundations for the transmission of precise instructions and the taking of appropriate actions.[12]

In this particular case, the war-normalizing intent behind the name given to the war not only missed its mark regarding the prevention of public criticism, but actually revealed the mechanism of naming itself, and the danger it presents, because of the confusion it had created in political and military upper echelons.

Now that we have completed our description of the complexity surrounding the term "operation" in Israeli discourse, we may turn to some cross-cultural aspects of military naming.

THE GLOBAL DISCURSIVE MARKET OF MILITARY NAMES[13]

This analysis of a corpus of Israeli military names, has in fact presented some concrete and methodological principles which may be applied to military naming practices in various contexts. A detailed list of names of military operations executed throughout the world since World War I is accessible at the click of a mouse ("List of military operations" from Wikipedia).

To demonstrate our method's universal applicability, several names have arbitrarily been chosen from the list "American military operations in Central America and the Caribbean (1951–1983)" found in the cited database. They include the following names: Fortune, Success, Golden Pheasant, Just Cause, Acid Gambit, Bushmaster, Sand Flea, Mongoose, Northwoods, Waverider, Peter Pan, Phibriglex, Power Pack, and Urgent Fury. Some semantic fields are easy to identify: animals (Golden Pheasant, Sand Flea, Mongoose), games (Gambit is a chess move) and characters/heroes from children' stories and comics (Peter Pan and Bushmaster). Two names may be classified as belonging to the semantic field of positive values (Fortune, Success).

Clearly, this sample is only presented here as a demonstration. It obviously does not permit the identification of all the dominant semantic fields employed, nor does it provide an analysis of the *functions* they activate. A significantly wider list of names would be required for such purposes (a full list of the American military operations throughout the world in any specific period or area). However, one of the most important factors in such a study would be adequate familiarity with American culture and history in addition to, for example, some knowledge of Caribbean culture and history. Once a full list of names would be compiled, a knowledgeable researcher could apply procedures similar to those used in the research presented here.

Lacking such a list and such information, I shall limit myself to pointing out some possible directions for future research of military naming practices in other cultures:

1. What are the *dominant semantic fields* used in the specific military naming conventions?
2. Do these *dominant semantic fields* activate the four *functions* of WND?
3. If not, what are the alternative principles involved?

4. If *symbolic annihilation* is practiced, what undesired components of military practices are these names meant to annihilate? (Consider the following possibilities: difficult consequences of the military practice, the division of legal responsibility between the political and the military, moral aspects associated with the use of such practices and so forth).

5. How does the local cultural apparatus impact the particular mechanisms involved in war-normalizing naming?

CONCLUSION

This chapter has focused on the Israeli discourse and has demonstrated that a considerable proportion of names in the Israeli military sphere are derived from two dominant semantic fields: Nature and the Bible. By assigning names from these semantic fields, the War-Normalizing naming activates the four *functions* of WND: Naturalization, Euphemization, Legitimization, and Symbolic Annihilation. These *functions* were used to depict the respective military practices as natural, positive and legitimate. Furthermore, such military names implied that those military practices were the result of the laws of nature, or the continuation of ancient traditions—and those two conceptions have contributed to the formation of a cultural ethos in Israel regarding the use of military power. In so doing, the names effectively "annihilated" considerations of those military activities' potentially negative physical, emotional, moral, and economical outcomes, as well as the contemplation of the possibility of asking questions related to human choices, decisions and assignment of responsibility concerning them.

It is reasonable to assume that for most people, military practices such as direct engagement or weaponry development and purchasing represent impenetrable and mysterious "black boxes." On the intuitive level, military actions with names like Operation Fountain of Youth are more likely to win public support than would actions with names like Beside a Young Soldier's Grave. From a different perspective, a war-normalizing naming may facilitate the penetration of the militaristic spirit into the civil arena and act as a vehicle for indirect influence. As an illustration, consider two Israeli practices: field trips made by high school students to military camps and outposts; and visits by high-ranking officers in schools for the purpose of recounting their military experiences in a positive light. As might be expected, the blatancy of such practices has indeed provoked criticism among parents and the public in general. In contrast, the subtle inculcation of positive attitudes toward the use of military power, perhaps the main purpose of military naming, has not aroused any critical public debate.

A comparison with the naming of streets may help clarify the force of war-normalizing naming. It is interesting to note that decisions over street names generally result from struggles between political actors intending to incise references to their ideologies or achievements, while the military has a monopoly over the naming of its own practices. Yet, both processes have much in common. They both shape the national collective memory (Pinchevski & Torgovnik, 2002), and both are "means of introducing history into social communication" (Azaryahu, 1996, 1997; Bar-Gal, 1987, 1989). Although everybody uses both street names and military names, it is essential to bear in mind that "hardly anyone pays attention [. . .] to the fact that they [the names] are associated with structures of power" (Azaryahu, 1996: 327). Both practices therefore enable "official" versions of history to penetrate the public's consciousness and speech.

NOTES

1. An earlier version of chapter 3 has been published in *Armed Forces and Society*, 36(5), 825–46: Gavriely-Nuri, Dalia (2010). *Rainbow, Snow, and the Poplar's Song: The "Annihilative Naming" of Israeli Military Practices.* http://afs.sagepub.com/search/results?fulltext= gavriely&x=0&y=0&submit=yes&journal_set=spafs&src=selected&andorexactfulltext=and. All rights reserved. © 2010 Sage Journals.

2. A list of Israeli operations is available at Wikipedia website (Hebrew version): '*Mivtza'ei Tzva Hagana Le'Israel*' [IDF military operations]. To confirm the validity of the Wikipedia website, I compared it with the official website of the IDF spokesperson and various Israeli military units, encyclopedias and lexicons pertaining to the IDF. The non-Hebrew reader can use the Wikipedia list of Israeli operations: http://en.wikipedia.org/wiki/List_of_military_ operations.

3. Indeed, the significance of *puma*, like that of most military names, is at least partly cultural-dependent. While for Israelis the Puma is a beautiful, quick and elegant animal, in other cultures, the puma is first and foremost a predator.

4. The Israeli government eventually concluded it could not finance completion of the aircraft's development independently, especially after being pressured by the US government to cancel a project that would compete with American weaponry exports.

5. The operation was depicted in Steven Spielberg's *Munich* (2005).

6. www.knesset.gov.il/main/heb/home.asp .

7. In another article, I claim that the word *peace* is an integral part of the Israeli just war rhetoric, a phenomenon that can be termed: Peace in the Service of War (PSW). See: Gavriely-Nuri (forthcoming).

8. www.mtholyoke.edu/acad/intrel/orwell46.htm.

9. "The Principles of Newspeak" available at:
www.newspeakdictionary.com/ns-prin.html.

10. Zisser (2009: 300) described Olmert's objections related in that speech, as being "very ambitious."

11. The Winograd Commission, The commission of inquiry into the events of military engagement in Lebanon 2006, is an Israeli government-appointed commission of inquiry which investigated and drew conclusions from the Second Lebanon War. The Commission harshly criticized key decision-makers, especially Prime Minister Eud Olmert, Defence Minister Amir Peretz, and Chief of Staff Dan Halutz. Many public figures called upon Olmert and Peretz to resign.

12. Translated by the author from the Hebrew version.

13. On the term "global discursive market," see chapters 1 and 2.

Chapter Four

War-Normalizing Framing

Wounded Soldiers on Israeli Television during the Second Lebanon War[1]

In the summer of 2006 Israel has initiated a war against Hezbollah—a Shi'a Muslim militant group based in Lebanon. During the 33 days of the war, more than 600 Israeli soldiers have been wounded and more than 2,000 Israeli citizens injured. This chapter explores another war-normalizing strategy, called the *war-normalizing framing*. It focuses on video clips of wounded Israeli soldiers and civilians, which were broadcast during the main news programs by the three networks of Israeli television.

Television is a crucial player in the struggle over the legitimacy of war. This is especially true in the case of the initiation of a new war. Television is "a form of public sphere [. . .], providing media publics with the opportunity to make judgments and deliberate over issues of common interest" (Chouliaraki, 2004: 130). For the majority of the public, news is the key source of information about war, and thus the ways in which it constructs the framing of war and battles have special importance (Wolfsfeld, et al., 2008: 402). "Framing" is referred to here as a *discursive element* that guides people toward "seeing" and interpreting an event in a particular way.

The topics of "framing" and "media framing" have evoked intensive research during the last decade (e.g., Bennett & Livingston, 2003; Bennet, Lawrence, & Livingston, 2006; Lakoff, 2004; McCombs & Ghanem, 2001; Reese, 2007; Scheufele & Tewksbury, 2007). Robert Entman, one of the leading exponents of framing analysis, depicts the key role of framing in the perception and interpretation of various aspects of reality:

Framing is an omnipresent process in politics and policy analysis. It involves
selecting a few aspects of a perceived reality and connecting them together in a
narrative that promotes a particular interpretation. Frames can perform up to
four functions: define problems, specify causes, convey moral assessments,
and endorse remedies [. . .] frames introduce or enhance the availability and
apparent importance of certain ideas for evaluating a political object. (Entman,
2010: 391; see also: Entman, 1993, 2003, 2004)

Many studies demonstrate how media framing constructs, shapes, and filters
reality while ignoring alternative or contrasting information (e.g. Chong &
Druckman, 2007; D'Angelo, 2002; Gamson & Herzog, 1999; Liebes & First,
2003; Reese, 2007; Vliegenthart & Roggeband, 2007; De Vreese, 2004). In
the sphere of news production, editors and journalists play key roles when
choosing a frame. Peri (2005:117) identifies three factors that influence journalists and editors in this process, arguing that these factors make their
choices more effective and less costly: first, frames are chosen according to
recommendations by politicians who are primary sources for information and
interpretation; second, frames are chosen according to the process of media
production and how they fit in it ("the logic of the media"); and third, frames
are chosen based on the audience's cultural infrastructure. In this chapter, I
shall focus on the first and last factors: the political and cultural motivations
for choosing a specific frame.

The main argument of this chapter is that the dominant framing that the
Israeli television used in its coverage of wounded soldiers during the Second
Lebanon War was a war-normalizing framing. A war-normalizing framing
activates one or more of the four *functions* of WND. This chapter will focus
on three specific issues:

1. How does *war-normalizing framing* work?
2. What are the specific components of the military practices it was
   meant to "normalize"?
3. How does a nation's cultural apparatus sustain the war-normalizing
   framing?

The typical television framing of wounded Israeli soldiers during the war is
referred to as the *Hero Code*—normally a short video clip emphasizing the
endurance of the wounded soldier and the medical staff's flawless teamwork.
At the same time, the *Hero Code* conceals any harsh pictures exposing bleeding organs, the suffering of the injured, and the disorder and confusion surrounding them while they are treated. In our terminology, the *Hero Code* is a
war-normalizing framing aimed mostly at euphemization and symbolic annihilation. The analysis of several *cultural codes* regarding the concept of the
Israeli soldier will show that the *Hero Code* also serves the *function* of
legitimization.

The analysis of the framing of wounded soldiers used in the news during the Second Lebanon War will also expose WND's silent power, which is yet to be discussed. We will see that the ability of WND to influence public opinion is mainly derived from its silent, latent properties. Even professional journalists, who are aware of the euphemistic character of the images of wounded soldiers, are not truly aware of WND's manipulative power. Being "invisible" is what makes WND a sophisticated cognitive-cultural mechanism for legitimizing war.

Many studies have paid much analytical attention to the role of journalism in times of war and crisis (Liebes, 1997; Neiger & Zandberg, 2004; Wolfsfeld, 1997, 2004; Wolfsfeld, et al., 2008; Zandberg & Neiger, 2005). Such studies have regarded the coverage of war and crisis as the acid test of government-media relations (Peri, 2005) and an extreme test of the role of journalism in a given society (Allan & Zelizer, 2004; Liebes & Frosh, 2006). This chapter will explore the media's role in times of war from a stance of critical discourse analysis and from a cultural perspective, and shall thus complete the picture using a less common perspective.

MEDIA COVERAGE DURING THE SECOND LEBANON WAR

The media coverage of war, warriors and battles—especially in visual images—is not only a critical prism through which the policy surrounding war is criticized; frequently, it is also in itself the target of public criticism. There is a common Hebrew phrase, originally coined on the first day of the First Lebanon War (1982), regarding the appropriate code of conduct for the media to adopt during wartime: "Silence, we are shooting." It reflects the idea or expectation that during battles, the media should take part in the national effort, and support the leaders by postponing criticism until the battles' end. Thus, achieving balance between patriotism and criticism, "between nation and profession" (Neiger, et al., 2010: 391; Zandberg & Neiger, 2005) is not a simple mission. Because of the special power of visual coverage, i.e., photographs and video clips (Anden-Papadopoulos, 2008; Hariman & Lucaites, 2003; Howe, 2002; Sylvester & Huffman, 2005), such a balance may become even more difficult to attain. In a discussion on the effect of the Abu Ghraib photographs, Anden-Papadopoulos (2008: 6) wrote:

> The photographs have themselves come to function as a critical prism through which elite and popular views on U.S. foreign policy are refracted, in the sense that the heretofore banned sight of American troops in the role of sadistic torturers has become an integral part of our understanding of the Bush administration's "war on terror."

The Second Lebanon War (2006) had begun with huge public support. Yet, by the time it ended it was widely criticized, mainly because of the way it was conducted. The finger of blame was directed at political and military leaders, but press and television writers were not spared either. Two opposing accusations were made against the Israeli media: that of being overly patriotic and that of not being patriotic enough. On the one hand, the media were accused of contributing to the creation of public euphoria on the first days of the war by only partially reporting what was really going on in Lebanon (The Dorner Committee Report, p. 9, below; see also Witztum, 2006). On the other hand, the public strongly criticized reports that had published the exact locations hit by Hezbollah missiles, reports which were later believed to provide the enemy with important intelligence information. This wave of accusations led to the submission of numerous complaints to the Israel Press Council. The criticisms accusing the media of providing intelligence information peaked following a report in one of the daily newspapers, which revealed that a thousand soldiers were parked next to a college in the small northern settlement Kfar Giladi. A day after the publication of the report, Hezbollah bombed the college, killing twelve soldiers and wounding many more.

Soon after the war ended, The Dorner Committee was established with the mandate to devise an ethical code to be followed by journalists during war. The Dorner Committee Report surveyed the long history of the Jewish-Israeli press since the British Mandate (1918–1948) and concluded: "Today the media are no longer insignificant, as they were before, to the government and the army, even in non-emergency cases" (p. 12).

A more balanced position was presented by IDF Spokesperson (during the war) Brigadier General Miri Regev in her testimony before the committee:

> The IDF understands that the media act as a live show arena, one that operates 24 hours a day. We adopt a policy of openness toward the media, within the limits of maintaining national security and safeguarding human life. (The Dorner Committee Report, p. 12)

In contrast to those positive evaluations that emphasize the freedom of the Israeli press during wartime, a July 2007 study by *Keshev* ("The Center for the Protection of Democracy") which analyzed about 9,000 news items published and broadcasted during the war stated:

> Except in a few isolated cases [. . .] the major Israeli media that covered the war were almost completely enlisted [. . .]. From time to time, alongside this support, emerged criticisms of the tactical elements in the conduct of the war, and those criticisms intensified as it became clear that the IDF could not win.

> But the wind that generally blew from the coverage of the war [. . .] was
> clearly non-critical, from the beginning of the war to its end. (p. 5)

Analyzing The Hero Code as a war-normalizing framing can help us see how
this *cultural code* helps the news channels report bad news (e.g., wounded
soldiers) in a way that is professional on the one hand, yet does not under-
mine the national morals on the other. In this way, it helps bridge the gap
between "nation and profession."

MEDIA COVERAGE OF THE WOUNDED SOLDIERS

Principles of Analysis

This research is based on an analysis of a corpus consisting of forty-seven
video clips of wounded soldiers and civilians televised in the news programs
broadcasted by the three main channels of Israeli television: 1, 2, and 10,
during the Second Lebanon War and during the years 1996–1997.[2] In the
first stage of the study, two groups of items were defined:

1. *Coverage of wounded soldiers* (twenty-four video clips). This group
   includes clips that were photographed during the Second Lebanon
   War, with a subgroup of clips collected from those televised ten years
   earlier, from 1996–1997.
2. *Coverage of citizens wounded during terror acts* (twenty-three video
   clips). This category contains short items broadcasted in parallel periods (2006, 1996–1997).

The analysis of each item was guided by Matthes and Kohring's (2008)
Cluster Analysis of Frame Elements. The research focused on the distinctive
dominant elements repeatedly used in the television coverage of wounded
soldiers as opposed to those used in the coverage of wounded civilians.
Considering the medium, that is, television, the research focused on those
components which formed the *audio-visual* thematic structure of the frames,
as well as on more basic components like "plot" and "heroes" (Howe, 2002;
Griffin, 2004; Griffin & Lee, 1995; King & Lester, 2005).

Using these analytical principles, the second stage of the research rated
each item (clip) from groups (1) and (2) separately according to seven elements:

1. Time and place of the event
2. Hero/main character: Israeli soldier or civilian
3. Other characters
4. Plot

5. Atmosphere and sound
6. Photographic technique
7. Typical accessories

Hero Code versus Victim Code

The comparison between the two different groups of video clips exposed a
binary encoding system—with wounded soldiers on the one hand and
wounded citizens on the other. While television coverage of wounded soldiers (during the years 1996–1997 and 2006) correlated quite considerably
with the *Hero Code*, items covering wounded civilians during the same time
periods complied with what will be referred to here as the *Victim Code*. This
was true whether the clips were produced by the state-owned Israel Broadcasting Channel (IBA Channel 1) or the commercial channels (Channel 2 and
Channel 10). Let us now focus on the components of these two codes.

The *Hero Code* is a short clip, usually less than one minute long. Its main
features are:

1. *Time and place*: A landing strip, usually at the Rambam Hospital—
    northern Israel's main hospital situated in Haifa, which treats all
    wounded soldiers from the northern front.
2. *Hero/main character*: A wounded soldier. The hero usually lies on a
    stretcher, appears calm or even asleep, normally with his eyes closed.
    He is covered with a blanket that conceals his injuries and is usually
    connected to a mobile infusion apparatus.
3. *Other characters*: A medical crew and soldiers, carrying or transport-
    ing the stretcher. A large label reading "paramedic" appears on the
    backs of the uniforms of some medical crew members. Very skilled
    staff is seen displaying a clearly visible high level of teamwork.
4. *Plot*: A rescue or, more precisely, an evacuation scene. It usually starts
    with a rescue helicopter landing on the hospital's airstrip. The
    wounded soldier is then taken out of the helicopter and through the
    entrance of the trauma unit of the hospital.
5. *Atmosphere and sound*: Apparent calm, an atmosphere contradicting
    the actions observed in the scene which normally shows the medical
    staff racing against time to save the wounded. The wounded soldier is
    very quiet. No voices are heard, nor are there any sounds coming from
    the urban environment in which the hospital is located. Sounds of
    helicopter propellers may puncture the silence. The pastoral atmos-
    phere is strengthened by focusing on natural elements, such as the sea
    and the sky.
6. *Photographic technique*: The long shot. The last picture is usually a
    fade-out of a helicopter flying against the background of a blue sky.

7. *Typical accessories*: A helicopter, the Israeli flag, uniforms, rank insignia and helmets. There is minimal medical equipment. The camera frame also captures natural objects, such as the sea, the sky, rocks, a hillside, and vegetation.

To complete the analysis of the *Hero Code*, we need to mention one popular scene that essentially realizes the main plot of this code, the evacuation scene. The evacuation scene is frequently followed by another scene televised on the next day's news: the happy-ending scene. This scene, a sequel to the previous day's coverage, is meant to prove that the soldier's rapid evacuation was a success and that the professional medical staff was able to save his life. In the sequel, the wounded soldier sits or lies comfortably on his hospital bed, dressed in civilian hospital pajamas (Israel does not maintain exclusive military hospitals). In contrast to the evacuation scene, the soldier is now shown talking and smiling; his face is also shown (zoom shot). Sometimes a fresh bandage is visible (e.g., a head bandage or a cast on his broken leg), but the general atmosphere transmits the message of an improved condition. Another repetitive element in the happy-ending scene is the visit of a high-ranking officer (sometimes, the chief of staff), or senior politician (such as the minister of defense). A short conversation is held before the camera. The visitors ask the soldier how he feels and inquire about some details concerning the circumstances of the injury. The soldier readily and easily cooperates. Despite his painful wounds, he does not complain; he is a true hero. Finally, the soldier shakes hands with his visitor as the camera cuts to another site, often the television studio.

An extreme example for the *Hero Code* is an exceptional item of television coverage of wounded soldiers. On 11 August 2006, during the course of the Second Lebanon War, Tomer Bohadana, a platoon commander in the IDF's Paratroopers Brigade, was seriously injured. All television channels broadcasted the pictures of his transfer to a rescue helicopter as well as all the daily newspapers, which featured them the following day. What was unusual about the scene was that he was photographed with his injuries clearly visible to the cameras. Despite his serious injuries, Bohadana was shown with his hand raised in a "V" sign of victory as the field surgeon clamped his hand on a haemorrhaging vein, an act that saved the soldier's life (after the scene was shot, Bohadana lost consciousness for thirty-six hours). Still, it appears that even in those unusual circumstances, the television networks continued to apply the *Hero Code*: The bleeding soldier was depicted before the cameras as both resourceful and resolute. The same was true for the field surgeon, who responded to the situation perfectly, just as the *Hero Code* predicted. A couple of days later, various media channels broadcasted another video clip of Bohadana. This time, Bohadana was sitting up in his hospital bed, typing on his laptop. This was the ultimate proof of victory: the victory of Bohadana the survivor and of the medical staff that saved his life. Tomer Bohadana became a national hero, with his picture immediately entering the national album as one of the purest symbols of the spirit of IDF's fighting during the Second Lebanon War.

The *Victim Code*, like the *Hero Code*, is also a short clip, but rather than a continuous plot, it is usually shown in staccato-like fragments, each running for no more than a couple of seconds:

1. *Time and place*: Wounded civilians are photographed at the site of their injury: a city's main street or a quiet neighborhood next to a bombed house, or in a hospital corridor after evacuation.
2. *Hero/main character*: An ordinary Israeli person: an old woman, a student, or a middle-aged man or woman. The victim's clothes are torn, with blood clotted on parts of their bodies and sometimes on their faces. The victim is frightened, confused, often panicked, and shouting for help.
3. *Other characters*: Mainly civilians standing or thronging about the victim; some are wounded, most are passive onlookers. Sometimes a policeman is shown, attempting to impose order. Hospital orderlies or rescue personnel occasionally appear at the camera frame's edges.
4. *Plot*: A string of events that brutally interrupt the routine of the ordinary life of an innocent person. The perfectly functioning medical crew, if shown, represents a subplot, an interior drama. The main story is that of the injured person and his attempt at coping with an externally imposed, sudden, and harsh reality.
5. *Atmosphere and sound*: Pictures taken from the bombed location show confused, helpless people seeking aid amid the rubble and chaos. The sounds heard are those of people often hysterically crying and shouting. Fear and insecurity are pervasive. Sometimes, the siren of an arriving ambulance is seen or heard.[3]
6. *Photographic technique*: Close-ups of faces and the victim's injured body; the devastated site.
7. *Typical accessories*: Blood, damaged personal belongings, torn clothing, and urban elements, such as buildings, cars, and pavements.

It is easy to see that the main difference between the *Hero Code* and the *Victim Code* is that the former "annihilates" the harsh aspects of the wounded soldiers. Why is the framing of the wounded soldiers an "annihilating framing"? More generally, why use two different codes in the news for the coverage of soldiers and civilians? Of the three explanations proposed, two are embedded in the characteristics of the media process—the technical aspect and the ethical dimension, whereas the third locates the *Hero Code* as an Israeli *cultural code* that is part of WND.

WHY IS THE FRAMING OF WOUNDED SOLDIERS AN "ANNIHILATING FRAMING"?

A. The Technical Explanation

Israeli soldiers are usually injured in the military arena, which is normally a special sphere, closed to all civilians, including journalists. In order to cover war-related battles and events, reporters and photographers need to obtain special permission from the military. Moreover, although battlefield injuries are certainly not unexpected, their exact location cannot be predicted. However, as aforementioned, the Israeli hospitals that treat wounded soldiers are civilian hospitals, and are therefore not closed military zones. As a result, the first place where reporters and photographers may meet the wounded soldiers is generally the hospital landing strip, and only at that moment can the broadcasting begin. Naturally, the first picture received by news editors is that of the rescue helicopter landing, a significant component of the *Hero Code*. However, this technical explanation of the *Hero Code* relates only to the time and place of the coverage. It does not explain the other components of the *Hero Code*, such as the systematic representation of order and control, an element that we refer to as creating the broadcast scene's "atmosphere" (element 5).

An interesting demonstration of the limits of this explanation was found in a rare, unedited video clip of wounded soldiers.[4] The event was a suicide bomb attack against soldiers waiting to hitchhike at a major intersection near Ashkelon on the morning of the February 25, 1996. Ashkelon is a relatively large city in Israeli terms. Since the event occurred in a civil space rather than a closed military zone, the television crew was able to begin filming the soldiers a few minutes after they had sustained injuries, exactly as in cases of wounded civilians. The unedited clip revealed elements that strongly contradict the *Hero Code* guiding military coverage: We could see the face of a wounded soldier with blood on his bandaged hand, blood dripping from the leg of another soldier, the frustration of waiting for the helicopter, the confusion until the medical staff person succeeded in connecting an infusion bag to the stretcher and the slow, chaotic evacuation. The footage shown on the special "breaking news" program broadcast at noon of the same day, a couple of hours after the event, indicated massive editing and presented the events in a very different light. In our terms, the video clip of the event clearly presented an activation of the familiar *Hero Code*.[5]

B. The Legal and Ethical Explanation

The publication of photographs in the Israeli press is regulated by the *Prohibition of Defamation Law*, the *Basic Law on Human Dignity and Freedom*, and Military Censorship regulations. No written or unwritten agreement was negotiated between military journalists and the IDF during the Second Lebanon War. By contrast, embedded journalists covering the activities of the U.S. Armed Forces are restrained by certain agreements regulating their work.[6] However, in order to enter a military sector or interview and photograph soldiers, permission does have to be issued by the Military Censor and the IDF Spokesperson.[7] "There is considerable competition over what little the IDF permits; hence, military journalists generally avoid confrontations with the IDF Spokesperson."[8] In addition, article 9A of the *Rules of Professional Ethics of Journalism* (Israel Press Council, 1996) states that:

> A newspaper and a journalist shall not publish the name, photograph, or other identifying details of a person who has died or who has been seriously injured in a war, accident, or other disaster, prior to information of the death or injury of the said person being brought to the knowledge of his next of kin by an authorized person, unless there are exceptional circumstances of public interest in immediate publication.

In the same vein, the report of the aforementioned Dorner Committee includes the following recommendation: "Respecting human rights and the right of privacy demands a prohibition against close-up photographs of wounded people" (p. 29).

The last two ethical restrictions do not differentiate between civilians and soldiers, yet our examination of the respective television coverage indicates the discriminatory *application* of those restrictions. In order to explain this behavior, we turn to WND.

C. The Discursive-Cultural Explanation: War-Normalizing Framing

The third explanation for the difference between the *Hero Code* and the *Victim Code* is the conscious or unconscious desire of journalists to "normalize" the concept of wounded soldiers, that is, to represent wounded soldiers as a minor disturbance to normal life. The *Hero Code* as a part of WND fulfills three of its four *functions*:

1. *Euphemization*: The *Hero Code* emphasizes the medical staff's flawless teamwork, and to an even greater extent, euphemizes the Israeli soldiers. Bodies of Israeli soldiers represent more than just the bodies of the individual soldiers, they become symbols. In order to understand this, a short survey of Israeli *cultural codes* regarding the concept of the male body is required. The cultural construction of the Israeli male body has accompanied the Zionist ethos since its formulation at the beginning of the twentieth century (Gluzman, 2007; Lubin, 2001; Yosef, 2001). While the Diaspora Jew had stereotypically been

depicted as weak, passive, and submissive, the new Israeli Jew—*the Sabra* depicted in Zionist ideology—more closely resembled the ancient Roman and Greek physical ideal: slender and flexible; tall and tanned; healthy, happy, and attuned to nature (Almog, 2000). The Sabra is ideologically motivated: He wishes to protect Israel's existential presence, and he is willing to sacrifice his life for that goal. The late Israeli Prime Minister Yitzchak Rabin, for example, was considered as one of the first in a line of ultimate Sabras. The perfect incarnation of the Sabra has come to be represented by the Israeli soldier. Israeli television attempts to preserve this myth of the perfect Israeli male body, and in effect intends to preserve its associated cultural and historic ethos, through the application of the *Hero Code*.

2. *Legitimization*: The *Hero Code*, together with the *Victim Code*, are two complementary parts of the same equation, which sustains and justifies the use of military power. The *Victim Code* emphasizes civilian victims and their suffering. Such exposure of civilian wounds and suffering implicitly points to the threat or danger that causes these wounds. Thus, the *Victim Code* sustains the ideological justification for the existence of a strong IDF to protect the citizens. At the same time, the *Hero Code* legitimizes the use of military power, demonstrating the relatively low cost of using this power.

3. *Symbolic annihilation*: Harsh pictures—exposing bleeding organs, the personal suffering of the injured, and the mess and confusion surrounding the care of the injured—are excluded from the *Hero Code*. The wounded soldiers, usually eighteen to twenty years old, have personally paid a huge price for the war, usually both physically and mentally. The injury does not end on the landing strip at the Hospital, as is usually depicted in the *Hero Code*, nor does it end in the above-mentioned "happy ending" scene a couple of days after the injury had been sustained. Frequently, for the wounded soldier the rehabilitation period is long, painful, and depressing. Omission of these difficult aspects of the cost paid by the individual soldiers is just one aspect of the symbolic annihilation. The *Hero Code* also prevents discussion over the basic underlying questions concerning the situation: How did the injury occur? Was the battle, or even the entire war, unavoidable? Above all, did the political and military leaders do their best to prevent such events in particular, and the war in general, from happening? The *Hero Code* completely ignores these questions, which are especially important with regard to wars initiated by Israel itself.

CONCLUSION

Understanding the *Hero Code* as part of WND enables us to see some interesting cultural aspects of WND that have not yet been discussed. I argue that
the *Hero Code* is so deeply established in the Israeli culture that sometimes,
the Israeli audience needs only one picture of a helicopter and a soldier to
conjure up the *Hero Code* in its entirety. For example, on July 20, 2006, in
the midst of the war, a picture was published in the most popular Israeli news
website *Ynet*, with a caption underneath it which read: "The evacuation of
wounded soldiers to Rambam Hospital this morning." In fact, the picture
showed no wounded soldier at all, only a helicopter (just before landing) and
three soldiers waiting on the landing strip at the hospital, one of whom was
speaking on his cell phone. I claim that by applying the *framing* of the *Hero
Code*, the reader is able to complete the missing details and "see" the
wounded soldiers although they are missing from the picture.

Moreover, I argue that the special power of the *Hero Code* as both a
cultural code and a war-normalizing framing, as well as the power of the
whole WND in general, is enhanced by the fact that the public is mostly
unaware of their existence. The indirect mechanisms of WND, in this case,
the *Hero Code*, intensify the normalizing message. In other words, the *Hero
Code*, like other latent war-normalizing strategies, is more effective precisely
because it is a "code" rather than a "full story."

Understanding the *Hero Code* as part of WND brings us back to our
former discussion about the public's expectation from the media during wartime to balance between "nation and profession." While a central part of the
public's criticism of the coverage of the Second Lebanon War was for being
overly patriotic (see also: Elliott & Elliott, 2003; Sylvester & Huffman,
2005), nobody complained about the activation of the euphemistic *Hero
Code*. In other words, sophisticated media attempts to influence public opinion by making use of latent codes like the *Hero Code*—an "overly patriotic"
type of coverage—were completely missed by the public, journalists and
scholars, and even by the specialists in The Dorner Committee and *Keshev*. It
appears that the Israeli media act as hidden or even unconscious agents of
WND by activating self-censorship which prevents sharp criticism of the
war. An interview with Colonel Ofer Kol, Media Head of the IDF Spokesperson's Unit, conducted two years after the Second Lebanon War (September 2, 2008) demonstrates the extent to which the *Hero Code* is part of the
Israeli ethos. Kol honestly stated:

> I assume that newspaper files contain photographs of wounded soldiers that
> have never been televised nor published. Why does this happen? Because they
> are everyone's sons. And if they are everyone's sons, we behave toward them
> as if they were our sons. Perhaps the media do not publish them in order to

protect morale. I think the public would be greatly irritated if they saw wounded soldiers in any condition other than bandaged. These are acts of self-censorship committed by the reporters themselves [. . .], the media understand that soldiers are special.

Within the analysis of WND, one more question may be raised: Is war-normalizing framing a general *discursive strategy* used beyond the case of wounded soldiers? The war-normalizing framing is also applied in the work of Israeli Air Force pilots, the most prestigious of all military specialties. Israeli television channels frequently show highly stylized video clips taken from a bomber's cockpit. These clips might show a target (for example, a building), but only from a bird's eye view: What the audience sees is a small dark "spot," which "disappears" following precision bombing. As in the case of the *Hero Code*, the televised coverage sterilizes the events by annihilating any hint of human suffering or any other damage. Similarly to the *Hero Code* and its emphasis on positive values such as bravery and friendship, the coverage of the aerial bombing demonstrates the positive dimensions of the topic: the professionalism and technological sophistication of the pilots rather than the destructive outcomes (the framing of aerial bombing will be covered in greater detail in the next chapter). In this last context, it is interesting to note that the Israeli television is not alone: during the first Gulf War, the photographs in the United States and European press were mainly of military technology (Machin, 2007: 124). These images reflected the importance of the superiority and precision of American technology (Griffin, 2004), while hiding the true role of the aerial bombardment of troops and civilians in the conflict.

NOTES

1. An earlier version of chapter 4 has been published in *Journalism*, 11(4), 409–23: Dalia Gavriely-Nuri and Tiki Balas (2010). *"Annihilating Framing": How Israeli Television Framed Wounded Soldiers during the Second Lebanon War* (2006). http://jou.sagepub.com/search/results?fulltext=gavriely&x=0&y=0&submit=yes&journal_set=spjou&src=selected& andorexactfulltext=and. It is published by permission of the publisher. All rights reserved. © 2010 Sage Journals. With special thanks to my coauthor, Dr. Tiki Balas.

2. We used the Archives of the Israel Broadcasting Authority (IBA Film Archive) and the virtual archive Infosite Searchable Archive . Out of a total of forty-seven clips, thirty-five clips were from the 2006 Lebanon War and twelve clips from the period 1996–1997. Among the thirty-five clips during the Second Lebanon War, we randomly selected seventeen events showing wounded soldiers and eighteen events showing ordinary citizens injured after a Katiusha attack. Unfortunately, the availability of hard copies of such clips in the years 1996–1997 preserved in the Israel Broadcasting Authority Archives was limited. From the dozens of events related to wounded soldiers and civilians that transpired in Israel during these years, we found only fourteen clips including soldiers wounded in border events, from which we then randomly selected and analyzed seven; from a list of ten terror events including wounded citizens, we randomly selected and analyzed five items.

3. For more about the representation of the home front in the Israeli media during the Second Lebanon War, see Liebes and Kampf (2007).

4. Israel Broadcasting Authority Archives, Item no. 9153/96.

5. Ibid, Item no. 8576/96-9.

6. Interview with Colonel Ofer Kol, Head of the IDF Spokesperson's Unit, September 2, 2008.

7. Interview with Yossi Bar Mocha, Chair, Association of Israel Journalists, Tel Aviv, August 20, 2008.

8. Interview with Rafik Halabi, former director, the News Division, IBA Channel 1 (the state's public television channel), August 21, 2008.

Chapter Five

War-Normalizing Metaphors

In the Context of The Second Lebanon War (2006)[1]

Military strategists stress the importance of controlling the high ground;
Political strategists stress the importance of controlling the metaphor.
—Katz and Mio (1996: 190)

THE SECOND LEBANON WAR: FROM THE ACTUAL
BATTLEFIELD TO THE COGNITIVE BATTLEFIELD

The initiation of the Second Lebanon War in the summer of 2006 created various evident challenges for the Israeli political discourse. Some of these challenges were derived from the general problem of rationalizing a new war in a democracy, while others arose as a result of Israel's cultural, historical, and political context (Levy, 2010). The first challenge was the need to justify the initiation of a new war in spite of memories of the first war in Lebanon (1982) and its aftermath, which are often associated with "the Lebanese mud." The second challenge consisted of justifying the massive bombing of Lebanon's civilian population and infrastructure, as an appropriate and pro-portional reaction to the damages sustained by Israel.

The high level of public support for the war (after two weeks of fighting, 82 percent of the public thought that the campaign waged by the IDF in Lebanon was justified; 71 percent even demanded that the IDF apply greater force [*Ynet*, July 28, 2006]) demonstrates the success of the political discourse to effectively and efficiently respond to those two challenges, at least during the first weeks of the war.

During the first days of the war, the Israeli political discourse used the most basic exclusion techniques to deal with the aforementioned political challenges. Essentially, it diminished the importance of the war and even ignored it—the political discourse simply denied the fact that Israel had initiated a new war. The title given by Israeli government to the massive bombing in South Lebanon was Operation Just Reward (*Mivtza Sachar Holem*), and this was the first official name of this war. A week later, another positive title replaced the first: Operation Change of Direction (*Mivtza Shinuy Kivun*). Defining the war as an Operation (*Mivtza*), which usually implies in the Israeli war jargon, an action limited in time and dimension (see discussion in chapter 3), obviously camouflaged the real dimensions of the IDF's actions and presented the war as a small, local and almost trivial event. Initially, the media followed the political leadership's rhetoric, and avoided rather systematically the use of the word "war." One salient example of this attitude was the phrase "The fighting in the north" which was persistently used in order to refer to the war in the popular evening news programs on Channel 2 (the most popular television channel in Israel). In the rare instances in which the word "war" was used, it remained a nameless war, a fact that gave it an abstract quality.

In fact, the name the "The Second Lebanon War" evolved spontaneously in the media after two weeks of fighting, and indicated the true proportions of the conflict. Most significantly, the Israeli government never formally declared the war. Only on March 21, 2007, seven months after the war had ended, and following considerable public pressure (especially by bereaved families), did Israel's Ministerial Committee for Symbols and Ceremonies decide to name the conflict a war (Ish-Shalom, 2010). The committee also decided to adopt the popular name: The Second Lebanon War (see chapter 3). Similarly, the government had also refused to declare a National Emergency as allowed by law and warranted by common sense, despite the severe circumstances endured by northern residents, and despite the obvious breaching of the population's normal routines.

During the thirty-three days of war, images of the war's progression and dimensions of destruction on both sides were broadcasted on television every evening. For the first time since the first Gulf War (1991) more than one million Israeli residents were compelled to spend their days in underground shelters due to the Katyusha rockets, which constantly fell within the area proximate to Israel's northern border (3,970 in total). In the initial days of the war, Hezbollah rockets hit Israel's northern settlements in response to Israel's aerial attacks. The fire then spread to the rest of the Galilee settlements, and finally rockets hit the city of Hadera, situated only 45 km from Tel Aviv. During the war, 44 Israeli civilians and 119 soldiers were killed (Zisser, 2009: 310). On the Lebanese side, 1,287 Lebanese citizens were killed and 974,334 became refugees, according to the official data published by the Lebanese government (Zisser, 2009: 9).

However, the Second Lebanon War was not fought solely in the actual battlefields; both sides also fought great battles on the cognitive front—over local and international public opinion. This resulted in what Zisser (2009: 321) calls "the battle over victory." Immediately after the declaration of a cease fire, Hassan Nasrallah, Hezbollah's secretary general, declared Hezbollah's victory and called it a "historic event" (*Al-Manar* TV channel, 22 September 2006, quoted in Zisser, 2009: 321). On the Israeli side, during the war it was extremely common to apply bumper stickers on cars, carrying the slogan: "We will win" (Kfir, 2006: 109). "The battle over victory" reached its tragic peak on the Israeli side during the last hours of the war. Toward the end of the war, the IDF launched a broad ground offensive in southern Lebanon that claimed thirty-four casualties. Many in Israel had criticized the decision to opt for a mainland-attack which they believed was a spin designed to create an image of victory (Zisser, 2009: 318).

Another "cognitive battle" was the battle fought over the choice of metaphors used to depict the war and its outcomes. This was not new. On May 26, 2000, the withdrawal of the IDF from Lebanon was followed by a festive victory demonstration of Hezbollah. One of the highest points of these festivities was marked by a speech given by Hasan Nasrallah, in which he made an insulting analogy that compared the resilience of the "spoiled" Israeli society to weak cobwebs (Liebes & Kampf, 2007).

Metaphors in the Arab-Israeli conflict (Mellor, 2009; Gavriely-Nuri, 2008, 2009a), a topic which has attracted almost no interest in the research community, will be the main subject of our following discussion. The metaphor of a cobweb is a good starting point for this discussion since it provides a good example of the power of metaphors within the context of this conflict. Six years after Nasrallah had coined this metaphor, at the beginning of the Second Lebanon War, the IDF launched Operation Steel-Web (*Mivtza Kurei Pladah*), demonstrating the sustained use of metaphors in the region.

As the war continued and public support slowly declined, new and recycled war metaphors began to appear more intensively in the Israeli political discourse. In this chapter, we will focus on the war-normalizing metaphors surrounding the Second Lebanon War.

It is important to remember that Israeli war discourse has a sizeable cultural inventory (Hall, 1983) of war-normalizing metaphors. This inventory has accumulated since 1948 (Gavriely-Nuri, 2009a), and has been expanded by the new metaphors applied in the discursive process of normalizing the Second Lebanon War.

The analysis in this chapter demonstrates the role that metaphors play in fulfilling the four *functions* of WND. It also attempts to contextualize these metaphors in the *global discursive market* of *war-normalizing metaphors*. Before beginning the analysis, I shall briefly summarize some general observations on the power of political metaphors. I shall then provide some defini-

tions of metaphor that will later be useful in the analysis of political metaphors.

THE POLITICAL POWER OF METAPHORS

Metaphors were traditionally studied by scholars in the fields of literature,
rhetoric, and linguistics. For many years, they were considered inappropriate
for the analysis of social and political events. Curticapean (2006: 17) suc-
cinctly described this attitude: "They were deemed incompatible with reason
(because metaphors get in the way of clear ideas and plain truth) or, at best,
garments of rational thought (ornaments which decorate texts without affect-
ing their meaning)."

However, advances in cognitive linguistics have altered the narrow perception of metaphors in the latter part of the twentieth century. In their
seminal study, *Metaphors We Live By*, Lakoff and Johnson (1980) chal-
lenged the traditional approach to metaphors and offered a coherent, systematic framework that became known as the *cognitive linguistic view of metaphor*. In general terms, this theory altered the status of the metaphor from
"art form" to "instrument," and then to "crucial device for the formation of
concepts and the conceptualization of reality." Metaphor thus came to be
perceived as inherent to human reasoning; more than a figure of speech, it
came to be viewed as a mode of thought. Lakoff and Johnson noted that
metaphors can "create social reality and guide future action," or, in other
words, they can behave like "self-fulfilling prophecies" (1980: 156). What is
most relevant for the current study is the understanding that "ideological
struggles are often a matter of fighting for one set of 'metaphors' to become
common sense and 'naturalized' as literal" (Goatly, 2002: 265).

The *cognitive linguistic view of metaphors* focused on *conceptual metaphors*—metaphors found in a culture's conceptual system and reflected in the
language employed by members of a linguistic community (Lakoff & Johnson, 1980: 139). Conceptual metaphors derive their significance and power
from the fact that they are so basic and essential for ordinary ways of thinking that they tend to go unnoticed. Due to the cognitive implications of
metaphorical connections, the adoption of new metaphors has the potential to
alter a culture's conceptual infrastructure and introduce new views of reality
(Lakoff & Johnson, 1980: 145). Researchers have undermined some of the
assumptions of the cognitive linguistic approach (Kennedy, 2000) and yet,
the idea of the power of coherent and systematic sets of metaphors has
remained intact.

Cameron (2007) argues that the coherence uniting a group of metaphors
may be of various types, including schematic, narrative, or thematic. Thus,
the terms "systematic metaphors" (Cameron, 2007), "metaphor scenarios"

(Musolff, 2004), or "metaphor themes" (Angus & Korman, 2002) all "provide insights into how the speakers foreground certain aspects of topics while backgrounding other aspects, and how they construct coherent explanations and narratives around the topic" (Cameron, 2007: 201).

Today, the political force and relevance of metaphors in decoding political discourse is no longer in question. Metaphors reflect and shape the way we think and feel about politics and about conflicts; they prime audiences and frame issues; they organize communities and motivate cooperation; they stimulate division and conflict; and they mobilize support as well as opposition (Beer & Landsheer, 2004: IX). As Chilton and Illyin put it (1993: 10):

> A new metaphor, or new use of a metaphor, can break up the rigid conceptual frames of an existing political order, introducing new options and stimulating political thought and imagination [. . .] once a significant new metaphor [. . .] has [. . .] captured public attention, politicians begin to seek to control and interpret it. Skillful manipulation of the metaphor can lead to manipulation of an emerging political discourse, providing new conceptual premises for the development and justification of policies.

Charteris-Black (2005: 4) claims that metaphors are essential ingredients of leadership, an argument he demonstrates using examples taken from Winston Churchill, Martin Luther King, Margaret Thatcher, Bill Clinton, and many others who "successfully exploited metaphor and myth in their use of rhetoric in the persuasive communication of ideology." Charteris-Black identifies four key rhetorical strategies for the creation of legitimation in political speaking and demonstrates how metaphor contributes to each of these. These are: establishing the speaker's ethos of ethical integrity; heightening the pathos or emotional impact of a speech; communicating and explaining political policies by developing and challenging political arguments; and the communication of ideology by the creation of political myth (Charteris-Black, 2004: 198). Mio (1997: 130) argues that metaphors "are also effective because of their ability to resonate with latent symbolic representations residing at the unconscious level." The analysis of metaphors can expose aspects of implicit perspectives or values latent in official ideology (Howe, 1988; Kendall & Kendall, 1993).

The role of culture, cultural codes, and cultural knowledge in the process of identification and interpretation of metaphors has attracted increasing attention over the past decade. Chilton (2004: 52) noted: "It is important to be aware that metaphorical mappings can enter into quite complex bundles of meaning that involve other cognitive factors, in particular frame representations that are in effect stores of structured cultural knowledge."

During the last fifteen years, there has been a growing recognition of the role of metaphor in shaping the conceptualization of war, the initiation of new wars, and the justification of political aggressiveness (Chilton, 2005,

1996; Dimitrova & Strömbäck, 2005; Erjavec & Volcic, 2007; Hartmann-Mahmud, 2002; Kennedy, 2000; Ivie, 1990; Lule, 2004; Yang, 2003). For example, the metaphors "iron curtain" and "cold war" conceptualized a conflict that lasted half a century and helped Americans and Europeans integrate this conflict as part of the Western common sense. At the beginning of the twenty-first century, metaphors play an even more significant role in the initiation and participation in wars (Steuter & Wills, 2008) since the "enemies" are often non-state players, difficult to define and locate (Carpentier, 2008), and since wars no longer follow the traditional plotline with a clear beginning and end.

Who was the "enemy" in 9/11? What was his goal? What was this enemy's connection, if any, to the Madrid train bombings in March 2004 and to the July 7, 2005, London bombings (often referred to as 7/7)? The *axis of evil* metaphor has helped clarify, to some extent, the enemy's identity, and connect between the terror acts carried out in the United States and London, and maybe also around the world. More significantly, it has thus helped justify the global War on Terror. War metaphors enable leaders not only to explain the purpose of wars, but also to conceal their real dimensions. In other words, *war-normalizing metaphors* may be perceived as cognitive, political and cultural constructions of war designed to influence public opinion so that it can more easily accept life in the shadow of war.

CONCEPTUAL FRAMEWORK AND DEFINITIONS

The "Political Metaphor"

The definition of "metaphor" has generated an enormous amount of research and studies over the course of history, from Aristotle and the ancient Greek philosophers and up to modern times. The Aristotelian approach to metaphor was based on the substitution of one name for another and was restricted to the study of the changed meanings of single *words*. It was the dominant approach until, during the twentieth century, it was realized that the basic semantic unit is larger than the word. Our analysis focuses on *political metaphors*, that is, metaphors that aim to promote a specific political agenda. Adopting the Cultural approach to Critical Discourse Analysis (CCDA) means that we will be more interested in decoding the metaphors' political and cultural cargo than understanding their linguistic structures. That being the case, the definition and clarification of the concept of metaphor is particularly important. I therefore suggest a straightforward definition of the political metaphor, which will best serve our discussion.

My definition of *political metaphor* is an encounter between two different semantic fields, or the echoing of these two semantic fields, with the condition that one of these fields is linked to political issues. The term "Echoing," in the first part of this definition, is inspired by Sperber and Wilson (1981) in their discussion of irony:

> There are echoic mentions of many different degrees and types. Some are immediate echoes, and others delayed; some have their source in actual utterances, others in thoughts or opinions; some have a real source, others an imagined one; some are traceable back to a particular individual, whereas others have a vaguer origin.[2] (Sperber &Wilson, 1981: 309–10, quoted in Livnat, 2004: 57)

In the second part of the definition, the concept of "semantic fields" is inspired by Kittay's The Semantic Field Theory of Metaphor (SFTM). This theory emphasizes that metaphor effects a transference of meaning, not between two terms, but between two structured domains of content, or "semantic fields."[3] Steinhart and Kittay (1994: 41) explain the claim of SFTM as follows:

> The cognitive force of metaphor results from the re-ordering of relations that hold among concepts in the [semantic] field of the topic by projecting onto them the relations that hold among the concepts in the [semantic] field of the source terms. These new relations allow for new understanding and new lines of implication among the concepts of the recorded topic field.

The identification of semantic fields is a culturally dependent process (Sovran, 2000: 34). Therefore, the identification and analysis of metaphors has no pretension of being universal. Rather, it is based on a familiarity with a specific language and culture, and hence this specific analysis shall be based on familiarity with the Hebrew language and the Israeli culture.

To complete the terminology regarding political metaphors, I will use the term *decoding* rather than the common term *mapping*. *Decoding a political metaphor* will be defined as exposing latent political and social powers, creating authority and domination, hierarchies, and mechanisms of exclusion, which are activated by the use of metaphor.

The suggested definitions have several specific advantages:

1. The definition of metaphor takes into consideration cultural codes and cultural knowledge of a specific cultural community. As such, it fits the CCDA, the general approach that is adopted in this study.
2. Identification of metaphor can be done not only by "professional" linguists but also by the members of a cultural community.
3. The definition of metaphor is dynamic because *semantic fields* "can be extended intuitively to any set of terms with a close relation in meaning, all of which can be subsumed under the same general label" (Akmajian, et al., 2001: 239–40).

4. The term *echoing* also enables a broad and flexible definition of metaphor, to include cases in which a clear-cut identification of the separate "organs" of the metaphor (commonly referred to as "source domain" and "target domain," or "tenor" and "vehicle") is not possible. I
   found this to be especially important when analyzing political metaphors.

Let us consider one example from *Ynet*, a popular Israeli news website, from
July 27, 2006 (during the days of the Second Lebanon War):
   "Minister Eli Yishai suggested turning the terrorist villages into a sandbox."
   This metaphor is an encounter between two semantic fields: the war
(echoed by "terrorist villages") and children's games or, more generally,
childhood (echoed by "sandbox"). *Decoding* this metaphor requires familiarity with the cultural knowledge that a sandbox is a popular children's play-
ground facility. I will later return to this metaphor.
   Kövecses (2002) has surveyed a selection of well-known metaphor dic-
tionaries to create an inventory of commonly used target and source domains
for English metaphors. He lists thirteen major categories, or in our terms,
semantic fields: the Human Body, Health and Illness, Animals, Plants, Buildings and Construction, Machines and Tools, Games and Sport, Money and
Economic Transactions, Cooking and Food, Heat and Cold, Light and Dark-
ness, Forces (such as gravitational, magnetic, electrical and mechanical), and
Movement and Direction (Kövecses, 2002: 16–20, quoted in Rash, 2005). As
noted before, Charteris-Black (2005) checked the domain source in a corpus
of speeches of Western leaders (Churchill, Clinton, and Bush, father and son,
among others). He found Journeys and Personification to be the most popular
source domain, whereas Weather, Sea, and Story were the least popular (p.
200). In this context, it may be interesting to examine the reservoir of semantic fields echoing in Israeli war metaphors and their specific goals.

War-Normalizing Metaphors

A *war-normalizing metaphor* is a political metaphor. It will be defined as a
discursive strategy that systematically uses certain semantic fields (e.g.,
sport, business) in order to exclude war from the discourse. The war-normalizing metaphors blur even war's most basic characteristic as a stressful event;
and at times even give it new and different characteristics. For example, the
WAR IS SPORT metaphor is widely used in the Israeli war discourse. The
metaphorical construction of war as a sport uses expressions such as "key
players" and "rules of the game." These expressions are also universally
found in the *global discursive market* of WND. Sport is a common war-
normalizing metaphor because of its flexibility and its ability to fit different

political aims and needs. In other words, the specific analogies derived from this metaphor depend on the specific political context. For example, following his father's example in 1991, George W. Bush made use of a team-sport vocabulary in speeches aimed at creating an international coalition against Iraq and other members of the *axis of evil* (Lakoff, 1991, 2005). I shall return to the WAR IS SPORT metaphor later.

Following Gentner (1982), I argue that an effective war-normalizing metaphor differs from other metaphors in the sense that such a metaphor goes beyond demonstrating that A is like B (as a "standard" metaphor does): A war-normalizing metaphor also points out that A *is not* like C. By comparing war to a game or a sporting match, war-normalizing metaphors make us forget what war basically implies: death, bereavement, anguish, and physical and mental destruction. In our terminology, *war-normalizing metaphors* not only fulfill the *functions* of euphemization, naturalization, and legitimization, but also the function of symbolic annihilation.

Going back to Eli Yishai's metaphor, which was mentioned earlier:

"Minister Eli Yishai suggested turning the terrorist villages into a sandbox."

This is, in fact, a literal translation of Minister Eli Yishai's words, which in a non-literal translation actually mean that he suggests razing the terrorist villages to the ground. However, *decoding* this cynical metaphor in the actual words with which it was uttered in the Hebrew language, reveals its significance, and uncovers at least two of its key *functions*: first, using the word "sandbox" gives the "war" (echoed by the terrorists' villages) a certain connotation of a naïve and childish activity, and by so doing, it symbolically annihilates the aggressiveness and harsh results of the suggested military action. The metaphor implies that after the terrorists' villages are turned into sandboxes, IDF fighters will be able to play in them like children. Thus, the IDF activity becomes a considerate act of responsibility for the welfare of small children, and any clue of killing or using weaponry is erased. The metaphor not only legitimizes war, but also emphasizes the positive goals of the military action. Indeed, it may be argued that such an interpretation ignores Eli Yishai's sarcasm in using this metaphor. Yishai's suggestion was clearly aggressive and obviously implied the total destruction of the terrorists' villages. However, I argue that in this specific case, the sarcasm does not change one important basic fact: the war discourse during the Second Lebanon War has systematically used certain *semantic fields* which distanced the war from the discourse, and, in our terminology, normalized it. This specific case, of a popular website (*Ynet*) quoting an Israeli minister, is only one example. Therefore, let us now focus on these semantic fields.

WAR-NORMALIZING METAPHORS IN THE
ISRAELI POLITICAL DISCOURSE, 2006

Corpus and Principles of Analysis

The corpus includes the online news pages of the two most popular online newspapers in Hebrew (*Ynet* and *Nrg*) and one printed newspaper (*Haaretz*, Israel's elite newspaper). These pages were surveyed every day during the thirty-three days of the war, from July 12, 2006, to August 14, 2006. The news pages included various kinds of texts in numerous contexts: news, speeches made by political leaders, interviews with high-ranking officers, analytical articles, columns and talkbacks.

The inclusion of talkbacks[4] in the corpus may require some further clarification. Talkbacks are very popular in Israel and represent one of the most accessible channels for average citizens to express their ideas and opinions. During the war, the news and opinion articles published in the online news websites which are included in the corpus could sometimes stimulate more than 500 talkbacks each. Friedman (2009) explored talkback discourse within the framework of the Palestinian-Israeli conflict in news websites (the English edition of Israeli *Haaretz*, and the English edition of *Al-Jazeera*). He wrote: "[The talkback] enable a lively, colorful, eclectic, and inclusive version of a public sphere, which facilitates heterogeneous opinions and attitudes, while favoring exhibitionism over engagement" (p. 2).

In addition, the corpus includes three complementary sources:

a. Random reviews of radio and television magazines, including the most popular news programs.
b. "Other voices," that is, media outlets voicing opposition to war, for example, Bloggers Against the War, and articles written by veteran Israeli leftists such as Uri Avneri.
c. Historical sources, primarily published protocols of sessions held by the Knesset during the week prior to the war's outbreak as well as Israel's previous wars (1956, 1967, 1973, and 1982).

It was found that a number of *dominant metaphors* were prevalent throughout the fragments and excerpts used in the corpus. *Dominant metaphors* echo specific *semantic fields* and fulfill two conditions:

1. The *semantic field* appeared in at least ten different metaphorical expressions.
2. The metaphor was used by at least two of the following groups: politicians, military officers, journalists, or citizens (talkbacks).

After the corpus was created, the metaphors included in it were decoded in two consecutive stages:

1. Analysis of the micro-context, that is, (1) identification of the *semantic fields* that each metaphorical expression activates or echoes, and (2) identification of the features that each metaphorical expression stresses and blurs (or ignores) regarding the concept of war;
2. Analysis of the macro-context, that is, analysis of the political *implications* of using the *dominant semantic fields* in the wider political context, in this case, the Israeli political discourse conducted in summer 2006.

One limitation of our research should be noted at this point. As is to be expected, the classification of the semantic fields in the corpus was not clear-cut. As Cameron (2007: 206) notes:

> A principled flexibility to the grouping of linguistic metaphors appears to be the most suitable approach with discourse data. The labeling of systematic groups should be at a level of generality appropriate to the research goals and to the actual discourse evidence, and there may be nesting of groups within groups. Some metaphors may fit into more than one group, reflecting the indeterminacy of human meaning making.

Following this logic, I classified the WAR IS A GAME metaphor as a subgroup of the WAR IS A SPORT metaphor. The metaphor WAR IS A HI-TECH CHALLENGE was analyzed in the section examining the WAR IS MEDICINE metaphor, because many metaphors relating to medicine included technological processes and hi-tech equipment.

Dominant Metaphors

Four *war-normalizing metaphors* have been identified in the corpus: the stereotypical worlds of women (WAR IS "WOMEN'S WORK"), health (WAR IS MEDICINE), sports (WAR IS A SPORT), and commerce (WAR IS BUSINESS). Other groups of metaphorical expressions, such as WAR IS SEX, WAR IS MUSIC, and WAR IS A CHILDREN'S GAME, were also used, but they did not meet our criteria and are therefore not included in the analysis of the dominant metaphors.

WAR IS "WOMEN'S WORK"

Research on metaphors and gender has accelerated during the last decade (Hegstrom & McCarl-Nielsen, 2006; Reuter, 2006). Janusz argues that metaphors in patriarchal systems are inherently subversive, and can therefore be used as powerful tools by feminists (Janusz, 1994: 290). In this section, I will invert this claim, and argue that metaphors referring to women's stereotypical activity are used as a subversive tool by the patriarchal system itself in order to normalize war. This is done by creating the connotation of war as a part of the stereotypical "normal" women's activity, taking place as far as possible from the battlefield. Using metaphors to connote war to the stereotypical women's sphere is a powerful mechanism that breaks widespread preconceived ideas associating "men" and "war," since historically, war has mainly been conceived of as involving and concerning men in particular. In another context but in a similar manner, Kittay (1988: 63) demonstrated how "[man] uses exclusively female activities as metaphors to help him structure his own relations to his exclusively male enterprises."

In the corpus examined here, a series of metaphors has indeed used the semantic field of the stereotypical "women's work," and linked the war in Lebanon to activities traditionally identified with women, such as cooking, cleaning, and looking after children. Here are some examples:

> Instead of attending to the father of an unruly child [referring to the state of Lebanon-DGN], we found ourselves running after the child—the Hezbollah. (*Nrg*, September 11, 2006)

> The population understands that if they want a long-term silence, we have no choice but to take care of the Hezbollah. (*Nrg*, July 13, 2006)

> Israel has to cleanse the south of Lebanon from effective missiles. (*Nrg*, August 11, 2006)

The Hebrew idiom "to run after the child" and the verbs "take care of" and "cleanse" as they are used in these examples, are taken from the vocabulary used to describe everyday activities in the domestic sphere, traditionally performed by women. Their use in the context of war cognitively relocates the war away from the battlefields and conflict zones and into the private and domestic spheres. In these private spheres, basic, positive and familiar maintenance activities are constantly taking place as part of everyday life. In other words, these simple domestic tasks are free from any intimation of the use of military power.

Another popular traditional "home-like" metaphor is the metaphor WAR IS A MEAL. Consider this example:

> Two main courses [of today's warfare] were damage to infrastructure and extensive blows to the rocket and missile bases. General Staff estimated that Peretz [Amir Peretz, Minister of Defense] would rather settle for the chicken. They were wrong. He wanted meat. (*Ynet*, July 21, 2006)

Food is not only a basic human need. It is also an expression of care, love, and support. A good meal aims to create joy, beauty, and satisfaction. Transferring war to the domestic area of cooking and eating *justifies* the war (food is essential for human existence), *naturalizes* it (eating is a natural need), and *euphemizes* and strengthens the role of military leaders and fighters (a good meal prepared by an expert chef or team).

In other words: *decoding* the political metaphor WAR IS "WOMEN'S WORK" exposes the various ways in which it dissociates or conceals the real meaning of "war" from the political discourse.

The WAR IS "WOMEN'S WORK" metaphor has deep historical roots and, what is equally important, a specific cultural background, yet to be studied. I shall later go back to two metaphors that were popular in Israel during the late 1960s, when a woman, Golda Meir, was Israel's prime minister: "Golda's Kitchen" and "Golda's shopping cart," both of which referred to military issues.

WAR IS A MEDICINE

The metaphorical encounter between the *semantic fields* "war" and "medicine" has deep historical roots in many languages and cultures (De Leonardis, 2008; Koteyko, et al., 2008; Rash, 2005; Wen-Yu & Ren-Feng, 2007). The MEDICINE IS WAR metaphor has been prevalent in Western biomedicine since the "discovery of infectious diseases in the 1880s, replacing the conceptual metaphor of DISEASE IS IMBALANCE which had been dominant since the times of Hippocrates" (Goatly, 2007: 49). The pair "war" and "medicine" commonly appeared in an inverse context to the one examined here, for example in the widely used metaphors "the war against Cancer" or "the war against AIDS" (Sontag, 1989; Williams Camus, 2009). In the last decade, "the war against illness" was also a popular phrase in the media coverage of avian flu (Koteyko, et al., 2008) and SARS (Wen-Yu & Ren-Feng, 2007). Koteyko, et al. (2008: 242) explain the political power of comparing medicine to war:

> These represent fundamental descriptive and explanatory structures that derive from culturally or phenomenologically salient objects or experiences, and which allow journalists, scientists, and policymakers to reduce the complexity of the threat posed by a disease and to promote risk-management strategies for the disease that appear to make instinctive or intuitive sense to experts and the public.

However, the MEDICINE IS WAR metaphor has provoked an increasing amount of criticism during the past two decades, calling for less problematic alternatives and greater attention to the implications of such metaphorization (e.g., Larson, et al., 2005; Sontag, 1989).

The metaphor WAR IS MEDICINE is complemented by a series of metaphors, such as: the ENEMY IS A DISEASE, the ENEMY IS POISON, or the ENEMY IS AN INSECT/PARASITE/VERMIN/BACTERIA (Rash, 2005: 77). Researchers (e.g., Chilton, 2005; Musolff, 2008) have previously shown the extensive use of the JEWS ARE A DISEASE metaphor in Hitler's *Mein Kampf*, and especially the metaphor of a "virus," as a part of the anti-Semitic national racist ideology.

Ironically, seventy years later the Israeli discourse surrounding the Second Lebanon War has created an encounter between the *semantic fields* surrounding the "enemy" with the semantic field surrounding "disease." In a frequently used variation of this metaphor, Hezbollah was described as a malady (usually cancer), whereas IDF commanders and soldiers were referred to as physicians. For example:

> Slowly but surely we will demolish this disease called [. . .] Hezbollah, then we will go on to Syria and Iran, together with the US and thus put an end to brutal, ugly Islamic fanaticism. (*Ynet*, 8 August 2006)

> Lebanon has to vomit this cancer [i.e., Hezbollah-DGN]. (*Ynet*, 14 July 2006)

> [We need to] isolate this deadly virus as well as terror. (Ibid.)

When the enemy is depicted as a disease or infection (a "deadly virus") then the war against it acquires the positive value of a remedy, and the army's task seems to be to provide a cure by purifying or sterilizing the infected area. Interestingly, the common verbs "to purify" and "to sterilize" also belong to the semantic field of housecleaning, which was previously categorized as belonging to the metaphor of "women's work." Thus, the combination between the metaphors WAR IS A MEDICINE and WAR IS "WOMEN'S WORK" adds yet another dimension to the metaphors, implying that war is a basic necessity and an essential and even natural act for human beings. In the words of Charteris-Black (2005: 197):

> Metaphors are especially effective when combined with other metaphors and that nested metaphors drawing on two or more source domains are likely to be more effective than those that draw of a single source domain because they create multiple arguments.

The fundamental images and attitudes these metaphors inspire suggest that the Second Lebanon War was unavoidable, that it was a "no-choice war," fought to protect human [Israeli] life. In this sense, these metaphors act as a part of WND, and fulfill the *function* of justification.

A complete *decoding* of the medical analogy as a political metaphor requires the clarification of one more metaphor to the already mentioned

WAR IS MEDICINE and ENEMY IS A DISEASE. This additional metaphor portrays the leader as a "doctor" (De Leonardis, 2008: 33) or, in a different variation, the fighters as the medical staff. The LEADER IS A DOCTOR portrays the leader as "the only one who is endowed with the proper knowledge and is thus allowed to 'cure' society" (Ibid.). In this way, the *semantic field* of MEDICINE not only *justifies* the war and the military and political leaders, but also *euphemizes* them, thus fulfilling another *function* of WND. It is important to note that in Jewish and Israeli culture, the practice of medicine is highly regarded and valued as one of the most prestigious professions. Thus, the semantic field of "medicine" has positive connotations which emphasize professionalism, knowledge and skills, and even high moral standards, which are then associated with the soldiers and their commanders.

In chapter 1 we clarified that the *function* of legitimization in various cultural war-discourses includes either the *jus ad bellum*, that is, criteria that are to be consulted before engaging in war, and the *jus in bello*, that is, how combatants should act after war had begun. Following this, we can see that the semantic field "medicine" is not only a part of the *jus ad bellum* discourse but also pertains to the *jus in bello* discourse. Consider for example the metaphor "surgical strikes." This metaphor, which was quite common in the Israeli discourse surrounding the Second Lebanon War, implies that like any good physician, Israel's military performs only precise and well-planned attacks or bombings on South Lebanon, causing minimal peripheral damage. This metaphor was extensively used not just for winning the hearts and minds of the Israeli public, but also as part of Israel's answer to the international criticism directed against its massive destruction of civilian property and infrastructure in Southern Lebanon.

Considering the accuracy of the "surgical strike," it is interesting to note that Israeli television channels frequently showed video clips taken from the cockpit of a bomber. These clips might show a target (e.g., a building), but only from a bird's-eye view: what the audience saw was a small, dark spot, then the spot's elimination following the precision bombardment. Focusing on the hi-tech military operations alluded to what we might expect of the sophisticated electronic equipment found in a hospital's operating theater and symbolically annihilated any undesired results of the bombardment from public consciousness.

WAR IS SPORT

Sport is a dominant war-normalizing metaphor because "sport" is a rich semantic field, easily adapted and therefore capable of fitting different political aims and needs; the specific analogies derived from it depend on the specific political context. Using analogies between war and sport should not be surprising since warfare, like sport, also requires great physical effort and involves strategic thinking, teamwork, preparedness, spectators, the glory of winning, and the shame of defeat (Lakoff, 1991).

> Sport is a social drama [. . .] but it is also a cultural drama, and it demonstrates how a group draws on rituals and symbols as well as language to face a crisis [. . .] questions of control, power, and supremacy are relevant, and the language of sport in all its slangy and facetious style offers us a fascinating window into the very soul of our existence. (Segrave, 1997: 218–19)

Echoing the semantic field "sport" may help make grim news about a war more palatable, and thus help the marketing of war news (Nadelhaft, 1994: 27); in our terms this may contribute to the *euphemization* of war. Political leaders throughout the world apply sport metaphors to portray war as a competitive, thrilling and positive event, an exhilarating challenge, a process entailing no danger and therefore a normal "pastime."

Let us point to some quite original variations on the general WAR IS A SPORT metaphor in the discourse surrounding the Second Lebanon War:

> The military still has not succeeded in destroying the organization's opening fivesome [referring to Hezbollah's leadership-DGN]. (*Protocol of Cabinet*, 27 July 2006)[5]

> The fastest, most effective tiebreaker is Nasrallah. (Ibid.)

These two examples are taken from the protocols of the Security Cabinet meeting. In both instances, damage to the enemy is described using images and vocabulary borrowed from the world of sport: killing Hezbollah's leaders is defined as damage to the "opening fivesome," that is, the opening players (the starting lineup) in a basketball game, whereas killing Nasrallah, Hezbollah's top leader, is conceived of as "tiebreaking."

Israel's chief of staff, Dan Halutz, has himself coined some original sport-related metaphors. A couple of days after the commencement of the fighting, he asked government ministers, "Don't pit us against a stop watch." (*Ynet*, 16 July 2006). At the end of the war, soon after signing the cease-fire agreement, he said: "We didn't knock them out but we won on points" (*Ynet*, 20 August 2006).

Describing "war" using vocabulary from the semantic field of "sport" provides the process of war (or the way it is conducted) with a clear logic by implying *clear goals* and *clear rules* in cases in which such goals and rules are, in reality, vague and unclear (Lakoff, 1991). In WND terminology, we can say that the WAR IS SPORT metaphor fulfills first and foremost the *function* of legitimization. It not only justifies the process of war, but also its fairness, by giving the appearance of a fair fight between two equal opponents. This function is especially important in cases of wars against small military organizations, such as the Hezbollah, as in the case of the Second Lebanon War. In addition to all its other *functions*, the semantic field "sport" may also enable leaders to censure war opponents by representing them as defeatist, cowardly, and even unpatriotic, afraid of taking part in the "national sport." In other words, in the Second Lebanon War discourse the WAR IS SPORT metaphor not only fulfilled the *functions* of legitimization and euphemization, but also contributed to the delegitimization of war opponents.

To summarize: *Decoding* the political metaphor WAR IS SPORT in the context of the Second Lebanon War exposes several representations of war which were constructed by the political discourse:

1. *War is goal-oriented*: Creating the impression that war has specific, achievable goals—the war in Lebanon is not endless, aimless, or vague in intent.
2. *Equalization of opponents*: Creating the impression of equality between obviously unequal opponents, in this case, the Israeli military versus the Hezbollah.
3. *Law and order*: Conveying an image of fighting according to defined "rules of the game."
4. *Professionalism*: All the players/fighters, and especially the military leaders, demonstrate consummate skill in the field.
5. *"Sporting spirit"*: Strengthening the national moral consensus to depict the Israeli war opponents as defeatists, lacking a "sporting spirit."

Needless to say that to some extent, most of these metaphorical constructions of war can also be found in other cultures, in other times, and regarding other wars.

WAR IS BUSINESS

Similar to the sport metaphor, the business metaphor is applied to provide the war with a clear rationale, in this case, an economic logic. Buying and selling valuable goods requires careful analysis of costs and benefits; investments are made to obtain profit in the short- and long-term. At the beginning of the war, Prime Minister Ehud Olmert was quoted as saying: "Can the air force deliver the goods?" (*Ma'ariv*, 20 July 2006). Here, we should again mention the war's initial name: *Fair Recompense Mission* (*Mivtza Sachar Holem*); the name creates an ironic analogy between the level of fighting and Hezbollah's due "payment."

During the Second Lebanon War, metaphors taken from the world of business were aimed to achieve two main goals. First, the metaphors were designed to make the war seem like a rational transaction, and second, they were meant to blur any moral questions concerning it. In WND terminology, the goals of the metaphors used in relation to the war were to fulfill the *functions* of legitimization and Symbolic annihilation. A new and popular metaphor was the "bank of targets," that is, the list of sites in Lebanon that the IDF planned to destroy. The equation was simple: each Hezbollah rocket that fell on Israel had a "price tag," which the IDF would reimburse by bombing sites from its "bank of targets." The term "price tag" (*tag mechir*), which has become very popular in the Israeli discourse since the war, appears also in the context of Prisoner-of-War (POW) discourse: the "price" of returning the two kidnapped soldiers, the proclaimed *casus belli*. Describing the process of obtaining the return of POWs in terms of a business "deal" or "transaction" was not new to the Israeli discourse. The most famous POW-related deal was the *Jibril Exchange* (1985), when 1,150 Palestinian prisoners were exchanged for three Israeli POWs. In 2006, politicians, military officers, and citizens would quarrel over "how many Hezbollah prisoners were worth one Israeli soldier" (see also chapter 6). From this perspective, the basic question became: was initiating a war and putting thousands of civilians and soldiers in danger worth the goal of bringing two POWs back? Knowing the costs, were they worth the benefits? Was the price "fair"?

Five years after the war, the father of the kidnapped soldier Gilad Shalit, appealed to Prime Minister Binyamin Netanyahu with the following words: "an IDF soldier is not real estate for which the market price is determined by supply and demand. Netanyahu, stop abuse in Gilad" (*Haaretz*, 1 August 2010). These words were the painful attempt of this poor father to call attention to the hypocrisy and weakness inherent in this artificial analogy, which compared his kidnapped son to a commodity or an object.

COMBINED METAPHORS

After illustrating various metaphors separately, we can now examine full paragraphs taken from the first speech delivered by Prime Minister Ehud Olmert after a week of fighting in Lebanon.[6] Parts of this speech appeared in all the main electronic and printed media in Israel, as well as abroad. The Analysis of one paragraph will demonstrate the key role that *war-normalizing metaphors* play in Israel's political discourse:

> The campaign we are engaged in these days is against the terror organizations operating from Lebanon and Gaza. These organizations are nothing but "subcontractors" operating under the inspiration, permission, instigation and financing of the terror-sponsoring and peace-rejecting regimes, on the *axis of evil* which stretches from Tehran to Damascus. Lebanon has suffered heavily in the past, when it allowed foreign powers to gamble on its fate. Iran and

Syria still continue to meddle, from afar, in the affairs of Lebanon and the Palestinian Authority, through Hezbollah and the Hamas.[7]

This section of the speech includes metaphors from the Israeli as well as the U.S. inventory of war metaphors. By appropriating the phrase *axis of evil* (indeed, quite a short axis, "from Tehran to Damascus") from G. W. Bush's rhetoric on the War on Terror, Olmert was attempting to make the Second Lebanon War part of a global war and connect Israel to the "correct" and "just" global camp. Olmert's description of a "suffering Lebanon" alludes to the "justice" of Israel's actions in helping this weak, victimized "female" of a country ("Lebanon" is a feminine noun in Hebrew). The reference to Lebanon as a victim builds on a well-remembered metaphor used by George Bush Sr. to justify America's involvement in the first Gulf War. According to Bush, the Iraqi villain had raped poor Kuwait (Lakoff, 1991); following this metaphoric line, Olmert claimed that "poor" Lebanon was a victim of gang rape, perpetrated by the Hezbollah.

Olmert's metaphors use the four *dominant semantic fields*. The terms "sub-contractors" and "terror-sponsoring" transform the relations maintained between Hezbollah, Iran and Syria into commercial relations, belonging to the metaphor WAR IS BUSINESS; the word "meddle" in the official English version is a translation of the Hebrew verb "livchosh" (to stir), which comes from the cooking inventory, the semantic field that we call "WOMEN'S WORK"; the word "afar" in the English translation misses the implications of the original Hebrew word: "remote control." The sentence in Hebrew is: "Iran and Syria still continue to stir [things up] by remote control." This allusion is derived from the world of hi-tech, associated with the metaphor WAR IS MEDICINE; and the expression "to gamble on its fate" is a variation of WAR IS A GAMBLE/GAME metaphor, and quite close to WAR IS SPORT.

In our terminology, this section from Olmert's speech is a part of WND and is intended to achieve its four *functions*.

The "Metaphorical Annihilation" of the Second Lebanon War

The metaphorical construction of the Second Lebanon War can be called a *metaphorical annihilation* of the war. Table 5.1 summarizes the four *functions* of this metaphorical construction.

Table 5.1. War-Normalizing Metaphors: *Dominant Semantic Fields* and the Four Functions

	Euphemization	Naturalization	Legitimization	Symbolic Annihilation
"WOMEN'S WORK"		++	++	++
MEDICINE	+	++	+++	++
BUSINESS	+	+	++	++
SPORT	++	+	++	++

The *metaphorical annihilation* of the Second Lebanon War altered the basic characteristics of the concept of war in two ways: First, it introduced new features or reused existing ones in the Israeli concept of war; second, it concealed or weakened some features of the war. Several of these changes are summarized in tables 5.2 and 5.3.

Table 5.2 emphasizes some relevant features of the dominant metaphors ("women's work," medicine, sport, and business): "normal," "essential to human existence" and "logical." These features are attached to the concept of war:

Table 5.2. Introducing New and/or Amplifying Existing Features of "War"

	Normal, Routine Part of Daily Life	Essential to Human Existence	Logical, Conducted According to Clear Rules
"WOMEN'S WORK"	++	++	+
MEDICINE	+	++	++
BUSINESS	++		++
SPORT	+	+	++

Table 5.3. Concealing or Weakening Features of the Concept "War"

War is	Destructive	Dangerous	Aggressive	Politically Oriented
"WOMEN'S WORK"				
MEDICINE		+	+	
BUSINESS				+
SPORT		+	+	+?

Table 5.3 indicates features considered characteristic of "war": war is perceived as "destructive," "dangerous," "aggressive" and "politically oriented."

Use of the four metaphors blurs or neutralizes the perception of these characteristic features.

As I mentioned at the beginning of this chapter, the metaphorical construction of "war" was required for dealing with two of the main moral issues arising from the Second Lebanon War: The need to justify a new war, and the need to justify the massive bombardment of Lebanon. Tables 5.1, 5.2, and 5.3 provide summary statements of the suggested solutions. For example, comparing war to essentials of medicine, fair sport, and the logic of business served to justify a new military campaign. Above all, these four metaphors were intended to make the war seem like a "normal" event and conceptually blurred its inherent "abnormal" aspects: death, bereavement, anguish, and destruction.

RECYCLING METAPHORS: HAS ANYTHING CHANGED BETWEEN 1967 AND 2006?

The metaphors employed in the metaphorical annihilation of the Second Lebanon War were by no means new. Forty years earlier, during the Six Day War (1967) and its aftermath, most of the above-mentioned semantic fields were used in the Israeli political discourse, as a part of the WND developed after this war. *Recontextualization* may provide an appropriate conceptual framework for the discussion on the reuse of metaphors (on recontextualization please also see the discussion in chapter 7). Recontextualization "involves a movement of discourse(s) (e.g., G. W. Bush's discourse) across practices, from one type of a practice (e.g., the Bush's administration practice) or context to another (e.g., Serbian nationalistic practices)" (Erjavec & Volcic, 2007: 127). Fairclough (2003: 139–40) developed some general principles for discussing recontextualization:

1. *Presence*: which elements of events or events in a chain of events are present; which ones are absent, which are prominent, and which are in the background?
2. *Abstraction*: what is the degree of abstraction or generalization of concrete events?
3. *Arrangement*: how are the events ordered?
4. *Additions*: what is added in representing particular events? (e.g., explanations, legitimizations or evaluations).

Semno explained that "the recontextualization of metaphors is a particularly interesting and complex phenomenon, as the relationship between source and target domains may be exploited very differently when a metaphor is adopted and developed in a different context from that in which it was originally introduced."[8]

Within the context of metaphors in the discourse surrounding two Israeli wars, I prefer the term *recycling* to the term *recontextualization*. The term *recycling metaphors* emphasizes an element of preservation and continuation, and is therefore more compatible with CCDA, the approach which guides the discussion in this book. Rather than differences and developments in the various appearances of metaphor, this term helps to expose the accumulative cultural reservoir of metaphors (see "WND's Global Market" in the first chapter), or more precisely, the reservoir of semantic fields that can be retrieved in similar political situations.

Let us now briefly focus on the political situation in Israel during the years 1967 to 1973 (chapter 8 provides a long discussion of this period). During this period, the Israeli-Arab conflict was characterized by different but intensive types of hostilities. The period began and ended in total wars: the Six Day War (1967) and the Yom Kippur War (1973). In between, a War of Attrition along the Egyptian frontier lasting eighteen months (1969–1970), was accompanied by dozens of terrorist attacks on the ground and in the air as well as by repeated shelling of Israeli border settlements.

To blur the harsh features of this security situation, the political discourse engendered *war-normalizing metaphors*. These metaphors enabled the Israeli society to perceptually integrate the continuing political conflict as well as periodic concrete military threats—into the flow of its daily existence. Aided by these *war-normalizing metaphors*, sitting Israeli governments were able to keep occupying the territories conquered in 1967 and reject at least ten peace initiatives offered by different countries without losing public support.

I will now exemplify the use of two metaphors during this period. The metaphors are taken from the aforementioned *semantic fields*: "women's work" and "sport." I shall then focus on some metaphors that were typical to the situation after 1967, and may be called *occupation-normalizing metaphors*.

War is "Women's Work" and "War is Sport"

In 1969, Golda Meir was appointed as the prime minister of Israel. She led an unyielding foreign policy and was considered a tough leader; one might say an Israeli version of Margaret Thatcher. Despite the stereotypical "masculine" qualities of her leadership, the image of Golda Meir etched in the Israeli collective consciousness was that of a woman presiding over her "kitchen cabinet," in the most literal of terms. The metaphor "Golda's kitchen" came into common usage in the political discourse during the years Meir served as prime minister (1969–1974). "Golda's kitchen," whether in her official residence in Jerusalem or in her private home in Tel Aviv, became the sanctuary where secret consultations were conducted with a permanent group of people who were very close to the prime minister. This "team," euphemistically nicknamed "Golda's kitchen cabinet" due to this venue, included government ministers as well as high-ranking officers. The informal, comfortable atmosphere, far from public or media view, allowed for very efficient deliberations. Naturally, security was the main issue discussed. Considering the range of topics, the metaphor "Golda's kitchen" camouflaged its function as a *war room*.

The metaphor "Golda Meir's shopping cart" also came into common usage in the political discourse during these years. It represents Meir's success in convincing American leaders to provide Israel with various kinds of advanced weaponry. Prior to every one of Meir's visits to the United States, she equipped herself with such a metaphorical "shopping cart" to be filled by items reflecting Israel's updated security needs.

These two metaphors were commonly used after the 1967 War, depicting the uncompromising policy of Meir's government after 1967 as "normal" activities of a "normal" housewife taking care for her family. Whereas the "kitchen" metaphor made banal the process of security-related decision-making by depicting it as a kind of "women's chatter," the "shopping cart" metaphor effectively blurred the escalating arms race in the Middle East.

Metaphors taken from the world of sport were also employed by Israeli leaders after 1967 primarily to stress war's nonviolent aspects. Consider the types of games chosen for comparison: With some exceptions, war was usually compared to chess or checkers, to running rather than to boxing. To illustrate, in a book published two years after the Six Day War, Israel's minister of defense at that time, Moshe Dayan, described the escalation that led to the outbreak of the war as if it were a round in a football match:

> We can describe the process in a style resembling a sportscaster's commentary while watching a goal. . . : [Alexei] Kosygin [the Soviet prime minister] passes the word to Atasi [Syria's president] who transfers it to Nasser [Egypt's president] who then passes it to Hussein [Jordan's king]: Hey, it's waaaar! (Dayan, 1969: 122)

Beyond the recycled metaphors, and in order to complete the picture, I shall now like to point out one innovation of the *war-normalizing metaphors* after 1967; namely, a series of metaphors regarding the occupation.

THE OCCUPATION-NORMALIZING METAPHORS

The *occupation-normalizing metaphors* depicted Israeli occupation echoing the semantic field of "tourism." In the aftermath of the Six Day War, Israel conducted an "open borders policy" in the occupied territories. The term referred to Israel's consent to allow Palestinians to cross the Jordan River (the post-1967 border between Israel and Jordan) in order to visit their families. The government also encouraged commercial relations with Jordanians although Jordan was still considered an enemy country. The phrase "open borders" metaphorically associated the guarded border crossing with a free passage, or with the idea of a world with no borders, and *symbolically annihilated* perceptions of the oppressive restrictions imposed on the Palestinians' freedom of movement under the occupation's military regime.

Another common metaphor referred to these trips as "summer visits," a term which gave the impression of a touristic event, a behavior resulting from freedom of choice for the purposes of having a good time. Moshe Dayan once provided an example of this metaphorical construction:

> Did you know that about 100,000 Arabs came here from neighboring and even distant Arab countries, in order to spend their vacations here [. . .] They decided to spend their summer holidays here, in the territories, under our occupational regime, of their own free will. (*Ma'ariv*, January 23 1972)[9]

Dayan, who was a master of irony and hyperbole, effectively used war-normalizing metaphors to paint an optimistic picture of reality. Words such as "holiday" and "spending time" portrayed the occupied territories as just another vacation site in Israel. Moreover, his texts conveyed the impression that Israel's occupation of the territories had improved the Palestinians' situation by bringing them the gift of Western progress. This kind of metaphorical construction avoids any direct reference to the basic fact that after 1967 Israel ruled over more than one million Palestinians in the occupied territories. (I will discuss Dayan's citation also in chapter 7.)

CONCLUSION AND OPEN QUESTIONS

What was the effect of the *metaphorical annihilation* of the Second Lebanon War in practice? How can we measure the influence of this effect on public positions in the short- and long-term? I leave these questions for future research. At this point, there may still be legitimate doubts as to the power of a set or even several sets of metaphors to dramatically change the political reality. Indeed, it is difficult to believe that depicting Saddam Hussein and the Iraqi army as villains raping helpless Kuwait might have played a key role in convincing the American public to support the first Gulf War (Lakoff, 1991). However, *war-normalizing metaphors* become relevant if they are conceptualized as part of general WND, and in this context, it will be much easier to see their influence on public opinion.

What is most interesting about the *metaphorical annihilation* of "war" is the observed subconscious cooperation of individuals who are not expected to actively take part in this discourse—the ordinary people. Once *war-nor-malizing* metaphors are incorporated into the political discourse, we discover them repeatedly in talkbacks written by common citizens. The adoption and circulation of these metaphors indicates the complex creation process of a "common sense"—the penetration of biased terminology into the fabric of the discourse that constructs what is considered to be "common knowledge."

Metaphorical annihilation, like the metaphorical construction of war or other core events, requires more than the manipulation of the masses by a hegemonic elite. Rather, its effectiveness is reflected by the collective effort to continue the discourse primarily by means of the disseminated metaphors. In other words, creation of war-normalizing metaphors and WND in general, is the joint work of leaders and citizens alike. This collaboration reaches its peak when war metaphors are unconsciously employed by people who are clearly not part of the consensus and even oppose the hegemonic military or political elite. For example, Brigadier General Menachem Einan, a member of the Winograd Commission, appointed by the government to investigate the initial conduct in the Second Lebanon War, used a phrase belonging to the metaphor WAR IS A GAME or SPORT: "The rules of the game after the withdrawal have reinforced the Hezbollah."[10] This automatic or unconscious use of the war-normalizing metaphor illustrates the power of a metaphor once it enters the political discourse.

Our short survey has shown that the same semantic fields were used in the construction of *war-normalizing metaphors* in different contexts, which in our case included the post-1967 War, and the Second Lebanon War, 2006. The same metaphors served different political needs: to initiate a new war (2006), and to preserve the results of another war (1967). The four *semantic fields* "women's work," medicine, sport, and business were also found in the Israeli political discourse surrounding the 1956 War and other wars. They were used by different political leaders, leftist and rightist alike, in different times and in order to support different specific agendas. It seems that war-normalizing metaphors are an independent language that is disconnected from any specific political context. The reservoir of war-normalizing meta-phors constitutes a rich and flexible language that can easily fit into different political contexts.

NOTES

1. An early version of chapter 5 was published in *Discourse & Society*: Dalia Gavriely-Nuri (2008). "The 'Metaphorical Annihilation' of the Second Lebanon War (2006) from the Israeli Political Discourse." *Discourse and Society, 19* (1), 5–20. http://das.sagepub.com/content/19/1/5. All rights reserved © 2008 Sage Journals.

2. www.phon.ucl.ac.uk/home/PUB/WPL/03papers/livnat.pdf.

3. About the origin and development of the theory of the *semantic field* and origins of the theory of the semantic field, see Terrence (2001): 1650–1662. See also discussion in chapter 3.

4. Talkbacks normally refer to comments about online articles, written by internauts, often appearing within the news site itself at the end of the article.

5. Published in *Yedioth Ahronoth*, 23 March 2007.

6. 17 July, 2006. The official English draft of the speech available at: www.pmo.gov.il/PMOEng/Communication/PMSpeaks/speechknesset170706.htm.

7. Ibid.

8. Elena Semino, "Metaphor and recontextualization." Plenary lecture at Specialized Seminar of Researching and Applying Metaphor Association (RaAM), 6 May 2011. The quotation appears in http://lancs.academia.edu/ElenaSemino/Talks.

9. Kenneth Harris, "A Few More Months Left" (In Hebrew).

10. A. Har'el et al. "*Winograd Commission* Member: The Rules of the Game after the Withdrawal Have Reinforced the Hezbollah," *Haaretz*, 23 March 2007.

Chapter Six

War-Normalizing Silencing

The Cultural Code of Captivity[1]

From 2006 to 2011, the Israeli soldier Gilad Shalit was held captive by the Hamas in the Gaza strip, and stood at the heart of an intensive Israeli discourse around one central question: How many Palestinians who were involved with terror acts against Israel and kept in Israeli prisons was one Israeli soldier "worth"? The ongoing discourse that appeared daily in newspapers and other media channels provided no obvious answers.

The Yom Kippur War (1973), which occurred four decades earlier, was arguably one of the most significant events in the painful history of captivity in Israel, and provides the context for later events. During the Yom Kippur War, 314 Israeli soldiers were captured by Egyptian and Syrian armies. This was the largest group of Israeli POWs since the establishment of the state. In contrast to the case of Gilad Shalit, once these soldiers returned to Israel, they were totally excluded from the discourse. This chapter follows what we may call the *silencing* of the Yom Kippur War ex-POWs. By examining this case, the chapter sheds light on several issues:

1. Silencing as another discursive strategy in WND
2. The Israeli Cultural Code of Captivity (CCC)
3. The connection between Cultural Codes and WND
4. The dynamic character of WND from a historical perspective
5. The anti-WND

THE SILENCING OF THE YOM KIPPUR WAR EX-POWS

Two marking events concerning the return of POWs have taken place during the years 1973 and 1974: First, the American POWs' return from Vietnam, and second, the Israeli POWs' return from Egypt and Syria. In the United States, massive media coverage turned the returning POWs into cultural heroes. They were invited to talk shows, interviewed in the newspapers, and filmed for documentaries and feature films (Gruner, 1993: 231–35). Israel also celebrated the return of its POWs, in official state ceremonies that acquired the character of national holidays. From the moment they stepped on the runway, the media engulfed the returning soldiers and dedicated full-page coverage in the daily press to their return. Yet, unlike the Americans, the Israeli POWs covered themselves in a thick cloud of silence soon after their return, and disappeared for a long time from the public eye and the public discourse. Between 1973 and 1993, more than 30 of the 591 American former POWs published their autobiographies (Gruner, 1993: 225–26); yet, among the Israeli former POWs, only 1 of the 314 chose to publish a book (Assaf Yaguri's autobiography, which was published in 1979).

A series of stories by Israeli ex-POWs, describing the time they spent in captivity, began to penetrate the public discourse only twenty-five years after the war (e.g., Ariel, 1999; Segev, 2001; Weiss, 1998). This trend peaked in the weekend supplement closing 2004, issued by *Yedioth Ahronoth*—Israel's highest-circulating newspaper at that time. The eighteen pages of coverage devoted to the POWs' experience not only provided a significant opportunity to examine the meaning of captivity within the Israeli culture but also exposed an interesting transformation in the Israeli culture in general.

I claim that the silencing of the Yom Kippur War ex-POWs is derived from CCC, and represents another motif in the Israeli WND that I refer to as a *war-normalizing silencing*. The main *function* of this silencing was *to symbolically annihilate* the harsh aspects of war, including the possibility of captivity for its participants. The characteristics of captivity and its costs are likewise annihilated: the mental and physical suffering, the anger directed by the POWs at themselves and at the political and military leadership for being captured and the shame and embarrassment integral to the POW experience in Israeli culture.

SILENCING AS A DISCURSIVE STRATEGY

In 1991, a full issue in the journal *Discourse and Society* (issue no. 2: 4) was devoted to the analysis of "silencing," so as to "consider some of the many ways men have muffled women's voices and writing, and some of the many ways women have struggled to tell stories" (Houston & Kramarae, 1991:

387). Houston and Kramarae exemplified some of the specific ways women have been silenced throughout history, such as by ridicule, enforcement of family hierarchies, male-controlled media, censorship, racism, and terrorism (Ibid.). The book *Discourse and Silencing* (edited by Lynn Thiesmeyer) published in 2003 extended the research field of silencing beyond gender issues and focused on silencing within legal discourse and national politics. This latter research provides the context for this chapter.

This chapter refers to "silencing" in a broad metaphorical context, including not only the opposite of "speaking" (Eades, 2000) but also the avoidance of various kinds of overt expressions, such as oral or written expressions and even the publishing of a book. Silencing may be imposed (in Hebrew: *Hashtaka*), or it may be the result of a choice (in Hebrew: *Shtika*). Glenn, for example, discusses imposed silence that "has long been considered a lamentable essence of femininity, a trope for oppression, passivity, emptiness, stupidity, or obedience" (2004: 2). Other researchers point to the power of chosen silence (e.g., Zerubavel, 2006). This chapter will describe and discuss "cultural silencing"—a different mode of silencing, which bridges the gap between the two kinds of silencing described.

It may be argued that the thirty years of silence of the Yom Kippur War ex-POWs stem from a combination of both choice and enforcement. In part, it was the ex-POWs' choice to remain silent. Yet, the main reason for this choice was derived from unwritten Israeli *cultural codes* that forced this silence upon them. Therefore, the ex-POWs' silencing is a *cultural silencing*, that is to say, it is derived from underlying, unwritten and even hidden *codes*, which the cultural community members adopt, sometimes unconsciously. As this chapter will demonstrate, a transformation that has been developing for almost three decades within the Israeli CCC was the main reason behind the ex-POWs breaking of this *cultural silencing.*

Let us briefly suggest some historical insights about the relationship between personal stories and historical memory before we apply the approach adopted in this book—CCDA (*Cultural approach to Critical Discourse Analysis*), and delve into a cultural discursive analysis of the silencing, and later the telling, of the POWs' stories. Such a historical perspective will locate our analysis within the context of the triad History-Culture-Discourse.

Understanding the relationship between personal stories and the historical memory within the Israeli discourse often begins with the narrative of the Holocaust. With respect to the Holocaust, Ginzburg claims:

> The historical narrative [of the Holocaust] would be incomplete without the personal stories told by the persecuted [. . .] Historiography that sterilizes personal stories silences the survivors' voices and imbues the narratives with abstract historical concepts, such as "policy" and "political measures," misses the historical truth. (Ginzburg, 2000:220)

Maurice Halbwachs (1992/1925) has laid the theoretical foundations for the comparison between personal stories and historical memory in his pioneering work *On Collective Memory*. Halbwachs argues that: "[. . .] the individual creates some kind of artificial milieu, external to every one of these personal thoughts, though encompassing them all—a collective space and time, a collective history" (Halbwachs, 1960: 59). According to this analogy, the autobiographies produced by the ex-POWs may be viewed as "personal thoughts" "encompassed" not only by a collective historical space but also by a collective cultural space. Kramarae (1991: 388) has argued that "silences are interpreted differently depending upon the culture, the status of the people involved, and the particular situation." Similarly, I argue that the silencing or telling of stories, as a *discursive strategy*, should be understood within both a cultural and a historical context. Such contextualization is crucial for understanding the dynamic relationships that connect the ex-POWs silencing with CCC and, finally, with WND.

THE CULTURAL CODE OF CAPTIVITY

The concept that this chapter introduces, *the CCC*, refers to an unwritten compendium of values and myths that form part of culture's foundation. It integrates cultural commands with cultural taboos and expresses the expectations that a given society has of POWs, the state, and the public in general. In the Israeli case, the CCC encompasses the following themes:

1. *Falling into Captivity*: The Israeli CCC advocates "fighting until the end" rather than being captured. The Israeli soldier is expected to never surrender unless special circumstances are involved. In such instances, submission is to be conducted in strict accordance with regulations.
2. *Behavior during Interrogation*: An Israeli soldier who falls into captivity never tells his interrogators anything other than his first name and rank. Israeli soldiers "bear up honorably" under all interrogations.
3. *Joint Detention*: This experience is characterized by cooperation and reciprocity. Prisoners develop a communal way of life while building a team that represents Israel with honor.
4. *The Return Celebration*: Return is a national holiday. Prisoners receive a warm welcome in official ceremonies.
5. *Return to Everyday Life*: Ex-POWs soon return to a normal life because captivity does not affect them beyond their physical scars.
6. *The Nation and the IDF*: These two institutions provide trustworthy support to the ex-POW and his family. Captivity occurs only after daring attempts of rescue, sometimes under extreme conditions. If a

soldier is captured, the government and the military will make tremendous efforts to negotiate for his exchange.

National myths, military legislation that deals with captivity and captivity stories relating POWs' experiences in previous wars are all integrated into the fabric of the CCC. One case in point is the story of Uri Ilan, an IDF soldier who had been captured by the Syrians in 1954. After his captivity, Uri Ilan committed suicide in order to avoid revealing secrets under torture, and left a note between his toes in which he wrote, "I did not betray." His moving story has been integrated into Israel's legacy of captivity.

POWS' PERSONAL STORIES AND THE CCC

For the purpose of examining the relationship between the CCC and the personal stories recounted by the Israeli ex-POWs, two corpora were defined:

1. *Initial stories.* A category containing all the stories told by the POWs as they appeared in Israel's three major daily newspapers (*Yedioth Ahronoth, Haaretz,* and *Al HaMishmar*)[2] during the week following the captives' return (POWs held in Egypt were released in November 1973, POWs held in Syria were released in June 1974), forming a total of thirty-six issues of the respective newspapers.
2. 2. *Stories after twenty-five years.* Stories recounted in personal interviews that were published in the national daily newspapers, and in military journals (e.g., the *Air Force Gazette*) after the twenty-fifth anniversary of the captives' return (1998), especially autobiographies and biographies, forming a total of thirty articles, three autobiographies, and one biography.

Additional complementary sources have also been used in order to validate the two main conclusions obtained from the research: I have conducted dozens of personal interviews with ex-POWs and their wives; and participated in four meetings of the prisoners' representative association Awake at Night *(Erim Ba'Laila).* In addition, many ex-POWs offered their personal journals or fragments thereof, written either during captivity or afterwards, yet these materials have remained private and unavailable for publication. The archives of the Israel Broadcasting Authority, which contain segments that deal with the Yom Kippur War, including short interviews with ex-POWs, served as another external source, which contributed to the research.

The main finding arising from this intensive research was that although, on the whole, the initial stories collectively agreed with the directives of the

CCC, the stories told twenty-five to thirty years later, generally did not. I shall now turn to present the research and its findings in more detail. As a first step, I shall present some of the stories themselves. First, I shall introduce some of the stories that comply with CCC, and then, I shall present some of the stories which do not. I shall later turn to a more in-depth analysis, using the theories and concepts guiding this book.

Stories that Comply with CCC

Falling into Captivity: Sixteen manned strongholds were distributed along the Suez Canal on October 6, 1973, the eve of the Yom Kippur War. All but one stronghold were abandoned or their soldiers taken captive. The *Mezach* ("Pier") stronghold held out longest: Only after a week, with just sixteen soldiers remaining fit out of the original forty-two, did its commander decide to surrender. The following is a description through the eyes of the stronghold's commander, Shlomo Ardinest:

> Ardinest watched the forlorn convoy. Despite the circumstances, his heart was filled with pride, pride over the Torah held in Hillel's hands. Following him were the wounded soldiers, who asked explicitly to walk on their own feet and not be carried on stretchers [. . .]. "No," reflected Ardinest, "my men aren't walking as sheep to the slaughter but as proud soldiers. (Michelson 1997: 129)

Interrogations: Withstanding interrogation is glorified by descriptions of how Israeli POWs succeeded in deceiving their captors. The captors are generally described as cruel and mentally inferior. The POW Avi (Abraham) Weiss, an intelligence officer, received a citation for endurance under capture:

> Second Lieutenant Abraham Weiss presented himself to his captors as a supply sergeant who had arrived to check the stronghold's battle rations. He maintained this cover story during his entire time in captivity. By doing so, Second Lieutenant Weiss effectively fooled his captors and avoided revealing any secrets. (*Yedioth Ahronoth*, October 10, 2003)[3]

Joint Detention: Joint detention is the phase most amenable to the dictates of CCC. Initial and subsequent stories repeatedly refer to the fellowship and reciprocity that characterized POWs' interactions during captivity. Many of these stories relate how simply meeting other Israeli POWs after a long, secluded, and difficult period caused great joy. Some POWs saw themselves as Israel's "ambassadors in exile," a status that, according to CCC, demands a display of national pride and solidarity in front of their captors. Soon after the POWs' return from Syria, Amiram Guy, an aviation crewmember, recounted:

It was an extraordinary Passover *seder*. The packages from home included everything: *matzoth*, IDF *Hagadot*, and *charoset*.[4] Only the wine was missing; instead, we drank coffee without sugar [. . .] At the end of the *seder* the "choir" sang. No, the Syrians didn't disturb us. They knew we had a holiday and didn't interfere. (*Yedioth Ahronoth*, June 2, 1974)[5]

The Return Celebrations: Owing to censorship, the newspaper editions published soon after the return of the POWs described mainly the joyous return celebrations. Pictures of ex-POWs descending the plane's ramp became part of the Israeli "national album." Military officers and distinguished personalities welcomed the returning POWs and the daily press published many short interviews with them over the next few days. In subsequent stories, told two decades later, the return celebrations were also repeatedly mentioned. For example, in his biography (1998), former captive Avi Weiss recalled a moving event from the celebrations for the returning POWs:

Prime Minister Golda Meir, and the President's wife, Nina Katzir, boarded the plane and began to kiss and hug the returned POWs. The IDF's Chief Rabbi, Mordechai Piron, presented them with a small prayer book. TV photographers crowded the runway. The woman officer at the plane's entrance exclaimed at that point: "Look how Israel's love engulfs you!" (Weiss, 1999: 86)

Return to Everyday Life: Some of the personal stories following the POWs' release are characterized by a "happy ending," as they depict the excellent financial and social status achieved by some ex-POWs. An article about Amiram Marcus, held captive by the Syrians, is a paean to the successful return to everyday life. Marcus opened a computer company, his dream while in prison (*Ma'ariv*, December 30, 1999).[6] Today he dreams of opening a branch in Damascus once peace is achieved. Another example is found in an interview with Dudi Senesh (*Anashim*, April 28, 1998)[7] a nephew of the mythic paratrooper Hanna Senesh,[8] which includes the following description: "Today Dudi Senesh, 44, is an optimistic man, a clinical psychologist (PhD), and an internationally recognized expert in child therapy." Stories of this kind describe the captive experience as a kind of a learning experience which strengthens the character, and which can later serve as a lever for success. Senesh himself admits:

I now understand better than others what it means to be in captivity, not necessarily my own war captivity, but captivity by disease or circumstances [. . .] What doesn't kill you makes you stronger. I learned to appreciate the fragility of life, not to take everything for granted. (Ibid.)

The Nation and the IDF: Despite the exhausting negotiations for the exchange and release of the POWs, most of the POWs' personal stories do not express any special gratitude to the country, the IDF, or its leaders. One exception is the biography written by Michelson. Michelson recounts the unsuccessful rescue attempt made by the Navy Seals. Before the operation, the Seals' commander had given his men a rousing pep talk:

> Surely you all know that the IDF, as we've always been told, does not desert its men on the battlefield. They were right. The IDF won't forsake its soldiers [. . .] this is a sacred principle in the IDF. We mustn't concede any opportunity to rescue our men. We must exhaust all the possibilities. (Michelson, 1997: 117)

Stories That Do Not Comply with the CCC

Falling into captivity: Twenty-five years after the prisoners' release, the CCC demonstrated in their stories is fragile and inconsistent. New narratives reveal the harsh hours before the fall into captivity. Some of them surrendered although their commanders did not give them orders to do so, since officer ranks often preferred to leave the decision of surrender to the men in the field. At most, surrender was conveyed by a spontaneous raising of hands or waving of a white cloth, free from formalities and contrary to CCC. Avi Weiss, one of the ex-POWs, narrates the story of the capitulation of the *Mefazeach* ("Nutcracker") stronghold:

> At this point the organized fighting ended and it became a battle of survival, every man for himself. [. . .] Everyone struggled to push their head through the [stronghold's] openings, gasping for air. People were fighting with each other, standing on top of one another. [. . .] At some point, completely spontaneously, with no order given by anyone, everyone poured outside. [. . .] We just came out because we couldn't breathe and because the Egyptians had thrown in tear gas grenades and the smoke was suffocating. (*Yedioth Ahronoth*, October 10, 2003)[9]

Interrogations: Later stories tell us that most of the POWs were unable to withstand the difficult interrogations. They revealed much of what they knew—even top secrets. One well known example is the story of Lieutenant Amos Levinberg, a member of an intelligence-gathering unit, who arrived at the *Hermon* stronghold (the most important stronghold in northern Israel) on the eve of the Yom Kippur War. Levinberg was gifted with a phenomenal memory and had gathered vast amounts of information on secret army bases, squadron numbers, elite reconnaissance platoons, and so forth. He was captured by the Syrians and submitted to severe psychological pressure. Apparently, he did not withstand the pressure, and filled volumes with the information he knew. With his return from captivity, demands were made that he be court-martialed for treason. However, he met with the chief of staff, and it was decided to simply discharge him (*Yedioth Ahronoth*, October 5, 2003).[10]

Joint Detention: In both the initial and the subsequent ex-POWs' stories, joint detention is repeatedly embellished in accordance with CCC standards. Very little criticism of fellow POWs has been expressed. Yaacov Ariel's story is an example of a readiness to reveal the truth found only among a minority of people: Despite many positive descriptions, Ariel does portray instances of egotistical and petty POW behavior (Ariel, 1999: 53).

The Return Celebration: Subsequent POWs' stories present a drastically different version of the press descriptions of joy and empathy surrounding the POWs upon their return to Israel. These stories recount how soon after the warm welcome and brief meeting with their families, the ex-POWs were taken to a harsh interrogation facility. They tell of their feelings of being forced to cope with the IDF's distrust in addition to the cruelty of captivity. David Abudaram, who was held by the Egyptians, related:

> On 16 November 1973 we landed to a great victory celebration. The beginning looked promising, filled with toasts and receptions [. . .] on the one hand, there were two weeks of festivities, we could eat for free in a million places; on the other hand, they didn't let us out of the [interrogation] facility. (*Ma'ariv* September 15, 2003)[11]

Return to Everyday Life: The dark side of returning to everyday life has only begun to come to light after more than twenty-five years of silence. Returning to Israel was, apparently, the first in a series of many arduous, and sometimes seemingly impossible steps reintegrating the ex-POWs into ordinary life. In his first interview after his return, Amiram Guy declared: "In the morning I have to go back to the hospital, but I also need to go and renew my country club subscription. [. . .] Come on, what's a [wounded] leg; you still need to continue and play tennis" (*Yedioth Ahronoth*, June 2, 1974).[12] Thirty years later, unemployed and suffering from many functional disorders, Amiram Guy told a very different story, acknowledging his difficulties.

Only after more than twenty years was it realized that a number of ex-POWs may have been suffering from post-traumatic stress disorder (PTSD) and neglected for years. Yoav Ben-David, an ex-POW, relates:

> I discovered horrific things about [. . .] dysfunctional returned prisoners, people who won't leave their homes, and others who do function [overtly] but whose [inner] life is hell; anger, frequent explosions of rage, many cases of seclusion and divorce in addition to people who are unable to form a family, not to mention extreme cases of people hospitalized in mental institutions. (Ibid.)

The Nation and the IDF: Only after twenty-five years were the accusations against the "Nation" and IDF for abandoning the POWs given voice. These accusations were directed against the IDF's high command and the Ministry of Defense, as well as against those institutions which, for more than two decades, were unable or unwilling to construct rehabilitation and monitoring systems for the ex-POWs. In 1979, Lieutenant Colonel Assaf Yaguri, the highest-ranking officer among the POWs, expressed an exceptional criticism. It was directed at all ranks, from his fellow commanders and the soldiers who fought beside him, to the entire nation, which according to him has betrayed its sacred values. The essence of his criticism consisted in the argument that the regiment that he commanded was denied help, which was one of the reasons for its capture:

> The sense of being abandoned that my regiment felt, attacking alone, was the most difficult. [. . .] I still believed that the IDF wouldn't forsake us. You don't just send a regiment into battle without any backup, or at least without trying to rescue it. There is a sacred tradition in the IDF that you don't abandon people on the battlefield. Nevertheless, the unbelievable did happen; we disappeared as if the ground had swallowed us, and no one cared. [. . .] [We felt] orphaned, isolated from values, norms and common standards, this feeling screamed out and is still echoing [within us]. (Yaguri, 1979: 12)

EXPLANATIONS FOR THE SILENCING OF EX-POWS

Why have the stories by the ex-POWs changed so drastically? What can explain their long silencing? The answers to both these questions stem from one single process. The reason for the refusal of the ex-POWs to tell stories that comply with CCC is also the main motive for their silencing. The coming section will clarify this process and offer several complementary explanations. Like the discussion in chapter 4 which dealt with wounded Israeli soldiers, the current discussion will reveal the explanatory power of WND in respect to various military issues.

1. *The military censorship*: We may simply explain the degree of compliance with CCC as owing to the strict military censorship imposed on the ex-POWs upon their return. Except for some sporadic short interviews in the newspapers, the censorship constrained the POWs' stories and kept them silent.
2. *Psychological factors*: Twenty-five years after their return, the maturing ex-POWs felt that they have greater freedom to transmit their internal truths, irrespective of the expectations of CCC. Some of the emotional wounds borne by ex-POWs have healed to some extent, and the sense of shame and guilt resulting from their inability to meet the expectations embodied in CCC also waned.
3. *Social "trend"*: This explanation derives from what we may call the Israeli trend of *shattering military myths*, a trend that has become

widespread during the past three decades. Within this context, it is possible to view the stories subsequently told by Yom Kippur War ex-POWs as an additional case of shattering the myths that were born out of prior narratives. War in general, and captivity in particular, provide fertile ground for the construction of myths (Katz & Keating, 1994; Hellman, 1986). Other factors which play a part in the constructions of myths include the shroud of secrecy enveloping certain events during the war, and the desire of commanders and soldiers to appropriate successes while disengaging from any failures which may have led to captivity. The confusion that raged immediately after the outbreak of the Yom Kippur War served as a convenient platform for nurturing myths concerning bravery and self-sacrifice. After three decades, certain flaws in those myths that had previously barely been recognized have lately penetrated the public discourse and raised questions regarding the myths' validity. The later stories of the ex-POWs form part of this "trend."

4. *The cultural aspect*: This explanation derives from an assumed transformation in CCC's content and influence in the years since the Yom Kippur War. Following the war, changes have been taking place within the CCC itself; in fact, a whole new *cultural code* has been created, and it places the POWs needs and distress at the center of attention. In more general terms, the new CCC has given more importance to human life than to the state. According to the new CCC more empathy is given to soldiers who prefer to live rather than fight until the last bullet, and to tell secrets rather than suffer unbearable tortures. Thus, the new CCC encourages the publication of stories that had previously been discouraged because they did not comply with the structures imposed by the previous CCC. This transformation is clearly illustrated by the fact that in early 2005, fifty-one years after becoming a prisoner, the ex-POW Meir Maor Mozes, who had been charged and convicted for revealing intelligence secrets to the enemy, was granted full pardon from the president of Israel. The lawyer who had served as the military prosecutor in his trial fifty years earlier, now stood beside Mozes in the public battle to clear his name. A more generally influencing event occurred in July 2005: the Knesset instituted a law that allocates a permanent monthly stipend to all living ex-POWs of Israel. In an official announcement, the *Knesset Security Committee* made the following statement: "the law is an expression of the debt of the State of Israel towards the ex-POWS [. . .] [it comes to atone] decades of negligence during which the ex-POWS did not receive recognition and appropriate treatment." Clearly, the CCC keeps changing all the time. This cultural explanation for silencing leads us to yet another *cultural discursive* explanation based on WND.

SILENCING, WND, AND ANTI-WND

Silencing the ex-POWs is a *war-normalizing strategy* that *symbolically anni-hilates* one of the most frightening scenarios for any fighter: that of being taken captive. At the same time this *discursive strategy*, together with the initial stories of the ex-POWs, strengthens the CCC. It depicts a euphemistic picture of the POW and of the situation of being held in captivity, by present-ing a set of clear and attractive values, such as the valor of the POWs, and the solidarity of the commanders and the whole nation. In this sense, the silenc-ing also fulfills the function of *euphemization*.

In this context, both the breaking of silence and the publishing of different stories may be perceived as parts of an *anti-war normalizing discourse (anti-WND)*. As such, they expose the harsh side of captivity as being an integral part of war. Such stories describe in detail the real meaning of being held in captivity: the torture, the humiliation, the shame, the guilt, and even the feeling of being abandoned by the state. Rather than legitimizing war, they legitimize the POWs who preferred survival to obedience to the *cultural code* of fighting until the last bullet. From their unusual perspective of per-sonal difficulties, the ex-POWs "rebelled" against the ethos of CCC and WND.

In chapter 8, I will argue that the first buds of the anti-WND in Israel started to appear in the Israeli war discourse right after 1967. I have already mentioned another example of the anti-WND in chapter 3: The insistence of bereaved families was the main reason for the Israeli Ministerial Committee for Symbols and Ceremonies decision to rename the conflict in Lebanon in 2006 the "Second Lebanon War" rather than to "normalize" it by using war-normalizing terms such as "operation" or "the fighting in the north." The groups that led the anti-WND discourse in both cases were those who most suffered from the negative consequences of war, and were therefore most aware of its "abnormalities." As such, the ex-POWs and the bereaved fami-lies were the two groups most interested in sharing their feelings and insights regarding the falsehood and artificiality of WND.

I shall conclude this chapter with two examples of the breaking of silenc-ing from the last decade. The first example is the group Breaking the Silence [*Shovrim Shtika*]—a group of soldier activists which solicited, collected, and disseminated dozens of testimonies by soldiers. The venture became known to the public in May 2004 through an exhibition of photographs shot by soldiers with their handheld cameras in the town of Hebron. These photo-graphs captured images of life under the occupation. Katriel (2009), and Katriel and Shavit (2011) have shown how these testimonies challenge the officially proclaimed ethic of combat and the legitimacy of the routine mili-tary practices of the Israeli Army (Katriel, 2009: 150–52):

> The soldiers' collective effort was designed to provide the evidentiary basis for countering the societal silencing and obfuscation that surrounded the occupation regime through speaking out in organized events of one form or another—public talks, press interviews, videotaped testimonies, small-scale meetings. Through this range of inscriptional activities, they sought to combat the "collective amnesia" (Zerubavel, 1995) that they felt threatened the memory of the second Intifada. They thus harnessed their individual memories and the experience of personal change for the goal of promoting public debate and thereby opening up the possibility of wider societal awareness and change. (Katriel & Shavit, 2011: 79–80)

Another recent example for breaking the silencing is *Waltz with Bashir,* a 2008 Israeli animated documentary written and directed by Ari Folman.[13] The film depicts Folman's search for the lost memories of his experiences as a nineteen-year-old soldier during the First Lebanon War (1982), and focuses on the days of the massacre in Sabra and Shatila.[14] At the beginning of the film, Folman is surprised to find that he remembers nothing from these days. As the film progresses, Folman realizes that his "amnesia" had stemmed from his feeling, at the time of the events, that as a soldier he was guilty of indirect contribution to the massacre (he was among the soldiers who were in charge of firing flares into the sky in order to illuminate the refugee camp for the Lebanese Christian Phalange militia who perpetrated the massacre inside). Folman's twenty-six years of silencing may remind us of the long silencing of the Yom Kippur ex-Pows. *Waltz with Bashir* emphasizes the psychological aspect of this process of silencing. The long silencing is shattered by an artistic production—a film—which creates a cathartic effect which may be compared to the effect produced by the flaw of autobiographies written in the last decade by the Yom Kippur War ex-POWs.

I claim that at the bottom of the process of silencing of the young soldier in Lebanon in 1982, and of that same process in the young soldiers who were captured in 1973, there is a strong unconscious desire to comply with the *cultural code* or even the cultural "directive" to take part in the "national sport" of *normalizing*-war. However, the strong artistic urges to write a biography, to make a film or to take photos (in the case of *Breaking the Silence*) seem to be a counter-force acting as an *anti-war normalizing* force. The question of whether these later examples could provide circumstantial evidence to the growing power of the anti-WND in Israel, and to the transformation of the Israeli military culture over the past decade, is yet to be explored.

NOTES

1. An earlier version of chapter 6 has been published in Dalia Gavriely-Nuri (2006). Israel's Cultural Code of Captivity and the Personal Stories of Yom Kippur War POWs, *Armed Forces and Society* 33: 94–105. http://afs.sagepub.com/content/33/1/94.full.pdf+html. All rights reserved © 2006 Sage Journals.

2. Publication of the newspaper *Al Hamishmar* ceased in 1995.

3. Ronen Bergman and Gil Meltzer, "The POW Who Talked (and Got a Citation for It)" (in Hebrew).

4. Charoset is a sweet, paste made of fruits and nuts eaten at the Passover Seder.

5. Josef Bar, "Many of Us Didn't Sleep Nights and Sang Sad Songs" (in Hebrew).

6. Alex Doron, "On a Clear Day You Can See Damascus" (in Hebrew).

7. Yitzchak Letz, "God, Oh God, Let It Be Over" (in Hebrew).

8. During WWII, Hanna Senesh volunteered to parachute into Hungary to help the Jews there escape. She was caught by the Nazis, tortured, and murdered.

9. Ronen Bergman and Gil Meltzer, "The POW Who Talked (and Got a Citation for It)" (in Hebrew).

10. Rami Tal, Ronen Bergman, and Gil Meltzer, "The Man Who Told Everything," *Yedioth Ahronoth*, Special Supplement: 30 Years after the Yom Kippur War (in Hebrew).

11. Liat Ron, "POW Forever" (in Hebrew).

12. Josef Bar, "Many of Us Didn't Sleep Nights and Sang Sad Songs" (in Hebrew).

13. The film won a Golden Globe Award for Best Foreign Language Film (2009). Also see: Morag (2011).

14. The Sabra and Shatila massacre was a massacre of Palestinian and Lebanese civilians, by a Lebanese Christian Phalangist militia. It took place in the Sabra and Shatila Palestinian refugee camps in Beirut, Lebanon, on September 1982, during the Lebanese civil war. The IDF surrounded the Palestinian refugee camps and controlled access to them. The Israeli government established the *Kahan Commission* to investigate, and in early 1983 the commission found that Israeli military personnel were aware that a massacre was in progress, without taking serious steps to stop it.

Chapter Seven

War-Normalizing Legislation

The Law of Decorations[1]

The central hypothesis of this chapter is that military decorations provide an effective cultural arena for the promotion and justification of the use of military force. In the terminology of this book, the central hypothesis is that military decorations are a complex *war-normalizing strategy*. Therefore, they are mainly aimed to achieve the four *functions* of WND: euphemizing, naturalizing, legitimizing the use of military power, and symbolically annihilating its inherent violence and harsh results.

The main theoretical claim here is that apart from paying a sincere homage to national heroes, the awarding of military decorations forms part of a complex social process of redistribution of symbolic capital. This process of redistribution is aimed to strengthen the fighters' status in particular and the national interest in general. In the Israeli case, the national interest would include strengthening the *cultural code* of the normalization of war.

In former chapters, WND was discussed via separate *discursive elements*: naming and metaphors; framing, which was explored through visual practice (video clips); and silencing, which was defined as the suppression of specific types of personal expression. In this chapter, we move on to a more complex *discursive strategy:* Military decorations are a conglomerate of *discursive practices*, which all aim to achieve the same goal—the normalization of war.

The symbolic arena of Israeli military decorations encompasses several *verbal* practices, for example: the text of The Law of Decorations for the IDF (1970) (here and after: "The Law of Decorations"); the long discussions prior to its legislation in the Israeli Knesset; and the explanatory narratives that accompany and justify each of the decorations awarded. It also includes some *operative* practices, such as the legislation process of the Law of Deco-

103

rations, the implementation of official awards ceremonies, and the material aspects of the decoration (i.e., the physical object).

While this book generally adopts the Cultural Approach to CDA (CCDA), for the purpose of discursive analysis of military decorations it will also adopt a historical perspective (e.g., Benke & Wodak, 2003; De Cillia, Reisigl, & Wodak, 1999; Van Leeuwen & Wodak, 1999). After a short introduction, the analysis in the first part of the chapter will focus on three practices:

1. The text of the Law of Decorations (1970)
2. The process of legislation of the law (1969–1970)
3. The awarding of decorations after the Yom Kippur War (1973)

I will show how these various practices represent different events in the Israeli timeline and work in cooperation, applying WND to the social reality.

The second part of the chapter will focus on the long text of the discussions in the Knesset on the subject of the legislation of the law in December 1969 and in January 1970. This analysis will illuminate the decorations as a sophisticated and dynamic social implementation for achieving various political, educational and psychological goals beyond WND. In this section, I will connect the decorations to the Holocaust, the ultimate Jewish-Israeli justification for the use of military power.

MILITARY DECORATIONS AS A "CULTURAL SITE"

The awarding of decorations to army fighters formed part of an entire state ceremonial, which may even be considered as a form of national ritual (Azaryahu, 1995; Turner, 1974). While religious rituals are intended to connect people with higher forces, modern nationalistic rituals are intended to link the members of a national community with the community's outstanding heroes or the supreme national values, such as liberty or independence. The design of national rituals is an illustration of a state's cultural planning (Kertzer, 1988). State rituals are part and parcel of a complex and deliberative process of solidifying and establishing the cultural arenas that support the socio-political order. In this particular Israeli case, the ritual is a ceremony. National flags accompany it, and explanatory texts are read aloud while the minister of defense and head of staff bestow the decorations upon the distinguished warriors.

There are two national practices aimed to define the "good Israeli citizen." We can compare the awarding of decorations to the awarding of the Israel Prize, the most significant and prestigious prize which the Israeli nation may grant one of its citizens. The state of Israel has been granting this prize every year since 1953 in an official ceremony in Jerusalem during the celebrations of Israel's Independence Day. Most of the Israel Prize recipients are awarded for their display of excellence in their scientific field of research. Both the decorations in the military sphere, and the Israel Prize in the civil sphere, indicate the qualities most appreciated by the state: bravery and wisdom, respectively. In so doing, they in fact encourage the characteristics believed to be the most essential for the existence of the state: bravery in battlefield—to physically protect the state; and wisdom in the civil sphere—to preserve and develop the Jewish-Israeli ethos known in the Israeli discourse as the (Israeli) "qualitative advantage" which supposedly counters the "quantitative (demographic) advantage" of its rivals.

The national decorations ceremony may be discussed using anthropological frameworks (e.g., Gledhill, 2009; Handelman & Katz, 1991; Kelly & Kaplan, 1990; Kertzer, 1988). It may also be interesting to look at this ceremony as a *cultural site* (Lomsky-Feder & Ben Ari, 1999: 12). Complementary to these anthropological and cultural perspectives, our analysis has viewed the national awards ceremony, as well as the act of legislation of the Law of Decorations, as a *discursive strategy*. Using the lenses of CCDA, it exposed the various ways in which this ceremony contributes to promotion of WND even after the shock sustained by the Yom Kippur War (1973).

A LEGAL-TEXT ANALYSIS OF THE ISRAELI LAW OF DECORATIONS

The Law of Decorations established three types of decorations: the *Decoration of Bravery* as the highest-ranking decoration, followed by the *Decoration of Valor* and the *Decoration of Exemplary Actions*. A legal-text analysis of the three categories illustrates the absolute definition of bravery from the legal point of view as that exhibited under circumstances of war or combat. In other words, only a war hero may be considered a hero according to the law.

Unlike a law proposed in 1954 (which will be discussed below), the 1970 law does not apply to acts of bravery performed by citizens. According to the 1970 law, only soldiers and military units are eligible for receiving these decorations. In addition, the two highest decorations are granted for acts performed during wartime or in fulfilling a duty during combat. Only the Decoration for Exemplary Actions, the third highest decoration, may be granted for acts not related to combat or not performed during combat. However, a prerequisite for the Decoration for Exemplary Actions is the presence of valor, usually demonstrated in the face of an enemy and not in the face of a natural catastrophe, for example. Neither does The Law of Decorations acknowledge any contributions made to national security via technological achievements. The suggestion to honor actions that promoted peace and add a "Decoration of Israel Peace" for exceptional actions to promote peace has also been rejected (Knesset Protocols, 1 December 1969).

In contrast, the various American laws concerning the awarding of medals generally display greater openness toward the awarding of medals to civilians for non-military actions (Anderson, 1986). On a number of occasions, the highest decoration—the Medal of Honor—was granted to citizens for outstanding feats performed in times of peace. For example, the Medal of Honor was awarded to Capt. Charles A. Lindbergh for his bravery, courage, and skill as a navigator during his historic non-stop flight from New York to Paris in May 1927.

Another significant contrast between the American and the Israeli distribution system is the difference between the officials who grant the decorations during the ceremonies. In the United States, the president, on behalf of the Congress, bestows the two highest decorations, whereas in Israel, the minister of defense, upon the recommendation of the head of staff, awards the Decoration of Bravery, while the head of staff bestows the other two decorations. A proposal to have Israel's president bestow all three decorations has been rejected (Knesset Protocols, 24 December 1954). Clearly, the position held by the person who awards the decorations sends a particular message about the martial nature of the Law of Decorations. It is this martial nature of the law which makes the Israeli institution of decorations such an interesting arena in which to examine the construction of the concept of "war," and more specifically, as another expression of WND.

THE LEGISLATION OF THE LAW OF DECORATIONS

Prior to the institution of the Law of Decorations, there were two previous attempts to establish an institutionalized awarding of decorations: one was an IDF initiative, and the other was a failed initiative of the Knesset.

During the 1948 War, intensive preparations were made for the granting of decorations. Multiple types of decorations were determined, and the various commanders were called upon to provide their recommendations.[2] The IDF archives cataloged dozens of letters of recommendations written by the commanders for their subordinates.[3] A vast correspondence surrounding the issue of decorations began between the superior commanders, which continued until 1952. This prolonged process generated only twelve "Badges of the Israeli Hero." No use was ever made of the remaining recommendations (Fried, 2000).

In 1954 renewed efforts were made to institute a law of military decorations. The "Law Proposal of Decorations for the IDF" sat untouched on the desk of the Knesset for sixteen years. The law proposal was disinterred in

December 1969. Unlike the two previous unproductive attempts, this time the law was expediently accepted within only two months, and a special committee began collecting recommendations for the distribution of the decorations.

What was the reason for the quick process of legislation in 1969–1970? In order to understand it, we must first understand the historical and political context in Israel during these years.

Right after the Six Day War, an insistent War of Attrition was waged by Egypt in an attempt to get back the Sinai Peninsula, which had been occupied by the Israeli army in 1967 (more information about the years 1967 to 1973 is provided in the next chapter). The War of Attrition was in stark contrast to Israel's swift victory in 1967, and it gave a new sense to the concept of "war." After 1967, the borders with Jordan (in the east) and Syria (in the north) also became "hot" borders, and there were hundreds of terrorism incidents on land and in the air. These harsh security conditions peaked during the years 1969 to 1970 and greatly discouraged the Israeli society at the time. To give an idea of the dimensions of insecurity it may be pointed out that during the sole month of May 1970, more than sixty Israelis, soldiers and citizens alike were killed.

At the same time, a sensible peace treaty became a realistic option for the first time since 1948. After Israel's victory in 1967, it had received an unprecedented number of peace propositions, some were public while others remain classified. With the country perceived as stronger than ever by itself and the world, many in the Israeli public believed it to be a favorable moment for the achievement of peace. These sentiments were echoed by anti-war protests around the globe, especially in the United States and France. Between 1967 and 1973, Israeli governments rejected at least ten peace initiatives proposed by different countries, including those proposed by the United Nations (Bavly, 2002).

The burgeoning of the "first sounds of peace" around Israel and abroad was another factor dimming the aura surrounding the concept of war, which was beginning to seem more and more difficult and undesirable. The Law of Decorations was part of the WND evoked in response to these developments.

The legislation of the Law of Decorations did not happen in a vacuum. It was part of a "festival of bravery," which may be perceived not only as a natural response to the victory in the 1967 War but also as part of a "festival of WND" aimed at improving the national "bad mood" during the years that followed this victory. A "victory march" took place on Independence Day in 1968, one year after the Six-Day War. It included a military air show by a fleet of 400 hundred jets, a display of American cannons alongside confiscated Russian cannons and the unveiling of the Israeli rifle "Galil" by paratroopers (Haber & Schiff, 1976). This march was the first-ever live show broadcast on Israeli television.

Let us focus now on the third point in time, which is very significant for the understanding of the Israeli institution of military decorations.

THE MASSIVE AWARDING OF DECORATIONS
AFTER THE YOM KIPPUR WAR (1973)

In May 1975, one year and six months after the Yom Kippur War, 296 decorations were awarded. This was the most massive awarding of decorations in Israel relating to one war.[4]

Table 7.1.   Number of Decorations Awarded per War up to Year 2006

War	Number of Decorations
1948 War	12
1956 War	28
1967 War	258
1969–1970 War	51
1973 War	296
1982 War	6
2006 War	18

The Yom Kippur War is registered in Israel's collective memory as a traumatic event for three reasons. First, Israel was caught completely off guard. The Yom Kippur War is recorded in the history of wars as one of the three largest strategic surprises of the twentieth century, besides the attack on Pearl Harbor and Operation Barbarossa, both of which took place in 1941. Second, during the first few days of the war, Israel faced immense danger, and many were wounded, killed or taken as POWs. The war ended after three weeks of fighting, but the price for Israel was very high: 2,569 casualties, more than 7,500 wounded soldiers, and 314 others taken as POWs. Those numbers are equivalent to as many lives lost per capita, as the United States suffered during almost a decade of fighting in Vietnam (Liebman, 1993). Third, for the first time in the history of Israel, a head of staff was dismissed from the IDF. The Agranat Committee, a National Commission of Inquiry, found him guilty of lack of military preparation at the outbreak of the Yom Kippur War. This contributed to an unprecedented crisis of confidence between the public and the military leadership.

Under such circumstances, we may view the intensified distribution of decorations for the warriors of the Yom Kippur War as part of a WND which was especially intended to euphemize the image of the IDF and its leading figures. The message was that despite its complete inferiority as a result of having been surprised at the outbreak of the war, the IDF managed to emerge victorious. The explanatory texts that accompanied each decoration awarded, euphemized the warriors using emotional descriptions of the situations and actions for which the decorations were granted. The decorations ceremony was the climax of the institutional mechanism aimed at supporting the warriors.

To complete the picture, we should mention that the Israeli television network, which began broadcasting two years after the Six-Day War, exposed the public to live images of the battlefields for the first time during the Yom Kippur War. Increasing doubts began to come up regarding the practicality of military force as well as its feasibility as a solution for the Israeli-Arab conflict. The Yom Kippur War exposed the Israeli society for the first time to the real price of the perpetual reality of "Life by the Sword." Barzilai (1992) claimed that following the Yom Kippur War, feelings of "War Fatigue" swelled within the Israeli society. He pointed to the fact that after this war, for the first time ever, there was a widespread demand for peace initiatives, not only among minority groups at the fringes of society, but also among central camps in the political system. The massive awarding of decorations after the Yom Kippur War may be perceived as an intent to counterbalance this fatigue.

We have focused on three different practices which illustrated how the awarding of decorations may be classified as part of WND: the text of the Law of Decorations, the process of legislation of the Law and the massive awarding of decorations after the Yom Kippur War. We shall now try to understand how the decorations contribute to the four *functions* of WND: euphemization, legitimization, naturalization and symbolic annihilation.

MILITARY DECORATIONS AND WND'S *FUNCTIONS*

The symbolic arena of military decorations as a conglomerate of practices fulfills the four *functions* of WND.

Euphemization

Granting decorations makes war a desired challenge, a unique opportunity for individuals to demonstrate superior qualities: bravery, resilience, and composure. Such bestowal emphasizes the "appealing" aspects of war: camaraderie in battle, enterprise, and leadership (Chambers, 2003; Cromer, 2004). Like military marches, decorations give the ethos of "life by the sword" an aura of majesty and glory. The *function* of euphemization is even revealed in the word chosen to describe the honor: the current term in Hebrew is "decorations," not "medals." The Hebrew word *itur* (decoration) is derived from the word *atara* (crown) and means beauty as well as ornament. In comparison, the origin of the word "medal" is the Latin word *metallum*, the root word of metal—the raw material from which the decoration is made.

Legitimization

The decorations in fact demonstrate to a certain degree the need for specific battles, and even the raison d'etre of wars. Acts of bravery can actually function as informal evidence for the existence of a threat, since they imply a dangerous and powerful enemy (clearly, if the enemies were weak or meaningless, our warriors would not seem so brave).

Moreover, the decorations may whitewash specific mistakes and failures of high-ranking or medium-ranking commanders. According to this claim, heroism and bravery sometimes become necessary specifically because of mistakes of the higher echelons, or unnecessarily dangerous acts. For example, the battle over the "Chinese Ranch" (in the area of the Suez Canal), one of the most notorious battles of the Yom Kippur War, is also a tragic memory burnt into the Israeli public consciousness. The lives of more than 40 paratroopers were lost in the course of this battle, and nearly 100 soldiers were injured. In the years that followed, an ever-increasing condemnation of this battle arose within the public, as well as questions concerning its necessity, organization and execution. It seems no coincidence that participants in this specific battle alone were granted more than thirteen decorations.

Naturalization

The basic premise of the institution of military decorations is the existence of wars. This premise does not leave room for questioning whether they are logical or wise. Naturalization, in this case, is part of the function of legitimization. The naturalization of war makes questions concerning the leadership's decision-making process marginal and even irrelevant. The massive awarding of decorations after the Yom Kippur War helped muffle difficult questions surrounding the circumstances of this war, for which Israel was ill prepared. Obviously, if war is turned into a given fact, questions regarding the responsibility for its occurrence are at least temporarily removed from public discussion.

Symbolic Annihilation

Military decorations help conceal, or at least balance, the darker aspects of war. It is not surprising that out of the 296 decorations bestowed on the Yom Kippur War's veterans, 116 were actually granted to dead soldiers. The decorations symbolically diminish the bad aspects of war, such as the bereavement of families or the suffering of wounded soldiers. In addition, and as we saw earlier, the decorations symbolically annihilate the responsibility of the leadership for unnecessary or misguided battles.

Thus, the WND as it is reflected in the text of the Law of Decoration, the act of legislation and in the massive awarding of decorations after the Yom

Kippur War, is revealed as a flexible, ready-made discourse that fits both the harsh days of the War of Attrition and the nationally traumatic period of the Yom Kippur War.

MILITARY DECORATIONS: BEYOND WND

The long debates in the Knesset in 1954 and in 1969 surrounding the legislation of the Law of Decoration will illuminate the process of awarding military decorations as a sophisticated arena for achieving political, educational and psychological goals. In other words, the institution of military decorations as a part of WND is not only an automatic discursive mechanism, it is also a subtle and dynamic discourse that can respond to various societal and political needs. I will focus on five of its goals, concerning the fighters' needs, the IDF and the nation.

a. *Psychological preparation of the soldiers for a continuous war*: The 1956 War and the 1967 War (the Six Day War) were very short wars, lasting eight days and six days, respectively. On the contrary, the War of Attrition, as implied by its name, was a long war and lasted for eighteen months, from March 1969 to August 1970 (some researchers even claim that this war lasted for almost three years, beginning immediately after the 1967 War). This situation created a new challenge for the IDF fighters. Contrary to former years, fighters who served in the army during this period spent all their mandatory service in war conditions. Knesset members were aware of this difficulty and perceived the decorations as a way of preparing the soldiers for the new situation. Here is what Knesset member Aharon Yadlin (Labor) said:

> What has changed to make the subject of medals so urgent an issue? Some basic psychological features of our struggle have changed. First of all, the length of the war [. . .] the young eighteen-year-old soldier enters the army in the anticipation that a state of war will characterize the entire period of his service. This has never happened before. (Knesset Protocols, 1 December 1969)

In the same Knesset debate, Knesset member Yoram Aridor (Herut/Liberals) demonstrated similar awareness to the didactic power of the decoration:

> Personal heroism and self-sacrifice are the foundations of the establishment of Israel [. . .] [and] the solidarity of a nation with its heroic sons must be made apparent to everyone [. . .] It is not the heroes who are in need of this; it is the nation who is in need of this [. . .] awarding the decoration will provide an official demonstration of the high esteem the

state has, not only for the hero himself, but also for the heroic spirit, and for the type of education which develops such a spirit.

b. *Material reward to the fighters*: The decoration is symbolic capital that can be easily exchanged for "real" capital, that is, for material advantages. The Knesset members expect that a fighter who has received a decoration will receive special prestige also in the civilian sphere. In other words, the status of being a "brave soldier" is worth money. Knesset member Uri Avnery, known for his ultra-leftist views, told this story:

> You probably remember the case of Nissim Mevorach, a heroic fighter who was later refused a post in a factory. There was also the case of the disabled paratrooper, who could not continue to live in his building in Jerusalem because the neighbors opposed to the adjustment of the building for his special needs. Unfortunately, there are many such cases, and the awarding of decorations to war heroes for their acts of bravery [. . .] is also needed because it promotes the attitudes which those people deserve [. . .] they who have done so much for the country. (Knesset Protocols, 1 December 1969)

The decoration represents a *cultural code*, that is, a network of shared values, norms, and beliefs which community members are familiar with and respond to. The decoration as a *cultural code* strengthens the connection between the army life and the civilian life, or more precisely, blurs the dichotomy between those two spheres.

c. *Improving the image of the IDF*: No less important than helping the fighter who receives the decoration, the Knesset members perceived the decoration as an opportunity to improve the image of the IDF. This point became especially important after the 1967 War, when the continuation of the occupation of territories began to evoke national and international criticism. In this context, Knesset member Uri Avnery said (1 December 1969): "I believe that the decoration is also necessary as a means of publicly recognizing heroism and thereby demonstrating the nature of the IDF before the eyes of all Israelis and before the eyes of the entire world." (Ibid.)

d. *Strengthening the national-historical narrative*: In 1969 Israel was a young nation—only twenty-one years old. Thus, the creation of a historical narrative and a historical ethos strengthened the social cohesiveness, and the national self-image. Drawing a line between the historical Jewish heroes and the heroes from more recent wars created a connection between the Jewish history and the young Israeli nation. In this context, Knesset Member Moshe Sne (The Israeli Communist Party, Maki) said:

The decoration also has great educational value as it connects between the past and the present [. . .] the Jewish bravery is a brilliant chapter in our history [. . .] the wars which we wage in our generation are independence wars and are therefore a continuation of the Jewish bravery in previous generations.

And Knesset Member Dov Milman (Gahal) explained (20 January 1970):

It must be admitted that Israel's courageousness did not begin in 1967 [. . .] it has a history of thousands of years, since the days of Samson to our day and age [. . .] and there must be a sense of continuity.

e. *Remembering the Holocaust*: In the long process of the legislation of the Law, many Knesset members offered a specific decoration for the commemoration of the Jewish fighters in the Warsaw ghetto rebellion in 1943. The Holocaust represents the ultimate threat to the Jewish nation, and takes us back to the functions of WND, especially legitimization.

DECORATIONS, LEGITIMIZATION, AND THE HOLOCAUST

The concept of *Recontextualization* provides an interesting tool for understanding how the institute of Israeli decorations incorporated the Holocaust into the Israeli narrative, and in so doing helped strengthen WND, especially in the case of the *Decoration of Bravery*: the highest-ranking decoration. Recontextualization may be understood as a relocation of a discourse from its original context/practice and its appropriation within another context/ practice, or as an incorporation of elements from one social practice/context to another (Erjavec & Volcic, 2007). Recontextualization can be used by the informants to legitimize and justify a specific ideology (Fairclough, 2003).

In the light of the above, and guided by Fried (2000), I will focus on the material aspects of the decorations, more specifically, on the yellow color of the ribbon of the Decoration of Bravery. In so doing, I shall demonstrate that even such a non-verbal practice may symbolically contribute to WND through the channel of visual language. The analysis of the color of this ribbon first requires an understanding of the historical context for choosing this color. The highest decoration—the Decoration of Bravery—is shaped like the Star of David, and at the front of it are a sword and an olive branch. The decoration is attached to a yellow ribbon.

Efraim Ben Arzi, who was the head of the National Committee for the Design of Decorations explained: "The choice of the yellow background for the highest decoration is intended as a counterbalance against the attempt to shame the Jewish people using this color" (Fried, 2000: 40).

The yellow badge is one of the most well-known symbols of the Holocaust. The German government first introduced mandatory yellow badges in Poland in November 1939, and Jews who failed to wear them risked death. The German government's policy of forcing Jews to wear badges, and then confining all who wore them to ghettos, aimed at isolate the Jews from the rest of the population. It enabled the German government to identify, concentrate, deprive, starve, and ultimately murder the Jews of Europe under its control.

Recontextualization of the yellow color, its relocation from its original context/practice (yellow badge), and its appropriation within another context/ practice (the Decoration of Bravery)—outlines a linear connection between the Holocaust and the valor of Israeli fighters. Such a recontextualization may suggest that the valiant Israeli fighters are the guarantee that another Holocaust will never happen again. This logic is deeply embedded in post-World War II Zionist thought and requires one important condition: preserving WND and the ethos of life by the sword. In other words: the yellow color is intended to remind Israelis of the continuous threats menacing the state of Israel's very existence, and the answers to such threats: brave soldiers, strong IDF, and preparations against the next war.

CONCLUSION

The starting point for the analysis of Israeli military decorations is the understanding that apart from paying a sincere homage to national heroes, military decorations also function as a complex *war-normalizing strategy*. The application of CCDA—the approach adopted in this book—reveals a rich symbolic arena for achieving various political, educational and psychological goals within the sphere of the military decorations. The analysis of Knesset discussions surrounding the legislation of the Law of Military Decorations demonstrated that Knesset members were fully aware of the power which the awarding of decorations has to prepare the fighters for a long war, improve their social status, and improve the general image of the IDF. At the same time, the Knesset members expected that the decorations would help engrave in the public's mind the national-historical narrative, as well as the memory of the Holocaust.

The analysis of WND in this book focused on four main *functions*: euphemization, naturalization, legitimization, and symbolic annihilation. In addition to these *functions*, the analysis of military decorations also points towards another *function*, which we may call the *ritualization* of war and military power. *Rituralization* shifts the public focus away from war and fighting towards the marginal, ceremonial aspects of military power. Military decorations, as well as military marches, are practices of ritualization. The *Scientification* of military power, war and fighting can be classified as another *function* of WND yet to be studied. This *function* focuses on the technological aspects of the use of military power, conforming to the principles of "exact science."

Applying Discourse analysis in general, and CCDA in particular to the study of Israeli decorations, exposed the latent symbolic power existing not only in verbal texts, but also in non-verbal texts and contexts. I claim that an integrated analysis focusing on both the verbal and non-verbal aspects of the discourse is the most effective type of critical analysis for understanding complex social phenomena. Objects that are usually studied by anthropologists and sociologists such as state ceremonies and rituals or visual symbols, are also logical objects for CDA and CCDA analysis. This process can also develop in the opposite direction: methodologies, strategies and approaches of CDA and CCDA may shed new light on "anthropological," "sociological" and other non-verbal objects.

NOTES

1. An early version of chapter 7 was published in *The Journal of Political Power* (Journal of Power): Dalia Gaviely-Nuri (2009) "It Is Not the Heroes Who Need This, but the Nation: The Latent Power of Military Decorations in Israel, 1948–2005." *Journal of Power, 2* (3), 403–21. www.tandfonline.com/doi/abs/10.1080/17540290903345880. It is published by permission of the publisher. Copyright © 2009 Taylor & Francis Group.

2. See, for example, a letter from Lieutenant General Yaakov Dori dated 11.3.1949 addressed to the commanders of various IDF units. The letter includes a "proposal to grant Badges of Excellence." The proposal includes, among other suggestions: a "Badge of the Israeli Hero," a "Badge of Protector of Heroes," a "Badge of Glory," and a "Badge of Courage." Tel Hashomer, Israel, The IDF and Security System Archives 683/1949 file 229.

3. See, for example, Tel Hashomer, Israel, The IDF and Security System Archives 553/1950 file 44; 2169/1950 file 125.

4. In April 1973, as part of Israel's jubilee celebrations, 527 decorations were granted. These included retroactive bestowals to warriors in former wars. This was done through the exchange of previously bestowed citations for decorations (see table 7.1).

Chapter Eight

WND and Anti-WND 1967–1973

This chapter has two goals:

1. To demonstrate how canonic and non-canonic Hebrew literature, and even children's magazines, adopted the unwritten rules of WND.
2. To demonstrate the existence of "ugly war" discourse, which is part of anti-WND.

The analysis focuses on the period between 1967 and 1973. In so doing, the chapter completes the analysis of WND in the Israeli setting, this time using the *Discourse-Historical Approach*, DHA (Reisigl & Wodak, 2001; Wodak & Weiss, 2005), which was earlier discussed in chapter 1 and later in chapter 7. After a short historical survey, the analysis will present examples of WND and anti-WND between 1967 and 1973.

ISRAEL AFTER THE SIX DAY WAR (1967)

Israel's victory in the Six Day War presented an extraordinary balance of cost effectiveness: "in return" for a mere six days of fighting and a few hundred killed—a price considered "tolerable"—Israel has won a series of unprecedented rewards. The victory tripled Israel's territory, created a dramatic improvement in its status within the region, and at the same time marked the end of the heavy recession and the beginning of six "fat" years. Yet, it soon became evident that the attempts to preserve the fruits of this victory, and specifically the wish to continue to hold on to the newly occupied territories, were taking a military, political, and moral toll: an insistent War of Attrition along the southern border (see chapter 7), terrorist attacks by land and from the air,[1] the need to manage an occupied population of over a million people, and increasing international pressure to withdraw from the occupied territories.

Consequently, in the aftermaths of the Six Day War, the Israeli public split into two opposing ideological camps. On the one hand, a substantial proportion of the population wished to retain the strategic assets acquired during this war, and above all, the occupied territories. On the other hand, a considerable number of Israeli citizens were willing to return these recently occupied territories within a framework of a peace treaty. The government's effective (although not declared) policy supported a continued occupation.

The military victory also represented a rhetorical challenge for the public discourse, a challenge that basically resulted from the difficulty of bridging the gap between Israel's traditional image as a "peace-seeking nation," and its new image as a strong and victorious nation, with an uncompromising security policy as its key priority.

In response to this challenge, a double-faced public discourse began to develop and made it possible to include, side by side, both the ethos of the quest for peace and the fruits of the victory. The externalized and expressed element of the discourse preserved the system of values sanctifying peace, and continued to present it as a national and political supreme goal; the second part of the discourse functioned as a "backyard" in which the advantages of continuing the state of war were discussed. This second part of the discourse takes us back to WND, and mostly to the *function* of euphemization. In this chapter I will call it "The Discourse of the Beautiful War."

Indeed, as we saw in the first chapter, WND has deep historical roots that go back to the beginning of Zionism at the end of the nineteenth century. However, after the Six Day War, a new and intensive WND emerged. The new WND enabled the Israeli society to perceptually integrate the ongoing political conflict and its destructive consequences, as well as periodic concrete military threats, into the flow of daily existence.

The Discourse of the Beautiful War illuminated the term "war" as a "very useful event," one that beautifies the fighters taking part in it and bestows a series of rewards even on those who only touch its periphery. War was depicted as an event restoring youth, and granting purpose to life. The very participation in war was portrayed as some sort of hard currency, exchangeable in civilian life for material rewards, an upgrade in social status, and a feeling of self-value.

The Discourse of the Beautiful War not only euphemized war, it also symbolically annihilated the corrupting nature of occupation, and blurred and diminished the war's negative outcomes, especially death and bereavement.

A series of cultural sites, beginning with the victory albums[2] that were published after the war, continuing with the military parades and intensive awarding of military decorations (see chapter 7) and ending with speeches by leaders, all rallied together to construct this discourse. Yet the main burden of constructing *The Discourse of the Beautiful War* fell on the shoulders of the "free" culture, which was supposedly not committed to the dominant ideology: the canonical and popular literature, children's and youth literature, poetry, plays, and the songs on the radio. This culture and especially the branches of popular culture—the discourse site least suspect to ideological imposition—repeatedly provided countless examples of the advantages that resided with an increased security ideology. It justified and explained the continued occupation, helped thwart the peace initiatives that kept cropping up, and acted toward preserving an ongoing state of "neither peace—nor war."

While the "free" culture was working to beautify war, the official governmental discourse, the leaders' discourse, was free to continue to publicly echo the ethos of "seeking peace." In its leaders' speeches, Israel is depicted time and again as a nation whose hand is continually extended, in vain, for peace (Gavriely-Nuri, 2010a).

The main bulk of this chapter is dedicated to the analysis of the appearances of *The Discourse of the Beautiful War* in Israeli culture after 1967, in a variety of literary genres. To some extent, I also point to the *functions* of naturalization and, as mentioned before, symbolic annihilation. For the purpose of the analysis, I defined a corpus of about 200 cultural products, which encompassed a wide variety of genres. The analyzed corpus includes:

1. *Leaders' speeches*: speeches, interviews, biographies and autobiographies of Prime Minister Golda Meir, Minister of Defense Moshe Dayan, Chief of Staff David Elazar, and others.
2. *Literature*: children's and youth literature by prominent writers (Yigal Mosinzon, Dvora Omer, Yemima Avidar-Tchernovitz, and others), as well as fifty-one issues of *Ha'aretz Shelanu* ("Our Country") children's magazine, from September 1970 until August 1971; adult literature (A.B. Yehoshua, Amos Oz, Rachel Eitan, Hanoch Levin, Dan Ben-Amotz, Nathan Shaham, and others).
3. *Songs and military band songs*: including the leading songs from the song festivals and the hit parades.

WND BETWEEN 1967 AND 1973

Euphemization of Fighters and Civilians

In a holiday interview in the newspaper *Ma'ariv* on the eve of the Jewish New Year in September 1972, Golda Meir, then prime minister, said:

> Once you skim off the upper foam, we have a wonderful nation! A wonderful nation! I go to gatherings, to meetings with the boys of the armored corps, the

artillery, the paratroopers, the pilots [. . .] look at these boys! The most magnif-
icent of men![3]

The reference to the fighters, the most splendid and amazing young people of
the new generation, appears not only in leaders' official speeches or interviews, but also in the writing of the Israeli children and youth. Thus, for
example, in *Ha'aretz Shelanu* youth magazine, in a page dedicated to articles
by young writers, Tova Judenfeld writes:

> To you the heroes of Israel, A song of glory I shall spell / Of your heroism I
> shall say, today, tomorrow, and every day / If you were injured coming to the
> people's aid / Don't ever lose hope or be afraid / Israel will know and the
> whole world too / That the heroes of the people are none but you. / [. . .] Of
> you the soldiers of Israel, courageous and brave / We shall always sing and
> rave![4]

The military bands were especially active in the creation of "The Beautiful
Fighter Discourse." The best of the period's artists rallied to glorify the
paratroopers, the armored corpsmen, the marines, and the divers. The beau-
tification of the fighter reached one of its peaks in the song "Sparks" (*On
Silver Wings*) which Naomi Shemer, one of the most popular Israeli song
writers, dedicated to the Air Force pilots. The pilot mentioned in the song
combined earthly powers with super-human powers and miraculous qualities.

Interesting in this context is the glorification of a special kind of "heroes
against their will," who are glorified especially by the Israeli leadership.
They are, in fact, the civilians who live close to the border, and find themselves on the front lines at the outbreak of war. Thus, for example, in her
speech to present *The national unity government* (1970), the prime minister,
Golda Meir, does not forget to mention them too:

> Our fortifications and posts have withstood enemy bombings. The residents
> near the borders in the east and the north have borne the brunt of the battle
> with the utmost courage, and continue to do so [. . .] no man deserted his place,
> and the children in the border settlements have adjusted to the bomb shelters
> *as a natural way of life*. (Alkalai, 1970: 9) (emphasis added)

The minister of defense, Moshe Dayan, repeated on the *function* of naturalization:

> The Jewish Settlements, Kibbutzim and Moshavim [in the Jordan Valley],
> adapted their ways of life to the state of war. With the help of the State and the
> army they built bomb shelters, and put the children to sleep in them; paved
> internal roads, to prevent mining; increased guard duties; built lighting and
> fencing. But in no place did they abandon even a single acre of their lands. The

vineyard of *Kibbutz Gesher* has become famous, a symbol. It was in the line of fire from the Legion's posts and fire was repeatedly opened on those who worked in it. Yet despite this it was not abandoned. (Dayan, 1976: 535)

Dayan emphasizes the need for an enduring adaptation to the state of war, and has high praise for those who bit their lips and carried on with their tasks. Assigning lofty values such volunteering, loyalty, and perseverance, symbolically annihilates the high price paid, physically and mainly emotionally, by the residents of the border settlements: adults and especially thousands of children who grew up during the war years.

Not only civilians who live in border settlements are exalted. An attitude recurs in leaders' speeches which depict terrorism as a part of "nature," and portray withstanding it as a sort of mental-spiritual challenge, a broadening of the individual's personality. An apt summary of this is found in the words of Golda Meir:

> But we have learned to endure terrorism, to protect our airplanes and passengers, to turn our embassies into little fortresses and to patrol our schoolyards and our streets. I have followed the caskets and visited the bereaved families of the victims of Arab terrorism, and I was filled with pride at being part of a nation able to sustain these blows. (Meir, 1975: 290)

War and terror are depicted as a special opportunity to demonstrate virtues that can be manifested only during conflict, such as bravery, survivorship, or a special type of solidarity.

Euphemization of "War"

"War" according to the 1967–1973 Israeli discourse yields a long line of benefits. First, it is represented as beneficial for the individual's identity, as an event which opens up possibilities, grants a feeling of belonging and rejuvenates. According to this discourse, even those who are only marginally involved in war enjoy its benefits. Thus, Yair Rosenblum's song "The Parachute Folding Girls," for example, tells of girls doing a boring job, far from the front and the glory. *The Beautiful War Discourse* provides them too with an opportunity to realize their romantic dreams.

The war can even vitalize and provide new excitements for those who for various reasons have left the circle of active life.[5] In A. B. Yehoshua's novel, *Early in the Summer of 1970* (1970), the War of Attrition rejuvenates an old teacher, the story's protagonist:

> Three years ago my time came to retire, and I indeed reconciled myself to the decree [. . .] but the war broke out suddenly, and the world around me became filled with the beating of cannons and distant cries. I went to the headmaster to announce that I'm not retiring, that I'm staying at school until the war is over.

After all, now, when the young teachers are constantly being recruited into the army, he shall be in great need of me. (Yehoshua, 1970: 6; translated by the author)

The war brings back more than the old man's youth. In A. B. Yehoshua's play, *A Night in May* (1969), which takes place in the days preceding the Six Day War, Amikam, a central character in the play, recounts:

Just a week ago I was walking around in Africa, such tranquility. And suddenly—the newspapers and a news broadcast I picked up. Something tugged at my heart. And I leave the airport and there are jeeps with machine guns passing on the roads. And it was like I'd returned to my youthful days. (Yehoshua, 1975: 305; translated by the author)

The war is seen as a desirable and helpful time out, a refuge from the grinding routine. Sometimes, it can supply a solution to situations which are usually perceived as inescapable. For the fighter, the war poses one supreme challenge: to survive situations of danger. In light of this challenge, the problems of daily life are dwarfed, feelings of a dead end and lack of meaning fade. In the book *Mom, I Hate the War*—a widely popular novel written by Yigal Lev after the Six Day War—the following description appears:

Rami wanted the war. He had just finished his compulsory military duty, and since then he has been wandering, out of work. Rami said, maybe to himself, maybe to me: "You won't believe this, but I'm dying for a war to break out. [. . .] I'm sick of everything. The food, the bed, the entertainment, I need something to shake me forwards. [. . .] I need the war, because I can't decide for myself." (Lev, 1967: 9; translated by the author)

Euphemization of Occupation

The occupation of territories is a difficult and central challenge facing *The Beautiful War Discourse*, and deserves a separate analysis going beyond the years 1967 to 1973 (Halperin, et al., 2010). In the corpus analyzed in this chapter, it is given normalizing descriptions, which mask its violent character and point out its benefits for the occupiers and the occupied alike. Thus, Golda Meir, for example, writes about the days following the war in her autobiography:

In every place we arrived in those summer days of elation, of no worries almost, we met the Arabs of the territories which we now ruled, we smiled at them, we bought their produce and we talked to them, and we shared with them—though not always in words—the vision of peace which suddenly seemed about to become reality, and we tried to convey to them our happiness at that we would all be able now to live normal lives together. (Meir, 1975: 268; translated by the author)

Putting things more ironically, the defense minister, Moshe Dayan, also retorts to those who opposed the occupation:

> Do you know that about one hundred thousand Arabs came here from the neighboring Arab countries, and even the farther ones, to spend their vacation here? [. . .] Of their own free will they choose to spend their summer vacations here, under our regime of occupation, in our occupied territories, under our regime of occupation. (*Ma'ariv*, January 23, 1972)[6]

Through exaggeration and repetition ("regime of occupation," "in our occupied territories," "regime of occupation"), Dayan tries to illuminate the dark side of occupation and present an optimistic, almost utopian, picture of good neighborly relations. The word "vacation" takes the sting out of the occupation. The occupied territory, under a military regime, is depicted as a tourist attraction, a natural continuation of the "summer visits" and "open bridges policy" which also recur in the period's discourse. According to the "normal" world of images suggested by Dayan, the Arabs come to Israel while adopting an Israeli-Western behavior code of summer tourism. Indirectly, Israel's contribution is implied, expressing itself in bringing the residents of the occupied territories and of the Arab states closer to Western society.

An expression of the harmony prevailing in the territories is given by Dayan in the book in which he summarizes the first two years after the war:

> On "the West Bank" a proper way of life prevails; all the mayors elected during the Jordanian rule continue to serve in their posts and to work in cooperation with the Israeli military governors; People passing in the streets of Nablus, Hebron, and Ancient Jerusalem can see that the markets and the shops are bustling with Israeli sightseers, who buy anything that comes to hand, and the grocers, as is the custom, shovel in the rising proceeds [. . .]; the city and state services—hospitals, buses, street cleaning, provision of water and electricity—are working as usual, maybe only with less bureaucracy. (Dayan, 1969: 122)

The symbolic annihilation of the harsh and violent elements of the occupation stands out especially in children's literature. Dvora Omer's[7] book, *Nunu-nu The Dog Goes to War* (1968), intended for young readers, suggests a simple solution to the complex reality created after the occupation. According to the worldview presented in the story, the moment the war ends those who were previously enemies immediately become good neighbors, and the state of enmity ends at once. On a visit to the Old City of Jerusalem the mother of the Maoz family says: "Here we are wandering where only a few weeks ago the enemy camped, and now everybody is smiling at us and offering food and drinks (for pay, of course), souvenirs, Chinese pencils, soap, jars made of Hebron glass, and bath sponges" (p. 61). When the Maoz family dog barks at an Arab passerby, the mother says: "This dog must get used to Arabs. You should see how he barks when he so much as sees an Arab on the street. This is wrong, and if there shall soon be peace, Nu-nu-nu must know Arabs and like them" (p. 100).

Contrary to these euphemistic descriptions, after 1967 a new anti-war voice begun to emerge, which undermined *The Beautiful War Discourse*. This nascent voice will be at the center of the next section.

ANTI-WND 1967–1973

The anti-war culture suggests an alternative to some of the fundamental claims arising from the corpus, though this alternative may seem relatively marginal. This is especially so if we compare the anti-war culture's scope, quantity and relative influence with, for example, its role during the period after the outbreak of the First Lebanon War in the summer of 1982. Another problem of the anti-war culture is the very fact that it too revolves around war and makes it its main theme, and this paradoxically contributes to the establishment of war as part of the normal routine. In this sense, it seems that even the voice representing the alternative to the dominant security ethos, does not escape its all-embracing influence. As a result, both WND and "anti-WND" mutually contribute to anchoring the possibility of war in the Israeli citizens' horizon, and establishing it as part of the default array of possibilities. Thus, war infiltrates the public consciousness as a habitual component, as a central layer in the Israeli vision of a "normal" life.

The importance of anti-WND is mainly the precise manner in which it publicly lays bare the double-faced discourse, which promotes peace with one hand, and preserves the state of war on the other. In his skit *Queen of a Bathtub* (produced by the *Cameri Theater* in April 1970), Hanoch Levin precisely mimics Prime Minister Golda Meir's "peace rhetoric," and demonstrates how peace becomes a term devoid of actual content:

> From this important podium I passionately call out to our cousins wherever they may be. We come in peace. The peace is all we desire. Bring us the peace. We want peace. All we need is peace. Give us peace. We seek peace. Give us peace. (Levin, 1987: 79; translated by the author)

The term "peace" receives automatic, sometimes metaphorical, associations, which expropriate the term from its concrete dimension—as a term which describes a specific type of international relations, or a legal term of specific content. "The yearning for peace," an expression found repeatedly in leaders' speeches, as well as the expression "the hand extended for peace," emphasize the literary, picturesque and idealistic elements of peace.

Besides pointing out the emptiness of the word "peace" and the expression "the yearning for peace," anti-WND also puts the consequences of war back at the center of discussions and warns against them. The novel *Don't Give a Damn* (the literal translation of the title is: "don't give a dick," a common slang phrase in Hebrew) was published a mere few months before the Yom Kippur War. In this novel, Dan Ben-Amotz[8] confronts in a direct and precise style the consequences of war for one injured soldier who must pay for them with his soul, body, and private finances. Rafi, the protagonist, is an Israeli paratrooper who is nineteen or twenty years old. He loses his whole world during a pursuit in the *Jordan Valley* as a result of being hit by a bullet in the back. This injury sets off a chain of losses: he becomes paralyzed from the hips down; he cuts off his very close relationship with his girlfriend Nira, claiming that he doesn't want to continue a relationship which society mutely forces her to stay in; he fights with his brother and parents; and he develops an obsessive preoccupation with photographs of injured and handicapped people. Eventually, his withdrawal from the world progressively disrupts his sanity.

The distress resulting from being the parent of a combat soldier is described in the book using the characters of the soldier's parents: "the horrible picture that wracked her [Dvora, Rafi's mother] sleep during the war, when Eli [Rafi's brother] was called to reserve duty with everybody else, would return to her again: a mangled body on a stretcher, a corpse wrapped in a sheet lowered slowly into the hole" (p. 88). The everyday reality of being paralyzed from the hips down is also tackled in the book:

> When in sitting position the invalid must be sure to pull himself up on his arms every ten minutes, to prevent scrapes and bumps from the chair's frame, and to especially beware hot water burns in the bath. After walking he must perform a meticulous general check of himself to see if the heels, and any leaning point that could suffer friction of pressure, were not harmed. (p. 102; translated by the author)

The war forces Nira, a twenty-year-old young woman, to face the complex reality of being the partner of a man who is paralyzed from the hips down. Under this single heading, lay many separate difficulties. The book chooses to illuminate with cruel honesty two of these difficulties: the ability of Rafi and Nira to have children, and the future of their sex life. These topics are normally perceived as taboo, and are therefore almost never mentioned in the corpus. Using the technique of combined registers, Nira reports the summary of a conversation she had with Rafi's doctor. The careful use she makes of medical jargon gives a tragic-comical impression:

> He can reach "erection" through "manipulation" of the genital area [. . .] he can't feel anything, but I'll be able to feel everything [. . .] if the sperm is alive, I will be able to conceive, both through natural sexual relations and through artificial insemination. (p. 101; translated by the author)

In summary, the novel is almost scientifically methodical in its treatment of a wide range of war consequences, by using three techniques. The first technique is detailed descriptions—an extremely precise depiction of the daily price paid by those injured in the war, with the whole ensemble of implications that their injury carries: physical, mental, social, and economic. The second technique is the use everyday lexica—anti-heroic, anti-cliché lexica, which seeks to deconstruct some of the language routines prevalent in the period's literature. This is opposed to the high and poetic language that is usually used in relation to bereavement, as we have seen. The third technique is the use of horror descriptions—descriptions aimed at hindering the reading and making it uncomfortable. Using these three techniques, the novel tries to pose *The Ugly War Discourse* as an appropriate response to *The Discourse of the Beautiful War,* which was the dominant discourse at the time it was published.

In the next chapter we will see the political outcomes of WND between the years 1967-1973. I shall argue that, surprisingly, WND has contributed to two opposing outcomes: on the one hand, Israel missed an exceptional opportunity to sign a peace treaty with its neighbors; and on the other hand it experienced one of the most traumatic events in its history—the outbreak of the Yom Kippur War in October 1973.

NOTES

1.   Seven hundred and two civilians and soldiers were killed in the hostilities from the end of the Six Day War until the end of the War of Attrition (Haber & Schiff, 1976).

2.   The numerous *victory albums* published immediately after the war, are a song of glory to the fighters and the fighting. About these albums and the criticism against them see Segev (2005) and Gan (2002).

3.   Dov Goldstein, "An Interview with the Prime Minister, Golda Meir," *Ma'ariv*, September 8, 1972 (in Hebrew).

4.   *Ha'aretz Shelanu* 1970, issue 13 (in Hebrew).

5.   George Mosse analyzed the experience of participating in *World War I* and argued that alongside the social significance and in addition to the feeling of fraternity and partnership, it also grants existential meaning: "while the men confronted mass death everywhere, another aspect of life in the trenches impressed them: the camaraderie of soldiers in a squad living together and depending upon each other for survival. This was seen as a positive experience at war's end, for even before the war many people had longed for some sort of meaningful community in the modern world as an antidote to a pervasive feeling of loneliness" (Mosse, 1990: 5).

6.   Harris, Kenneth, "A Few More Months Left" (in Hebrew).

7.   Dvora Omer is one of the most prolific and popular children's writers in Israel. In 2006, she was awarded the Israel Prize, for her lifetime achievement and special contribution to society and the State.

8.   An Israeli writer, 1923–1989.

Conclusion

How WND Led to The Yom Kippur War (1973)

Since Israel's establishment in 1948, WND has been in use throughout different periods, ranging from periods of total war to periods of relative peace. I argue that after it had been used for so long, WND has become a fundamental part of the Israeli public discourse concerning both peace and war. Moreover, it has become an integral part of the Israeli identity. WND affects Israeli society, the Israeli regime and the daily life of Israelis. Above all, it quietly influences Israel's security policy and its relations with its neighbors. Another significant insight is that after so many years, the WND no longer serves the needs of neither the hegemony, nor the civilians. This mechanism has taken on a life of its own. It promotes and sustains an independent agenda of what we may call a *culture of ongoing war*.

In this concluding chapter, I shall focus on two issues which illustrate future possibilities for research on the subject of WND:

1. The influence of WND on the Israeli political reality
2. The *Normalizing Discourse* beyond the context of war

WND BETWEEN PEACE AND WAR

The intensive WND which was employed after the Six Day War (see chapter 8) blurred the distinction between "peace" and "war." Thus:

1. It contributed to a pattern of systematically missing opportunities for the establishment of peace treaties between Israel and its opponents.
2. It helped pave the way toward the outbreak of the Yom Kippur War.

WND was instrumental in the creation of the misperception that the political situation after 1967 was normal, giving the illusion of relative peace. Otherwise, it would be hard to understand the many repeated missed opportunities for peace negotiations (Bavly, 2002). WND helped the Israeli government at the time maintain public support while rejecting at least ten peace initiatives offered by different countries, including those proposed by the United Nations (Ibid.).[1]

Equally tragic was the fact that, in the six years following the Six Day War, WND became habitual, self-evident, and self-explanatory. It contributed to the misinterpretation of a series of visible and direct preparations for the Yom Kippur War initiated by Egypt and Syria (Bar-Joseph, 2005). These preparations were not perceived as dangerous or immediate threats, and were interpreted as "normal." Israel therefore ignored its enemies' preparations for the Yom Kippur War, which included:

1. The urgent departure of Soviet military experts prior to the war;
2. The massive reinforcement of Arab military forces and their deployment in attack positions;
3. The neutralization of the mine field west of the Suez Canal, which cleared the way for the passage of military forces; and
4. The dismantling of the dirt batteries along the Suez Canal to facilitate the passage of artillery forces.

Astonishingly, these and many other obvious preparations did not set off any alarm bells, and were not perceived as signs indicating possible military attack. To a great extent, WND had dulled their potential sting. Instead, the events were interpreted as "normal" Egyptian military exercises; similar to those that had been routinely taking place since the Six Day War. On the Syrian front, the war preparations were interpreted as a "normal" response to an unsuccessful air combat a few weeks earlier. Such combats were quite usual, and erupted every now and again between the Israeli and Syrian armies with no major consequences to either side. They were called "days of combat" and formed part of the reality in the zone during those years.

The intensive use of WND between the years 1967 and 1973 has contributed to the creation of a distorted and faulty notion of "war." By normalizing the threat, it in fact prevented the swift and appropriate defensive action, which was in fact required on 6 October 1973. The Yom Kippur War is registered in the Israeli public memory as a traumatic event (see chapter 7). It is recorded in the history of wars as one of the three largest strategic surprises of the twentieth century, besides the attack on Pearl Harbor and Operation Barbarossa.

The analysis of WND in the context of the surprise attack that triggered the Yom Kippur War presents only one example of the complex relationship between this discourse and the recurrence of Israeli wars. I leave the systematic analysis of this issue for future research. At this point, I shall only raise one more question: What was the contribution, if any, of WND to the success or failure of the *peace process* Israel took part in? At the moment, I can only suggest that WND is one of the crucial factors determining the Israeli public's attitude toward peace. The stronger the WND, the weaker the public's readiness for reconciliation is, and vice versa. Contrary to the years following the Six Day War, after the Yom Kippur War, WND was perhaps at one of its lowest points in Israeli history. For the first time since the establishment of the state, this traumatic war demonstrated the "abnormality" of war in terms of casualties, disruption of normal life, etc. It is not surprising then that this war, which seriously weakened WND, led to the first peace treaty between Israel and one of its most bitter enemies.

BEYOND WARS: THE NORMALIZATION OF POVERTY AND OF OTHER INCONVENIENT ISSUES

The Normalizing Discourse (ND), the analytical tool suggested in this book for the analysis of war, may also be applied to other disturbing social issues. By "disturbing social issues" I refer to controversial social issues that can potentially be subjected to ND, using the *discursive strategies* that were presented in this book. Poverty, diseases, corruption, earthquakes, global warming, ethnic minorities and disabled people can all be "normalized" using euphemization, naturalization, legitimization, and symbolic annihilation.

I shall now focus on one of those issues as a specific example: the normalization of "poverty" within the Israeli culture. The issue of poverty is intensively normalized by Israeli television during periods prior to the major Israeli holidays. Before the major Israeli holidays (Jewish New Year and Passover), Israeli television channels never fail to present a moving story demonstrating the "pretty side" of poverty: NGOs and other groups of volunteers who collect food products and deliver them to poor people so that they may celebrate the festive dinner (the eve of the New Year and the eve of Passover) with the rest of "Am Yisrael" (the Jewish people). In the last few years, this construction of "poverty discourse" has been so popular in the Israeli media that, like the *Hero Code* of the wounded soldiers, it has become a *cultural code*. This code not only euphemizes the solidarity and responsibility of the Israeli society; it also symbolically annihilates the darker sides of poverty and, more importantly, it excludes from the discourse the more essential questions such as, for example: What do these poor people eat a day or two before or after the eve of the holiday? Or, why are there hundreds of thousands of people in Israel who cannot afford to buy food?

In a similar vein, Soffer, et al., point to "the social invisibility of people with disabilities in Israel" (2010: 691). Their studies also show that one of the most mediated images of individuals with disabilities in the Israeli press is that of high-achieving individuals with disabilities who set high standards that others fail to meet. In our terminology, Soffer, et al., have demonstrated that two *functions* of the ND, euphemization and symbolic annihilation, are dominant in the Israeli media discourse concerning disabled people.

It is important to note that "social problems" are not the only issues which may be subjected to ND. Controversial ideologies and suppressive policies may also be subjected to it. Rojo and Van Dijk (1997) exemplified the power of normalizing discourse in relation to racism. They explored the discursive strategies used by the Spanish Secretary of the Interior, Mayor Oreja, to legitimize and naturalize (or, generally speaking, in our terminology, "to normalize") his decision to expel 103 Africans from the Spanish enclave of Melilla in 1996. Their discussion on "normality" clarifies the special power of ND in civilian contexts:

> One major political strategy of legitimization used by the Secretary to empha-size that this operation was not in any way new, exceptional or otherwise merely his own initiative. The Secretary does this first by emphasizing that all actions of himself and the authorities are not only legal, but also standard procedures [. . .]. Thus, his claim that the present operation is nothing special and nothing new is a strong reminder for the members of the committee that they in fact share the responsibility for the action. Also in his description of the treatment of the migrants he uses the words "habitual" and "usual" to empha-size that the action was normal, and hence legitimate. (p. 537)

In yet another context, Wodak and van Leeuwen (2002) have demonstrated how the globalization rhetoric enables politicians and bureaucrats to propose economic and social adjustments by "reifying and naturalising globalisation, thus providing arguments that make change appear inevitable and necessary" (2002: 348).

Harsh collective or individual memories may also be subjected to ND. Benke and Wodak (2003) explored "How Austrian 'Wehrmacht' Soldiers Remember WWII" and more specifically how Nazi war crimes had been conceptually "purified" in retrospect. In the terminology used in this book, it may be said that they analyzed the *discursive strategies* that enabled the normalization of a "disturbing" history. In a similar context, Achugar ana-lyzed the discursive manifestations of conflicts over the memory of the mili-tary's actions during the last dictatorship in Uruguay (1973–1985). She re-vealed how the military institution manipulated the discourse in order to justify its violation of human rights in the past and construct its identity in relation to ethical norms (Achugar, 2007, 2008). Achugar (2007) quoted

Walton's saying: "History is not simply a record of these events, it is a justification for them" (Walton, 2001: xvii).

These examples of ND, which relate to various social, ideological and historical issues in various cultures, prove that a systematic analysis of ND is yet to be explored. In the last section, I shall return to the War-Normalizing Discourse and suggest more directions for future research.

FUTURE RESEARCH

The main purpose of this book was to introduce WND as an analytic tool for the analysis of war discourses, using the analysis of the Israeli case as an example. The choice of focusing on the *cultural* discursive aspect of WND, and consequently to apply CCDA (Cultural Approach to CDA), meant that some other interesting aspects of WND have not been discussed at length. Those aspects include, for example:

1. *Sociological aspects and questions of identity*: For example, what is the specific contribution of political leaders, journalists, military commanders or citizens to the creation of WND and which discursive sites (speeches, newspapers, songs, films, talkbacks, etc.) do they use for its creation?
2. *Historical factors*: For example, the historical changes in WND since the establishment of Israel (1948).
3. *Psychological aspects*: For example, exploring WND and its relation to the Israeli public's attitudes towards the initiation of new wars or towards new peace initiatives.
4. *International relationships*: What is the impact of WND on Israel's foreign policy? Is WND a catalyst of new wars or does it in fact contribute to a more moderate use of military power?
5. *Alternative discourses*: What are the alternatives to WND, if any, and who uses them?
6. *Beyond the Israeli WND*: Assuming that WND is not an Israeli invention: To what extent do other cultures use this discourse? What are the main *functions* and *discursive strategies* that they use in the process?

These important questions deserve future research.

One objective guiding much critical research is the need to uncover the political cultures and national histories that sustain and disseminate problematic social practices. As this book has demonstrated, the Israeli war discourse provides ample opportunity for developing analytic tools promoting this objective. The approach that has been proposed and applied throughout this book to the cultural analysis of discourse is the *Cultural Approach to*

Critical Discourse Analysis (CCDA). The *War-Normalizing Discourse* (WND) was another important analytical tool, which I have introduced and used for my research. I hope that these analytic tools will provide a framework for other scholars to apply in their research on war discourses, as well as in the broader field of CDA.

NOTE

1. But see, for example, Gazit (1997: 97): "Sadat was not yet willing in 1971–1973 to make any compromise whatsoever, insisting on every detail of the collective Arab stand. The implication of this is that the diplomatic moves of the United States or Israel in 1971 had no real chance of success."

Glossary

- **WND** = War-Normalizing Discourse
- **CCDA** = Cultural Approach to CDA
- **IDF** = Israel Defense Forces

WND'S KEY TERMS

- **War Normalizing Discourse (WND).** A set of linguistic, discursive and cultural devices aimed at blurring the anomalous character of war by transforming it into an event perceived as a "natural" or "normal" part of life. WND fulfills at least one of *four "functions."*
- **WND's Four "Functions."** Euphemization, Naturalization, Legitimization, *Symbolic annihilation.*
- **Symbolic Annihilation**. One of the four *"functions."* A total exclusion of war from the discourse or some of its components by omitting or blurring its basic negative characteristics, such as death and economic damages.
- **War-Normalizing Strategies**. *Discursive strategies* aimed at normalizing war by fulfilling one of the *four "functions."* For example: war-euphemizing *metaphors*, war-naturalizing names (or naming).
- **The WND Matrix**. The "multiplication table" of WND including all the *war-normalizing strategies*. The Matrix combines vertical *discursive elements and* horizontal *functions*.

133

- **WND's Global Market**. Appearances of WND in various national war discourses. WND's global market is open to all political leaders and exists for "trading" *war-normalizing strategies*.

CCDA'S KEY TERMS

- **CCDA**. Cultural Approach to Critical Discourse Analysis (CDA). CCDA aims to uncover the cultural and cross-cultural codes embedded in discourse.
- **Cultural Code**. A network of shared values, norms and social beliefs that, due to their constant repetition in set combinations, constructs a cultural community's "common sense."

Table G.1. Names of the Israeli Wars[1] (In Israeli Discourse)

1948 War	The War of Independence The War of Liberation
1956 War	The Sinai Operation The Kadesh Operation
1967 War	The Six Day War
1969–1970 War	The War of Attrition
1973 War	The Yom Kippur War
1982 War	The First Lebanon War Operation Peace for the Galilee Operation Snow
2006 War	The Second Lebanon War
2008 War	Operation Cast Lead

1. It is important to note that this table regards as war any acts (such as the peace for Galilee operation or the Cast Lead operation) that in terms of scope, duration and outcome can be regarded as wars, even if not declared by Israeli government as a war.

Bibliography

Achugar, Mariana (2007). Between Remembering and Forgetting: Uruguayan Military Discourse About Human Rights (1976–2004). *Discourse and Society 18*, 521–47.

Achugar, Mariana (2008). *What We Remember: The Construction of Memory in Military Discourse*. Amsterdam/Philadelphia: John Benjamins.

Aday, Sean (2005). The Real War Will Never Get on Television: Analysis of Casualty Imagery in American Television Coverage of the Iraq War. In Philip Seib (Ed.). *Media and Conflict in the Twenty-First Century* (pp. 141–56). New York: Palgrave Macmillan.

Aditi, Bhatia (2008). Discursive Illusions in the American National Strategy for Combating Terrorism. *Journal of Language and Politics 7* (2), 201–27.

Akmajian, Adrian, Demers, Richard A., Farmer, Ann K., & Harnish, Robert M. (Eds.) (2001). *Linguistics: An Introduction to Language and Communication*. Cambridge: MIT.

Albakry, Mohammed (2004). U.S. "Friendly Fire" Bombing of Canadian Troops: Analysis of the Investigative Reports. *Critical Inquiry in Language Studies, 1* (3), 163–78.

Alimi, Eitan Y. (2007). *Israeli Politics and the First Palestinian Intifada*. Routledge: New York.

Alkalai, Reuven (Ed.) (1970). *The Prime Minister's Office Government Yearbook*. Jerusalem: Publicity Services (in Hebrew).

Allan, Stuart, & Zelizer, Barbie (2004). Introduction: Rules of Engagement: Journalism and War. In Allan Stuart & Barbie Zelizer (Eds.), *Reporting War: Journalism in Wartime* (pp. 3–21). New York: Routledge.

Almog, Oz (2000). *The Sabra: The Creation of the New Jew*. Berkeley: University of California Press.

Alterman, Nathan (1941). *Joy of the Poor: Poems*. Tel Aviv: Machbarot Lesifrut (in Hebrew).

Alterman, Nathan (1944). *Plague Poems*. Tel Aviv: Machbarot Lesifrut (in Hebrew).

Anden-Papadopoulos, K. (2008). The Abu Ghraib Torture Photographs: News Frames, Visual Culture, and the Power of Images. *Journalism, 9* (1), 5–30.

Anderson, Jeffrey W. (1986). Military Heroism: An Occupational Definition. *Armed Forces and Society, 12*, 591–606.

Angus, Lynne, & Korman, Yifaht. (2002). Conflict, Coherence, and Change in Brief Psychotherapy: A Metaphor Theme Analysis. In S. Fussell (Ed.), *The Verbal Communication of Emotions: Interdisciplinary Perspectives* (pp. 151–66). Mahwah, NJ: Lawrence Erlbaum Associates.

Arazi, Abraham (1982). *And These Are the Names of the Sons of Israel*. Tel Aviv: Lesharshim (in Hebrew).

Arian, Asher (1995). *Security Threatened: Surveying Israeli Opinion on Peace and War*. Cambridge: Cambridge University Press.

135

Ariel, Yaakov (1999). *The Road to Damascus: Memories of Captivity*. Tel Aviv: Sifriat Poalim (in Hebrew).

Avneyon, Eitan (Ed.) (2000). *Word for Word—Thesaurus of the Hebrew Language*. Tel Aviv: Eitav (in Hebrew).

Azaryahu, Maoz (1995). *State Rituals: Independence Celebrations and the Commemoration of the Fallen in Israel, 1948–1956*. Ben-Gurion University in the Negev (in Hebrew).

Azaryahu, Maoz (1996). The Power of Commemorative Street Names. Environment and Planning. *Society and Space, 14*. 311–30.

Azaryahu, Maoz (1997). German Reunification and the Politics of Street Names: The Case of East Berlin. *Political Geography, 16* (6), 479–93.

Azaryahu, Maoz (1999). The Independence Day Military Parade: A Political History of a Patriotic Rritual. In Edna Lomsky-Feder and Eyal Ben Ari (Eds.), *The Military and Militarism in Israeli Society* (pp. 89–116). New York: State University of New York Press.

Barak, Dudu, Heller, Dalia, & Shiloni, Amnon (Eds.) (1983). *Soldiers Embarked on Their Way: 101 Songs of the Military Bands*. Tel Aviv: Ministry of Defense Publishing House (in Hebrew).

Bar-Gal, Yoram (1987). Names for Tel Aviv's Streets: A Chapter in Urban Cultural History (1909–1933). *Katedra, 47*, 118–31 (in Hebrew).

Bar-Gal, Yoram (1989). Cultural-Geographical Aspects of Street Names in the Towns of Israel. *Names, 37* (4), 329–43.

Bar-Joseph, Uri (2005). *The Watchman Fell Asleep: The Surprise of Yom Kippur and Its Sources*. Albany: State University of New York Press.

Bar-Joseph, Uri (2006). Last Chance to Avoid War: Sadat's Peace Initiative of February 1973 and Its Failure. *Journal of Contemporary History, 41* (3), 545–56.

Bar-Lev, Zev (2007). Mrs. Goldberg's Rebuttal of Butt, et al. *Discourse and Society, 18*, 183–96.

Bar-Tal, Daniel (1983). *The Masada Syndrome: A Case of Central Belief*. Jerusalem: The International Center for Peace in the Middle East.

Bar-Tal, Daniel (1998). Societal Beliefs in Times of Intractable Conflict: The Israeli Case. *International Journal of Conflict Management, 9* (1), 22–50.

Bar-Tal, Daniel (2000). *Shared Beliefs in a Society: Social Psychological Analysis*. Thousand Oaks, CA: Sage.

Bar-Tal, Daniel (in press). *Intractable Conflicts: Psychological Foundations and Dynamics*. Cambridge: Cambridge University Press.

Bar-Tal, Daniel, & Oren, Neta (2000). *Ethos as an Expression of Identity: Its Changes in Transition from Conflict to Peace in the Israeli Case*. Jerusalem: Leonard Davis Institute for International Relations, The Hebrew University.

Bar-Tal, Daniel, & Teichman, Yona (2005). *Stereotypes and Prejudice in Conflict: Representation of Arabs in Israeli Jewish Society*. Cambridge: Cambridge University Press.

Bar-Tal, Daniel, Raviv, Amiram, Raviv, Alona, & Dgani-Hirsh, Adi (2009). The Influence of the Ethos of Conflict on Israeli Jews' Interpretation of Jewish-Palestinian Encounters. *Journal of Conflict Resolution, 53* (1), 94–118.

Barthes, Roland (1972). *Mythologies* (trans. Annette Lavers). London: Cape.

Barthes, Roland (1977). *Image-Music-Text*. London: Fontana.

Barzilai, Gad (1992). *Democracy in Wars*. Tel Aviv: Sifriat Poalim (in Hebrew).

Bavly, Dan (2002). *Dreams and Missed Opportunities*. Jerusalem: Karmel (in Hebrew).

Beer, A. Francis, & De Landtsheer, Christ'l (2004). Introduction. Metaphors, Politics, and World Politics. In Francis A. Beer & Christ'l De Landtsheer (Eds.), *Metaphorical World Politics* (pp. 5–58). East Lansing: Michigan State University Press.

Bellamy, Alex J. (2004). Ethics and Intervention: The "Humanitarian Exception" and the Problem of Abuse in the Case of Iraq. *Journal of Peace Research, 41* (2), 131–47.

Ben-Amotz, Dan (1973). *Don't Give a Dick*. Tel Aviv: Bitan (in Hebrew).

Ben-Eliezer, Uri (1998). *The Making of Israeli Militarism*. Bloomington: University of Indiana Press.

Ben-Eliezer, Uri, & Robbins, Joyce. Gender Inequality and Cultural Militarism—The Significance of the Partial Containment of the IDF's Women Soldiers. In Haggith Gor (2005). *Militarism in Education* (pp. 245–75). Tel Aviv: Bavel (in Hebrew).

Benford, Robert D., & Snow, David A. (2000). Framing Processes and Social Movements: An Overview and Assessment. *Annual Review of Sociology, 26*, 611–39.

Benke, Gertraud, & Wodak, Ruth (2003). The Discursive Construction of Individual Memories: How Austrian "Wehrmacht" Soldiers Remember WWII. In J. R. Martin & Ruth Wodak (Eds.), *Re/Reading the Past: Critical and Functional Perspectives on Time and Value* (pp. 115–38). Amsterdam: John Benjamins.

Bennett, Lance W. (1990). Toward a Theory of Press State Relations in the U.S. *Journal of Communication, 40*, 103–25.

Bennett, Lance W. & Livingston, Steven (2003). Editors' Introduction: A Semi-Independent Press: Government Control and Journalistic Autonomy in the Political Construction of News. *Political Communication, 20* (4), 359–62.

Bennett, Lance W., Lawrence, Regina G., & Livingston, Steven (2006). None Dare Call It Torture: Indexing and the Limits of Press Independence in the Abu Ghraib Scandal. *Journal of Communication, 56*, 467–85.

Ben-Zvi, Avraham (1979). *Surprise Attacks as a Research Field*. Ontario: Peace Research Institute.

Berg, Herbert (2005). Mythmaking in the African American Muslim Context: The Moorish Science Temple, the Nation of Islam and the American Society of Muslims. *Journal of the American Academy of Religion, 73* (3), 685–703.

Billig, Michael, & McMillan, Katie (2005). Metaphor, Idiom and Ideology: The Search for "No Smoking Guns" Across Time. *Discourse and Society, 16* (4), 459–80.

Bishara, Marwan (2001). *Palestine/ Israel: Peace or Apartheid, Occupation, Terrorism and the Future*. New York: St. Martin's Press.

Bitan, Dan (1996). Myths of Fighting Bravery in the Early Days of Zionism. In David Ohana & Robert Wistreich (Eds.), *Myth and Memory* (pp. 169-86). Tel Aviv: Hakibbutz Hameuchad (in Hebrew).

Boltanski, Luc (1999). *Distant Suffering: Morality, Media and Politics* (trans. Graham Burchell). Cambridge: Cambridge University Press.

Bosmajian, Haig A. (1984). Dehumanizing People and Euphemizing War. *Christian Century* (1984), 1147. www.religiononline.org/showarticle.asp?title=1442.

Bourdieu, Pierre (1977). *Outline of a Theory of Practice*. Cambridge: Cambridge University Press.

Bourdieu, Pierre (1986). *Distinction: A Social Critique of the Judgment of Taste*. London: Routledge.

Bourdieu, Pierre (1993). *The Field of Cultural Production: Essay on Art and Literature*. Cambridge: Polity Press.

Bourdieu, Pierre (1998). *On Television*. New York: The New Press.

Bridgeman, Cathleen A. (2000). *What Kind of Peace Is This? Metaphor in the U.S. Press Coverage of Israeli-Palestinian Negotiations*. Unpublished doctoral dissertation. Program of Linguistics: University of South Carolina.

Bridgeman, Cathleen (2002). Playing at Peace: Game Metaphors in Discussions of the Israeli-Palestinian Conflict. *British Journal of Middle Eastern Studies, 29* (2), 165–67.

Brownfield-Stein, Chava (2010). Visual Representations of IDF Women Soldiers and 'Civil-Militarism' in Israel. In Gabriel Sheffer & Oren Barak (Eds.), *Militarism and Israeli Society* (pp. 304–28). Bloomington: Indiana University Press.

Buttny, Richard, & Donald, Eliis G. (2007). Accounts of Violence from Arabs and Israelis on Nightline. *Discourse and Society, 18* (2), 139–61.

Cameron, Lynne J. (2007). Patterns of Metaphor Use in Reconciliation Talk. *Discourse and Society, 18* (2), 197–222.

Carpentier, Nico (2008). Dichotomized Media Discourse of War: The Construction of the Self and the Enemy in the 2003 Iraq War. In Nico Carpentier & Erik Spinoy (Eds.), *Discourse Theory and Cultural Analysis: Media, Arts and Literature* (pp. 29–54). New York: Hampton Press.

Cavin, Margaret, & Hale, Katherine (1997). Metaphors of Control toward a Language of Peace: Recent Self-Defining Rhetorical Constructs of Helen Caldicott. *Peace and Change, 22* (3), 243–64.

Chambers, Ross (2003). The War of the Words: The Rhetoric of "Operation Iraqi Freedom" (an informal survey). *Culture, Theory and Critique, 44* (2), 171–81.

Charteris-Black, Jonathan (2004). *Corpus Approaches to Critical Metaphor Analysis*. Houndmills, Basingstoke, Hampshire: Palgrave Macmillan.

Charteris-Black, Jonathan (2005). *Politicians and Rhetoric: The Persuasive Power of Metaphor*. New York: Basingstoke: Palgrave, Macmillan.

Chilton, Paul (1984). Orwell, Language and Linguistics. *Language and Communication, 4* (2), 129–46.

Chilton, Paul (1985). Words, Discourse and Metaphors: The Meanings of Deter, Deterrent, and Deterrence. In Paul A. Chilton (Ed.), *Language and the Nuclear Arms Debate* (pp. 27–103). London: Pinter.

Chilton, Paul (1987). Metaphor, Euphemism and the Militarization of Language. *Current Research on Peace and Violence, 10* (1), 7–19.

Chilton, Paul (1996a). The Meaning of Security. In Francis A. Beer & Robert Hariman (Eds.), *Post-Realism: The Rhetorical Turn in International Relations* (pp. 193–216). East Lansing: Michigan State University Press.

Chilton, Paul (1996b). *Security Metaphors: Cold War Discourse from Containment to Common European Home*. New York: Peter Lang.

Chilton, Paul (1998). *Orwellian Language and the Media*. London: Pluto Press.

Chilton, Paul (2002). Do Something! Conceptualizing Responses to the Attacks of 11 September 2001. *Journal of Language and Politics, 1* (1), 181–95.

Chilton, Paul (2004). *Analysing Political Discourse: Theory and Practice*. London: Routledge.

Chilton, Paul (2005a). Missing Links in Mainstream CDA: Modules, Blends and the Critical Instinct. In Ruth Wodak & Paul Chilton (Eds.), *A New Agenda in (Critical) Discourse Analysis—Theory, Methodology and Interdisciplinary* (pp. 19–51). Amsterdam/Philadelphia: John Benjamins.

Chilton, Paul (2005b). Manipulation, Memes and Metaphors: The Case of *Mein Kampf*. In Louis de Saussure & Peter J. Schulz (Eds.), *Manipulation and Ideologies in the Twentieth Century* (pp. 5–45). Amsterdam: John Benjamins.

Chilton, Paul A., & Ilyin, Mikhail (1993). Metaphor in Political Discourse: The Case of the "Common European House." *Discourse and Society, 4* (1), 7–31.

Chilton, Paul A., & Schäffner, Christina (2002). Introduction: Themes and Principles in the Analysis of Political Discourse. In Paul A. Chilton & Christina Schäffner (Eds.), *Politics as Text and Talk: Analytic Approaches to Political Discourse* (pp. 1–41). Amsterdam: John Benjamins.

Chilton, Paul, & Lakoff, G. (1995). Metaphor in Foreign Policy Discourse. In Christina Schäeffner & Anita Wenden (Eds.), *Language and Peace* (pp. 37–60). Dartmouth: Aldershot.

Chong, Dennis, & Druckman, James N. (2007). A Theory of Framing and Opinion Formation in Competitive Elite Environments. *Journal of Communication, 57* (1), 99–118.

Chouliaraki, Lilie (2004). Watching September 11: The Politics of Pity. *Discourse and Society, 15* (2–3), 185–98.

Chouliaraki, Lilie (2006a). *The Spectatorship of Suffering*. London: Sage.

Chouliaraki, Lilie (2006b). The Aestheticization of Suffering on Television. *Visual Communication, 5* (3), 261–85.

Chouliaraki, Lilie (2007a). Introduction: The Soft Power of War: Legitimacy and Community in Iraq War Discourses. In Lilie Chouliaraki (Ed.), *The Soft Power of War* (pp. 1–10). Amsterdam: John Benjamins.

Chouliaraki, Lilie (2007b). Spectacular Ethics: On the Television Footage of The Iraq War. In Lilie Chouliaraki (Ed.), *The Soft Power of War* (pp. 143–59). Amsterdam: John Benjamins.

Cohen, Stuart A. (2008). *Israel and Its Army: From Cohesion to Confusion*. London: Routledge.

Cromer, G. (2004). *A War of Words: Political Violence and Public Debate in Israel*. London: Frank Cass.

Curticapean, Alina (2006). Power, Metaphor and the Power of Metaphor. Presented in ECPR Joint Sessions of Workshops, Nicosia, April 25–30, 2006.

D'Angelo, Paul (2002). News Framing as a Multiparadigmatic Research Program: A Response to Entman. *Journal of Communication, 52* (4), 870–88.

Daniel, Dor (2001). *Thank You for That Positive Report—Newspapers under the Influence*. Tel Aviv: Bavel (in Hebrew).

Dor, Daniel (2004). *Intifada Hits the Headlines: How the Israeli Press Misreported the Outbreak of the Second Palestinian Uprising*. Bloomington: Indiana University Press.

Dayan, Moshe (1969). *New Map Different Relations*. Tel Aviv: Ma'ariv Library (in Hebrew).

Dayan, Moshe (1976). *Milestones: Autobiography*. Jerusalem: Idanim (in Hebrew).

De-Cillia, Rudolf, Reisigl, Martin, & Wodak, Ruth (1999). The Discursive Construction of National Identities. *Discourse and Society, 10*, 149–73.

Deetz, Stanley (1984). Metaphor Analysis. In William B. Gudykunst & Young Yun Kim (Eds.), *Methods for Intercultural Communication Research*, (pp. 215–28). Beverly Hills: Sage.

De-Leonardis, Fabio (2008). War as a Medicine: The Medical Metaphor in Contemporary Italian Political Language. *Social Semiotics, 181*, 33–45.

De-Vreese, Claes H. (2004). The Effects of Frames in Political Television News on Issue Interpretation and Frame Salience. *Journalism and Mass Communication Quarterly, 81* (1), 36–53.

De-Vreese, Claes H. (2005). The Spiral of Cynicism Reconsidered. *European Journal of Communication, 20* (3), 283–301.

De-Vreese, Claes H., & Boomgaarden G., Hajo (2005). Projecting EU Referendums: Fear of Immigration and Support for European Integration. *European Union Politics, 6*, 59–82.

De-Vreese, Claes H., & Boomgaarden G. Hajo (2006). Media Message Flows and Interpersonal Communication—The Conditional Nature of Effects on Public Opinion. *Communication Research, 33* (1), 19–37.

Dimitrova, Daniela V., & Strömbäck, Jesper (2005). Mission Accomplished? Framing of the Iraq War in the Elite Newspapers in Sweden and the United States. *The International Journal for Communication Studies, 67* (5), 399–417.

Dolev, Diana (2005). A Feminist Look at the Hebrew University Campus on Mt. Scopus. In Haggith Gor, *Militarism in Education* (pp. 187–205). Tel Aviv: Bavel (in Hebrew).

Don-Yehiya, Eliezer (1993). Memory and Political Culture: Israeli Society and the Holocaust. *Studies in Contemporary Jewry, IX*, 139–61.

Drulak, Peter (2006). Motion, Container and Equilibrium: Metaphors in the Discourse about European Integration. *European Journal of International Relations, 12* (4), 499–531.

Dunmire, Patricia L. (1997). Naturalizing the Future in Factual Discourse: A Critical Linguistic Analysis of a Projected Event. *Written Communication, 14* (2), 221–63.

Dunmire, Patricia L. (2007). "Emerging Threats" and "Coming Dangers": Claiming the Future for Preventive War. In Adam Hodges & Chad Nilep (Eds.), *Discourse, War, and Terrorism* (pp. 19–43). Amsterdam: John Benjamins.

Dunmire, Patricia L. (2009). 9/11 Changed Everything: An Intertextual Analysis of the Bush Doctrine. *Discourse and Society, 20*, 195–222.

Eades, Diana (2000). I Don't Think It's an Answer to the Question: Silencing Aboriginal Witnesses in Court. *Language in Society, 29*, 161–95.

Eagleton, Terry (1991). *Ideology: An Introduction*. London: Verso.

Edwards, Jason A. & Valenzano, Joseph M. (2007). Bill Clinton's "New Partnership" Anecdote: Toward a Post-Cold War Foreign Policy Rhetoric. *Journal of Language and Politics, 6* (3), 303–25.

Edwards, John & Martin, J. R. (2004). Introduction: Approaches to Tragedy. *Discourse and Society, 15* (2–3), 147–54.

Elliott, Deni, & Lester, Paul Martin (2003). Manipulation: The Word We Love to Hate (Part 2). *News Photographer, 58* (9), 12–13.

Elwood, William N. (1995). Declaring War on the Home Front: Metaphor, Presidents and the War on Drugs. *Metaphor and Symbol, 10* (2), 93–115.

Entman Robert M. (2010). Media Framing Biases and Political Power: Explaining Slant in News of Campaign 2008. *Journalism, 11* (4), 389–408.

Entman, Robert M. (1993). Framing: Toward a Clarification of a Fractured Paradigm. *Journal of Communication, 43* (4), 51–58.

Entman, Robert M. (2003). Cascading Activation: Contesting the White House's Frame after 9/11. *Political Communication, 20* (4), 415–32.

Entman, Robert M. (2004). *Projections of Power: Framing News, Public Opinion, and U.S. Foreign Policy.* Chicago: The University of Chicago Press.

Erez, Yaacov, & Kfir, Ilan (Eds.) (1982). *The IDF and Its Corps—The Encyclopedia of Military and Security.* Tel Aviv: Maariv (in Hebrew).

Erjavec, Karmen, & Volcic, Zala (2007). "War on Terrorism" as a Discursive Battleground: Serbian Recontextualization of G. W. Bush's Discourse. *Discourse and Society, 18* (2), 123–37.

Fairclough, Norman (1989). *Language and Power.* London: Longman.

Fairclough, Norman (1995). *Critical Discourse Analysis: The Critical Study of Language.* London: Longman.

Fairclough, Norman (2000). Discourse, Social Theory and Social Research: The Discourse of Welfare Reform. *Journal of Sociolinguistics, 4,* 163–95.

Fairclough, Norman (2003). *Analyzing Discourse: Textual Analysis for Social Research.* London: Routledge.

Fairclough, Norman (2007). Blair's Contribution to Elaborating a New "Doctrine of International Community." In Lilie Chouliaraki (Ed.), *The Soft Power of War,* (pp. 39–60). Amsterdam: John Benjamins.

Fairclough, Norman (2009). *A Dialectical-Relational Approach to Critical Discourse Analysis in Social Research.* In Ruth Wodak & Michael Meyer (Eds.), *Methods of Critical Discourse Analysis* (pp. 162–86). London: Sage.

Fairclough, Norman & Wodak, Ruth (1997). Critical Discourse Analysis. In Teun. A. van Dijk (Ed.), *Discourse as Social Interaction* (pp. 258–84). London: Sage.

Ferrari, Federica (2007). Metaphor at Work in the Analysis of Political Discourse: Investigating a "Preventive War" Persuasion Strategy. *Discourse and Society, 18* (5), 603–25.

First, Aant, & Avraham, Eli (2004). *Media Representation of the Arab Population in the Hebrew Media: Comparison between the Coverage of the First Land Day (1976) and the Al-Akza Intifada (2000).* Tel Aviv: Tel Aviv University, Tami Steinmetz Center for Peace Research (in Hebrew).

Fisher, Solomon J. (1985). Speaking of No One: The Logical Status of Fictional Proper Names. *Names, 33,* 145–57.

Foucault, Michel (1969). *The Archaeology of Knowledge.* London: Routledge.

Foucault, Michel (1972). *Power/Knowledge.* New York: Pantheon.

Fountaine, Susan, & McGregor, Judy (2002). Reconstructing Gender for the 21st Century: News Media Framing of Political Women in New Zealand. *ANZCA,* On-line Journal: http://praxis.massey.ac.nz/fileadmin/praxis/papers/JMcGregorSFountainePaper.pdf.

Fousek, John (2000). *To Lead the Free World: American Nationalism and the Cultural Roots of the Cold War.* Chapel Hill: University of North Carolina Press.

Fowler, Roger, & Kress, Gunther (1979). Critical Linguistics. In Roger Fowler, Bob Hodge, Gunther Hess & Tony Trew (Eds.), *Language and Control* (pp. 185–213). London: Routledge.

Frank, David, & Rowland, Robert S. (2002). *Shared Land/Conflicting Identity: Trajectories of Israelis & Palestinian Symbol Use.* East Lansing: Michigan State University Press.

Fried, Shelli (2000). The Yellow Background of the Decoration of Bravery: The Meeting Point between the Jewish Holocaust and Israeli Heroism. *Zemanim, 70,* 35–47 (in Hebrew).

Friedman, Elie (2009). *Talking Back in the Israeli-Palestinian Conflict: Rational Dialogue and Reconciliation or Emotional Shouting Match and Confrontation?* MA thesis, Bar-Ilan University.

Gamson, William A. (1992). *Talking Politics.* Cambridge: Cambridge University Press.

Gamson, William A., & Herzog, Hanna (1999). Living with Contradictions: The Taken-for-Granted in Israeli Political Discourse. *Political Psychology, 20* (2), 247–66.

Gamson, William A., & Modigliani, Ander (1987). Media Discourse and Public Opinion on Nuclear Power: A Constructionist Approach. *American Journal of Sociology, 95* (1), 1–37.

Gavriely-Nuri, Dalia (2006). Israel's Cultural Code of Captivity and the Personal Stories of the *Yom Kippur War* ex-POWs. *Armed Forces and Society, 33*, 94–105.

Gavriely-Nuri, Dalia (2007). The Beautiful War—Representations of War in Israeli Culture 1967–73. *Tarbut Demokratit, 11*, 51–76 (in Hebrew).

Gavriely-Nuri, Dalia (2008). The "Metaphorical Annihilation" of the *Second Lebanon War* (2006) from the Israeli Political Discourse. *Discourse and Society, 19* (1), 5–20.

Gavriely-Nuri, Dalia (2009a). Friendly Fire: War-Normalizing Metaphors in the Israeli Political Discourse. *Journal of Peace Education, 6* (2), 153–69.

Gavriely-Nuri, Dalia (2009b). "It Is Not the Heroes Who Need This, but the Nation"—The Latent Power of Military Decorations in Israel, 1948–2005. *Journal of Power, 2*, 403–21.

Gavriely-Nuri, Dalia (2009c). Appropriated Militarism—The Case Study of "Jerusalem of Gold." *Politika, 19* (19), 41–60 (in Hebrew).

Gavriely-Nuri, Dalia (2010a). If Both Opponents "Extend Hands in Peace" Why Don't They Meet? Mythic Metaphors and Cultural Codes in the Israeli Peace Discourse. *Journal of Language and Politics, 9* (3), 449–68.

Gavriely-Nuri, Dalia (2010b). The Idiosyncratic Language of Israeli "Peace": A Cultural Approach to Critical Discourse Analysis (CCDA). *Discourse and Society, 21* (5), 1–22.

Gavriely-Nuri, Dalia (2010c). Rainbow, Snow, and the Poplar's Song: The "Annihilative Naming" of Israeli Military Practices. *Armed Forces and Society, 36* (5), 825–42.

Gavriely-Nuri, Dalia (2010d). Saying "War," Thinking "Victory": The Mythmaking Surrounding Israel's 1967 Victory. *Israel Studies, 15* (1), 95–114.

Gavriely-Nuri, Dalia. (2012). Cultural Approach for Critical Discourse Analysis. *Critical Discourse Studies, 9* (1): 77–85.

Gavriely-Nuri, Dalia (forthcoming). Talking "Peace," Going to "War": Peace in the Service of the Israeli Just War Rhetoric. *Critical Discourse Studies.*

Gavriely-Nuri, Dalia, & Balas, Tiki (2010). "Annihilating Framing": How Israeli Television Framed Wounded Soldiers during the Second Lebanon War (2006). *Journalism, 11* (4), 1–15.

Gentner, Dedre (1982). Are Scientific Analogies Metaphors? In David S. Miall (Ed.), *Metaphor: Problems and Perspectives* (pp. 32–106). Brighton: Harvester Press.

Gerbner, George (1972). Violence in Television Drama: Trends and Symbolic *Functions.* In George A. Comstock & Eli A. Rubinstein (Eds.), *Media Content and Control: Television and Social Behavior* (pp. 128–87). Washington, DC: U.S. Government Printing Office. Available at: www.asc.upenn.edu/gerbner/Asset.aspx?assetID=1562.

Gertz, Nurith (1996). *A Nation in the Family of Nations—Journalism and Literature in the War of Independence in Captive in Its Dream.* Tel Aviv: Am Oved (in Hebrew).

Gertz, Nurith (2000). *Myths in Israeli Culture: Captives of a Dream.* London: Vallentine Mitchell.

Gethard, Gregg (2006). How Soccer Explains Post War Germany. *Soccer and Society, 7*, 51–61.

Ginzburg, Shai (2000). Shaul Friedlander: Between History and Autobiography. *Teoria Uvikoret, 17*, 217–22 (in Hebrew).

Gledhill, John (2009). Power in Political Anthropology. *Journal of Power, 2* (1): 9–34.

Glenn, Cheryl (2004). *Unspoken: A Rhetoric of Silence.* Carbondale: Southern Illinois University Press.

Gluzman, Michael (2007). *The Zionist Body: Nationalism, Gender and Sexuality in Modern Hebrew Literature.* Tel Aviv: Hakibbutz Hameuchad (in Hebrew).

Goatly, Andrew (2007). *Washing the Brain—Metaphor and Hidden Ideology.* Amsterdam/Philadelphia: John Benjamins.

Goffman, Erving (1974). *Frame Analysis.* New York: Harper & Row.

Golani, Motti (2002). *Wars Don't Happen on Their Own—On Memory, Power and Choice.* Tel Aviv: Modan (in Hebrew).

Gor, Haggith (2005). What Did You Learn at Kindergarten Today, My Sweet Child?: Militaristic Education in the Pre-School Ages. In Haggith Gor (Ed.), *Militarism in Education*, (pp. 88–108). Tel Aviv: Bavel (in Hebrew).

Gordon, W. Terrence (2001). The Origin and Development of the Theory of the Semantic Field. In Sylvain Auroux, E. F. K. Koerner, Hans-Josef Niederehe & Kees Versteegh (Eds.), *History of the Language Sciences*, (pp. 1650–62). Berlin: Walter de Gruyter.

Graham, Phil, Keenan, Thomas, & Dowd, Anne-Maree (2004). A Call to Arms at the End of History: A Discourse: Historical Analysis of George W. Bush's Declaration of War on Terror. *Discourse and Society, 15* (2–3), 199–221.

Gramsci, Antonio (1971). *Selections from the Prison Notebooks*. London: Lawrence & Wishart.

Griffin, Michael (2004). Picturing America's "War on Terrorism" in Afghanistan and Iraq: Photographic Motifs as News Frames. *Journalism, 5*, 381–402.

Griffin, Michael & Jongsoo, Lee (1995). Picturing the Gulf War: Constructing an Image of War in *Time, Newsweek*, and *U.S. News and World Report*. *Journalism and Mass Communication Quarterly, 72*, 813–25.

Gruner, Elliot (1993). *Prisoners of Culture*. New Brunswick: Rutgers University Press.

Ha'aretz Shelanu (Magazine), 1970–1971 (in Hebrew).

Haber, Eitan & Schiff, Zeev (1976). *Israeli Security Lexicon*. Tel Aviv: Zmora Bitan Modan (in Hebrew).

Hadari, Yona (2002). *Messiah Riding a Tank: Public Thought in Israel between the Sinai Operation and the Yom Kippur War 1955–1975*. Jerusalem: Shalom Hartman Institute (in Hebrew).

Halbwachs, Maurice (1960). *Autobiographical Memory and Historical Memory: Their Apparent Opposition In The Collective Memory*. New York: Harper.

Halbwachs, Maurice (1992). *On Collective Memory*. (Lewis A. Coser ed., trans.). Chicago: University of Chicago Press (originally published in 1925, in French).

Hall, Stuart (1980). Encoding/Decoding. In Stuart Hall, Dorothy Hobson, Andrew Lowe & Paul Willis (Eds.), *Culture, Media, Language* (pp. 128–38). London: Hutchinson.

Hall, Stuart (1982). The Rediscovery of Ideology: Return of the Repressed. In Michael Gurevitch, Tony Bennett, James Curran, & Janet Woollacott (Eds.), *Culture, Society and the Media*. (pp. 56–90). London: Methuen.

Hall, Stuart (1983). *Ideology in the Modern World: Transcript of an Address and Discussion Held at La Trobe University on April 14th, 1983*. Edited by Mavis Robertson.

Hall, Stuart (1992). The West and the Rest: Discourse and Power. In Stuart Hall & Bram Gieben (Eds.), *Formations of Modernity* (pp. 275–331). Cambridge: Polity Press.

Hall, Stuart (1997). The Spectacle of the "Other." In Stuart Hall (Ed.), *Presentation: Cultural Representations and Signifying Practices* (pp. 223–79). London: Sage.

Halperin, Eran, Bar-Tal, Daniel, Sharvit, Keren, Rosler, Nimrod, & Raviv, Amiram (2010). Socio-Psychological Implications for an Occupying Society: The Case of Israel. *Journal of Peace Research, 47* (1), 59–70.

Handelman, Don, & Katz, Elihu (1998). State Ceremonies in Israel: Remembrance Day and Independence Day. In Don Handelman (Ed.), *Models and Mirrors: Towards an Anthropology of Public Events* (pp. 191–233). New York: Berghahn.

Harel, Amos, & Issacharoff, Avi (2004). *The Seventh War*. Tel Aviv: Miskal (in Hebrew).

Harel, Amos, & Issacharoff, Avi (2008). *Spider Webs*. Tel Aviv: Miskal (in Hebrew).

Hariman, Robert, & Lucaites & John Louis (2003). Public Identity and Collective Memory in U.S. Iconic Photography: The Image of "Accidental Napalm." *Critical Studies in Media Communication, 20*, 35–66.

Hartmann-Mahmud, Lorry (2002). War as Metaphor. *Peace Review, 14* (4), 427–32.

Haugaard, Mark (2006). Power and Hegemony in Social Theory. In Mark Haugaard & Howard H. Lentner (Eds.), *Hegemony and Power—Consensus and Coercion in Contemporary Politics* (pp. 45–66). Lanham, MD: Lexington Books.

Haugaard, Mark (2009). Power and Habitus. *Journal of Power, 1* (2), 189–206.

Hegstrom, Jane L., & McCarl-Nielsen, Joyce (2006). Gender and Metaphor: Descriptions of Familiar Persons. *Discourse Processes, 33* (3), 219–34.

Hellmann, John (1986). *American Myth and the Legacy of Vietnam*. New York: Columbia University Press.

Herman, S. Edward & Chomsky, Noam (2002). *Manufacturing Consent*. New York: Pantheon.

Herzog, Hanna (2004). Family-Military Relations in Israel as a Genderizing Social Mechanism. *Armed Forces and Society, 31* (1), 5–30.

Hever, Hanan (2001). *Suddenly the Sight of War—Nationalism and Violence in Hebrew Poetry in the 1940's*. Tel Aviv: Hakibbutz Hameuchad (in Hebrew).

Hodges, Adam, & Nilep, Chad (2007). Introduction: Discourse, War and Terrorism. In Adam Hodges & Chad Nilep (Eds.), *Discourse, War and Terrorism* (pp. 1–17). Amsterdam: John Benjamins.

Honko, Lauri (1984). The Problem of Defining Myth. In Alan Dundes (Ed.), *Sacred Narrative: Readings in the Theory of Myth* (pp. 41–52). Berkeley: University of California Press.

Horowitz, David (1985). The Constant and the Variant in the Perception of Israeli Security. In Aharon Yariv (Ed.), *A War of Choice*, Tel Aviv: Tel Aviv University (in Hebrew).

Houston, Marsha, & Kramarae Cheris (1991). Speaking from Silence: Methods of Silencing and of Resistance. *Discourse and Society, 2* (4), 387–99.

Howe, Nicholas (1988). Metaphor in Contemporary American Political Discourse. *Metaphor and Symbol, 3* (2), 87–104.

Howe, Peter (2002). *Shooting Under Fire: The World of the War Photographer*. New York: Artisan.

Hülsse, Rainer & Spencer, Alexander (2008). The Metaphor of Terror: Terrorism Studies and the Constructivist Turn. *Security Dialogue, 39* (6), 571–92.

Inbar, Efraim (1990). Attitudes towards War in the Israeli Political Elite. *Middle East Journal, 44* (3), 432–37.

Inbar, Efraim (2007). How Israel Bungled the Second Lebanon War. *Middle East Quarterly, XIV* (3), 57–65.

Ish-Shalom, Piki (2010). Defining by Naming: Israeli Civic Warring over the Second Lebanon War. *European Journal of International Relations* (first published online 7 October 2010).

Ivie, Robert L. (1990). Cold War Motives and the Rhetorical Metaphor: A Framework of Criticism. In Martin J. Medhurst, Robert L. Ivie, Philip Wander & Robert I. Scott (Eds.), *Cold War Rhetoric: Strategy, Metaphor, and Ideology* (pp. 71–80). New York: Greenwood Press.

Ivie, Robert L. (2004). The Rhetoric of Bush's "War" on Evil. *KB Journal, 1* (2004). Online Journal: http://kbjournal.org.

Ivie, Robert L. (2007). Fighting Terror by Rite of Redemption and Reconciliation. *Rhetoric and Public Affairs, 10* (2), 221–48.

Janusz, Sharon (1994). Feminism and Metaphor: Friend, Foe, Force? *Metaphor and Symbolic Activity, 9* (4), 289–300.

Kariithi, Nixon, & Kareithi, Peter (2007). IT'S OFF TO WORK YOU GO! A Critical Discourse Analysis of Media Coverage of the Anti-Privatisation Strike in South Africa in October 2002. *Journalism Studies, 8* (3), 466–80.

Katriel, Tamar (2009). Inscribing Narratives of Occupation in Israeli Popular Memory. In Michael Keren & Holger Herwig (Eds.), *War Memory and Popular Culture: Essays on Modes of Remembrance and Commemoration* (pp. 150–65). Jefferson, NC: McFarland Publishers.

Katriel, Tamar & Shavit, Nimrod (2011). Between Moral Activism and Archival Memory: The Testimonial Project of "Breaking the Silence." In Motti Neiger, Oren Meyers & Eyal Zandberg (Eds.), *On Media Memory—Collective Memory in a New Media Age* (pp. 77–87). New York, Palgrave Macmillan.

Katz Keating Susan (1994).*Prisoners of Hope: Exploiting the POW/MIA Myth in America*. New York: Random House.

Katz, Albert, N. & Scott Mio, Jeffery (Eds.) (1996). Metaphor: *Implications and Applications*. Mahwah, NJ: Lawrence Erlbaum Associates.

Kellner, Douglas (2007). Bushspeak and the Politics of Lying: Presidential Rhetoric in the "War on Terror." *Presidential Studies Quarterly, 37* (4), 622–45.

Kelly, John D., & Kaplan, Martha (1990). History, Structure, and Ritual. *Annual Review of Anthropology, 19*, 119–50.

Kemble, Robert C. (2007). Mutations in America's Perceptions of Its Professional Military Leaders—A Historical Overview and Update. *Armed Forces and Society, 34* (1), 29–45.

Kendall, Julie E., & Kendall, Kenneth E. (1993). Metaphors and Methodologies: Living beyond the Systems Machine. *MIS Quarterly, 17* (2), 149–71.

Kennedy, Victor (2000). Metaphors in the News: Introduction. *Metaphor and Symbol, 15* (4), 209–11.

Keren, Michael (1991). *The Pen and the Sword*. Tel Aviv: Ramot (in Hebrew).

Kerlinger, Fred N. (1984). *Liberalism and Conservatism: The Nature and Structure of Social Attitudes*. Hillsdale, NJ: Lawrence Erlbaum.

Kertzer, David I. (1988). *Ritual, Politics, and Power*. New Haven: Yale University Press.

Keshev—The Center for the Protection of Democracy in Israel (2007). *War Until the Last Moment: The Israeli Media During the Second Lebanon War*. Jerusalem (in Hebrew).

Kfir, Ilan (2006). *The Earth Has Trembled*. Tel Aviv: Ma'ariv (in Hebrew).

Kielwasser, Alfred P. & Wolf, Michelle A. (1992). Mainstream Television, Adolescent Homosexuality, and Significant Silence. *Critical Studies in Mass Communication, 9* (4), 350–73.

Kimmerling, Baruch (1993). Patterns of Militarism in Israel. *European Journal of Sociology, 34*, 196–223.

Kimmerling, Baruch (2008). Patterns of Militarism in Israel. In Baruch Kimmerling (Ed.), *Clash of Identities: Explorations in Israeli and Palestinian Societies* (pp. 132–53). New York: Columbia University Press.

King, Cynthia, & Lester, Paul Martin (2005). Photographic Coverage during the Persian Gulf and Iraqi Wars in Three U.S. Newspapers. *Journalism and Mass Communication Quarterly, 82* (3), 623–37.

Kinney, K. Katherine (2000). *Friendly Fire: American Images of the Vietnam War*. Oxford: Oxford University Press.

Kittay Feder, Eva (1987). *Metaphor: Its Cognitive Force and Linguistic*. Oxford: Oxford University Press.

Kittay Feder, Eva (1988). Woman as Metaphor. *Hypatia, 3* (2), 63–86.

Kittay Feder, Eva (1989). *Metaphor: Its Cognitive Force and Linguistic Structure*. Oxford: Clarendon Press.

Koteyko, Nelya, Brown, Brian, & Crawford, Paul (2008). The Dead Parrot and the Dying Swan: The Role of Metaphor Scenarios in UK Press Coverage of Avian Flu in the UK in 2005–2006. *Metaphor and Symbol, 23* (4), 1–35.

Kövecses, Zoltàn (2002). *Metaphor: A Practical Introduction*. Oxford: Oxford Press.

Kövecses, Zoltàn. (2006). *Language, Mind and Culture: A practical introduction*. Oxford: Oxford University Press.

Kruglanski, Arie W. (2008). Martha Crenshaw, Jerrold M. Post, and Jeff Victoroff. Talking about Terrorism. *Scientific American Mind, 19* (5), 58–65.

Lakoff, George (1991). Metaphor and War: The Metaphor System Used to Justify War in the Gulf. Presented on January 30, 1991, the University of California at Berkeley. Available at: ww2.iath.virginia.edu/sixties/HTML_docs/Texts/Scholarly/Lakoff_Gulf_Metaphor_1.html.

Lakoff, George (1995). Metaphor, Morality, and Politics, or, Why Conservatives Have Left Liberals in the Dust. *Social Research, 62* (2), 177–13.

Lakoff, George (2004). *Don't Think of an Elephant*. Vermont: Chelsea Green Publishing.

Lakoff, George. (2005). *War on Terror, Rest in Peace*. www.rockridgeinstitute.org/research/lakoff/gwot_rip.

Lakoff, George & Johnson, Mark (1980). *Metaphors We Live By*. Chicago: University of Chicago Press.

Larson, Brendon M. H., Nerlich, Brigitte, & Wallis, Patrick (2005). Metaphors and Biorisks: The War on Infectious Diseases and Invasive Species. *Science Communication, 26*, 243–68.

Lazar, Annita & Lazar, Michelle (2004). The Discourse of the New World Order: "Outcasting" the Double Face of Threat. *Discourse and Society, 15* (2–3), 223–42.

Lazar, Annita & Lazar, Michelle (2007). Enforcing Justice, Justifying Force: America's Justification of Violence in the New World Order. In Adam Hodges and Chad Nilep (Eds.), *Discourse, War and Terrorism* (pp. 45–63). Amsterdam: John Benjamins.

Leibman, Charles S., & Don-Yehia, Eliezer (1983). *Civil Religion in Israel: Traditional Judaism and Political Culture in the Jewish State*. Berkeley: University of California Press.

Leibovits, Inbal, & Katriel, Tamar (2010). On the Rhetoric of Going to War. *Israel Studies in Language and Society, 3* (2), 56–85 (in Hebrew).

Lemish, Dafna (2004). Exclusion and Marginality: Portrayals of Women in Israeli Media. In Karen Ross & Carolyn M. Byerly (Eds.), *Women and Media* (pp. 39–59). Malden: Blackwell.

Lev, Yigal (1967). *Mom, I Hate the War*. Tel Aviv: Bitan (in Hebrew).

Levin, Hanoch (1986). *The Eternal Patient and His Beloved*. Tel Aviv: Hakibbutz Hameuchad (in Hebrew).

Levin, Hanoch (1987). *What Does the Bird Care 79*. Tel Aviv: Hakibbutz Hameuchad (in Hebrew).

Levy, Yagil (2003a). Social Convertibility and Militarism: Evaluations of Military-Society Relations in Israel in the Early 2000's. *Journal of Political and Military Sociology, 31* (1), 71–96.

Levy, Yagil (2003b). *The Other Army of Israel—Materialist Militarism in Israel*. Tel-Aviv: Yedioth Ahronoth Books. Series: Tapuach (in Hebrew).

Levy, Yagil (2007a). *From the "People's Army" to the "Army of the Peripheries."* Jerusalem: Carmel Publishing House. Series: Tmunat Matzav (in Hebrew).

Levy, Yagil (2007b). *Israel's Materialist Militarism*. Madison, MD: Rowman & Littlefield.

Levy, Yagil (2010). The *Second Lebanon War*: Examining "Democratization of War" Theory. *Armed Forces and Society, 36* (5), 786–803.

Lewis, Bernard (1975). *Recovered History: Remembered, Invented*. Princeton: Princeton University Press.

Liebes, Tamar (1997). *Reporting the Arab-Israeli Conflict: How Hegemony Works*. London: Routledge.

Liebes, Tamar, & First, Anat (2003). Framing the Palestinian-Israeli Conflict. In Pippa Norris, Keren Montague & Marion Just (Eds.), *Framing Terrorism* (pp. 59–74). New York: Routledge.

Liebes, Tamar, & Frosh, Paul (Eds.) (2006). *Meeting the Enemy in the Living Room: Terrorism and Communication in the Contemporary Era*. Tel Aviv: Hakibbutz Hameuchad (in Hebrew).

Liebes, Tamar, & Kampf, Zohar (2004). The P.R. of Terror: How New-Style Wars Give Voice to Terrorists. In Stuart Allan & Barbie Zelizer (Eds.), *Reporting War: Journalism in Wartime* (pp. 77–95). New York: Routledge.

Liebes, Tamar & Kampf, Zohar (2007). *From "Spider Web" to "Fortified Wall" and Back: The Changing Positions of the Israeli Home Front During the Second Lebanon War. The Media in the Lebanon War Series*. Tel Aviv: The Rothschild-Caesarea School of Communication, Tel Aviv University (in Hebrew).

Liebman, Charles S. (1993). The Myth of Defeat: The Memory of the *Yom Kippur War* in Israeli Society. *Middle Eastern Studies, 29*, 399–418.

Lissak, Moshe (2001). "The National Security Ethos" and the Myth of Israel as a Militarist Society. *Tarbut Demokratit, 4–5*, 187–211 (in Hebrew).

Livnat, Zohar (2004). On Verbal Irony, Meta-Linguistic Knowledge and Echoic Interpretation. *Pragmatic and Cognition, 12* (1), 57–70.

Livnat, Zohar (2011). Making Analogy Work in the Public Arena. *Language and Politics, 10* (2), 227–47.

Lomsky-Feder, Edna, & Ben Ari, Eyal (1999). Introduction: Cultural Construction of War and the Military in Israel. In Edna Lomsky-Feder & Eyal Ben Ari (Eds.), *The Military and Militarism in Israeli Society* (pp. 1–36). New York: State University of New-York Press.

Lomsky-Feder, Edna, & Ben-Ari, Eyal (2010). The Discourse of "Psychology" and the "Normalization" of War in Contemporary Israel. In Gabriel Sheffer & Oren Barak (Eds.), *Militarism and Israeli Society* (pp. 280–304). Bloomington: Indiana University Press.

Lorda, Clara Ubaldina & Elisabeth Miche (2006). Two Institutional Interviews: José María Aznar and Jacques Chirac on the Iraq Conflict. *Discourse and Society, 17* (4), 447–72.

Lubin, Orly (2001). The Boundaries of Violence: The Boundaries of One's Body. *Teoria U'vikoret, 18,* 103–38 (in Hebrew).

Luks, Samantha (1975). Political Ritual and Social Integration. *Sociology, 9* (2), 289–308.

Lule, Jack (2004). War and Its Metaphors: News, Language and the Prelude to War in Iraq, 2003. *Journalism Studies, 5,* 179–90.

Maasen, Sabine & Weingart, Peter (1995). Metaphors—Messengers of Meaning. A Contribution to an Evolutionary Sociology of Science. *Science Communication, 17* (1), 9–31.

Maasen, Sabine & Weingart, Peter (2000). *Metaphors and the Dynamics of Knowledge.* New York: Routledge.

Machin, David (2007). Visual Discourses of War: Multimodal Analysis of Photographs of the Iraq Occupation. In Adam Hodges & Chad Nilep (Eds.), *Discourse, War and Terrorism* (pp. 123–42). Amsterdam: John Benjamins.

Machin, David & van-Leeuwen, Theo (2007). Computer Games as Political Discourse: The Case of Black Hawk Down.In Lilie Chouliaraki (Ed.), *The Soft Power of War* (pp. 119–41). Amsterdam: John Benjamins.

Mapu, Avraham (1929). *Complete Works of Avraham Mapu.* Tel Aviv: Dvir (in Hebrew).

Martin Rojo, L. & Van-Dijk, Teun A. (1997). "There Was a Problem, and It Was Solved!" Legitimizing the Expulsion of "Illegal" Immigrants in Spanish Parliamentary Discourse. *Discourse and Society, 8* (4), 523–67.

Martin, J. R., & Rose, David (2003). *Working with Discourse: Meaning Beyond the Clause.* London: Continuum.

Matthes, Jorg, & Kohring, Matthias (2008). The Concept Analysis of Media Frames: Toward Improving Reliability and Validity. *Journal of Communication, 58,* 258–79.

Mazid, Bahaa-eddin, M. (2007). Presuppositions and Strategic *Functions* in Bush's 20/9/2001 Speech—A Critical Discourse Analysis. *Journal of Language and Politics, 6* (3), 351–75.

McCartney, Paul T. (2004). American Nationalism and U.S. Foreign Policy from September 11 to the Iraq War. *Political Science Quarterly, 119* (3), 399–423.

McClosky, Herbert, & Zaller, John (1984). *The American Ethos: Public Attitudes toward Capitalism and Democracy.* Cambridge: Harvard University Press.

McCombs, Maxwell, & Ghanem, Salma (2001). The Convergence of Agenda Setting and Framing. In Stephen D. Reese, Oscar H. Gandy & August E. Grant (Eds.), *Framing Public Life* (pp. 67–80). Lawrence, NJ.

McDougall, Alex (2009)."State Power and Its Implications for Civil War in Colombia." *Studies in Conflict and Terrorism, 32* (4), 322–45

Meir, Golda (1975). *My Life.* Tel Aviv: Ma'ariv (in Hebrew).

Mellor, Noha (2009). War as a Moral Discourse. *International Communication Gazette, 71* (5), 409–27.

Meron, Dan (1992). *Before the Silent Brother: Studies in the Poetry of the War of Independence.* Jerusalem: Open University & Keter (in Hebrew).

Messaaris, Paul & Abraham, Linus (2001). The Role of Images in Framing News Stories. In Stephen D. Reese, Oscar H. Gandy & August E. Grant (Eds.), *Framing Public Life* (pp. 215–25). Lawrence: NJ.

Michelson, Menachem (1997). *Hillel from the Mezach Stronghold.* Tel-Aviv: Miskal (in Hebrew).

Mio, Jeffery S. (1997). Metaphor and Politics. *Metaphor and Symbol, 12,* 113–33.

Miron, Dan (1992). *Before the Silent Brother: Studies in the Poetry of the War of Independence.* Jerusalem: Open University & Keter (in Hebrew).

Mitsikopoulou, Bessie, & Koutsogiannis, Dimitris (2007). The Iraq War as Curricular Knowledge: From the Political to the Pedagogic Divide. In Lilie Chouliaraki (Ed.), *The Soft Power of War* (pp. 93–117). Amsterdam: John Benjamins.

Morag, Raya (2011). *Waltzing with Bashir: Perpetrator Trauma and Cinema.* London: I. B. Tauris.

Morek, Ernst L. & Pincus, Faith (2000). How to Make Wars Acceptable. *Peace and Change, 25* (1), 1–21.

Mosheer, Amer M. (2009). "Telling-It-Like-It-Is": The Delegitimization of the Second Palestinian Intifada in Thomas Friedman's Discourse. *Discourse and Society, 20* (1), 5–31.

Mosse, George (1990). *Fallen Soldiers: Reshaping the Memory of the World Wars*. New York: Oxford University Press.

Murphy, John (1978). How to Name a New Product. *Marketing* 100 (September 1978).

Musolff, Andreas (2004). *Metaphor and Political Discourse: Analogical Reasoning in Debates about Europe*. Basingstoke: Palgrave Macmillan.

Musolff, Andreas (2007). What Role Do Metaphors Play in Racial Prejudice?: The Function of Antisemitic Imagery in Hitler's *Mein Kampf. Patterns of Prejudice, 41* (1), 21–44.

Musolff, Andreas (2008). What Can Critical Metaphor Analysis Add to the Understanding of Racist Ideology? Recent Studies of Hitler's Anti-Semitic Metaphors. *Critical Approaches to Discourse Analysis across Disciplines (CADAAD), 2* (2), 1–10.

Musolff, Andreas (2010). *Metaphor, Nation and the Holocaust: The Concept of the Body Politic*. New York: Routledge.

Nadelhaft, Matthew (1993). Metawar: Sports and the Persian Gulf War. *Journal of American Culture, 16* (4), 25–33.

Naor, Arie (2005). "Behold, Rachel, Behold": The Six Day War as a Biblical Experience and Its Impact on Israel's Political Mentality. *The Journal of Israeli History, 2*, 229–50.

Nave, Hannah, & Menda-Levy, Oded (Eds.) (2002). *A Day of Battle and Its Eve and the Day After: The Representation of the War of Independence in Hebrew Literature and Culture in Israel*. Tel Aviv University (in Hebrew).

Neiger, Motti & Zandberg, Eyal (2004). Days of Awe: The Praxis of News Coverage of Violent Conflict. *The European Journal of Mass Communication, 29*, 429–46.

Neiger, Motti, Zandberg, Eyal, & Meyers, Oren (2007). *The Rhetoric of Criticism: Challenging Criticism, Reaffirming Criticism, and Israeli Journalism during the Second Lebanon War. The Media in the Lebanon War Series*. Tel-Aviv: The Rothschild-Caesarea School of Communication, Tel Aviv University (in Hebrew).

Neiger, Motti, Zandberg, Eyal, & Meyers, Oren (2010). Communicating Critique: Toward a Conceptualization of Journalistic Criticism. *Communication, Culture & Critique, 3*, 377–95.

Norris, Pippa, Montague, Keren & Just, Marion (2003). Introduction: Understanding Crisis Coverage Framing Terrorism. In Pippa Norris, Keren Montague & Marion Just (Eds.), *Framing Terrorism* (pp. 3–26). New York: Routledge.

Nye, Joseph S. (2004). *Soft Power. The Means to Success in World Politics*. New York: Public Affairs.

Ohana, David, & Wistrich, Robert S. (Eds.) (1997). *Myth and Memory*. Jerusalem: Hakibbutz Hameuchad & Van Leer Institute (in Hebrew).

Omer, Dvora (1983). *Nu-nu-nu The Dog Goes to War*. Tel Aviv: Amihai (in Hebrew).

Ortony, Andrew (1979). Metaphor: A multidimensional problem. In Andrew Ortony (Ed.), *Metaphor and Thought* (pp. 1–16). Cambridge: Cambridge University Press.

Orwell, George (1946). *Politics and the English Language*. Available at: www.mtholyoke.edu/acad/intrel/orwell46.htm. Chouliaraki, 119–41. Amsterdam: John Benjamins.

Pardo Laura (2010). Latin-American Discourse Studies: State of the Art and New Perspectives. *Journal of Multicultural Discourses, 5* (3), 183–92.

Paterson, T. E. (1998). Political Roles of the Journalist. In Doris Graber, Denis McQuail, & Pippa Norris (Eds.), *The Politic of News, The News of Politics* (pp. 17–32). Washington: CQ Press.

Peled-Elhanan, Nurit (2010). Legitimization of Massacres in Israeli School History Books. *Discourse and Society, 21*, 377–404.

Peri, Yoram (1983). *Between Battles and Ballots: Israeli Military in Politics*. Cambridge: Cambridge University Press.

Peri, Yoram (2005). *Brothers at War: Rabin's Assassination and the Cultural War in Israel*. Tel Aviv: Bavel (in Hebrew).

Pinchevski, Amit & Torgovnik, Efraim (2002). Signifying Passages: The Signs of Change in Israeli Street Names. *Media, Culture & Society, 24*, 365–88.

Rabinow, Paul (Ed.) (1984). *The Foucault Reader*. London: Penguin.

Rapaport, Amir (2007). *Friendly Fire*. Tel Aviv: Maariv (in Hebrew).

Rash, Felicity (2005). Metaphor in Adolf Hitler's *Mein Kampf. Metaphorik*.de 09/2005. www.metaphorik.de/09/rash.pdf.

Reese, Stephen D. (2007). The Framing Project: A Bridging Model for Media Research Revisited. *Journal of Communication, 57* (1), 148–54.

Reinhart, Tanya (2006). *The Road Map to Nowhere: Israel/Palestine since 2003*. London: Verso.

Reisigl, Martin & Wodak, Ruth (2001). *Discourse and Discrimination: Rhetorics of Racism and Antisemitism*. London: Routledge.

Reuter, Martina (2006). The Significance of Gendered Metaphors. *Nordic Journal of Women's Studies, 14* (3), 151–69.

Richardson, John E. (2007). *Analysing Newspapers*. New York: Palgrave Macmillan.

Rivlin, Gershon, & Prat A., Amram (Eds.) (1986). *David Ben-Gurion, The Man and the IDF*. Tel-Aviv: Ministry of Defense (in Hebrew).

Rokeach, Milton (1960). *The Open and Closed Mind*. New York: Basic Books.

Said, Abdul Aziz & Funk, C. Nathan (2003). Making Peace with the Islamic World. *Peace Review 15* (3), 339–48.

Schäffner, Christina & Wenden, Anita L. (Eds.) (1995). *Language and Peace*. Dartmouth: Aldershot.

Scheufele, Dietram A., & Tewksbury, David (2007). Framing, Agenda Setting, and Priming: The Evolution of Three Media Effects Models. *Journal of Communication, 57* (1), 9–20.

Schiff, Zeev, & Yaari, Ehud (1985). *Israel Lebanon's War*. New York: Simon & Schuster.

Scollo, Michelle (2011). Cultural Approaches to Discourse Analysis: A Theoretical and Methodological Conversation with Special Focus on Donal Carbaugh's Cultural Discourse Theory, *Journal of Multicultural Discourses, 6* (1), 1–32.

Schudson, Michael. (1995). *The Power of News*. Cambridge: Harvard University Press.

Schudson, Michael. (2003). *The Sociology of News*. New York: Norton.

Schwartz, Barry (1982). The Social Context of Commemoration: A Study in Collective Memory. *Social Forces 61*, 374–402.

Segev, Arie (2001). *I Didn't Complete the Assignment*. Tel Aviv: Halonot (in Hebrew).

Segev, Tom (2005). *1967: And the Country Changed Its Countenance*. Jerusalem: Keter (in Hebrew).

Segrave, Jeffrey O. (1997). A Matter of Life and Death: Some Thoughts on The Language of Sport. *Journal of Sport and Social Issues, 21* (2), 211–20.

Segrave, Jeffrey O. (2000). The Sports Metaphor in American Cultural Discourse. *Culture, Sport, Society, 3* (1), 48–61.

Sela, Avraham (2010). National Security: The Case of Israel's Security Zone in South Lebanon. In Gabriel Sheffer & Oren Barak (Eds.), *Militarism and Israeli Society* (pp. 67–94). Bloomington: Indiana University Press.

Semino, Elena. M. (1996). Politics Is Football: Metaphor in the Discourse of Silvio Berlusconi in Italy. *Discourse and Society, 7* (2), 243–69.

Shah, Dhavan V., Watts, D., Domke, Mark, & Fan, P. David. (2002). News Framing and Cueing of Issue Regimes: Explaining Clinton's Public Approval in Spite of Scandal. *Public Opinion Quarterly, 66*, 339–70.

Shaked, Gershon (1999). *Hebrew Fiction 1880–1980*. Tel Aviv: Hakibbutz Hameuchad (in Hebrew).

Shamir, Moshe (1947). *He Walked through the Fields*. Merhavia: Sifriyat Hapoalim (in Hebrew).

Shapira, Anita (1994). History and Memory—The Case of Latrun, 1948. *Alpayim, 10*, 9–41 (in Hebrew).

Shapira, Anita (2003). *The Dove's Sword—Zionism and Power 1881–1948*. Tel Aviv: Am Oved (in Hebrew).

Shapira, Anita (2005). *The Bible and Israeli Identity*. Jerusalem: Magnes.

Shaw, Martin (2002). Risk-Transfer Militarism, Small Massacres and the Historic Legitimacy of War. *International Relations, 16* (3), 343–59.

Sheffer, Gabriel, & Barak, Oren (Eds.) (2010). *Militarism and Israeli Society*. Bloomington: Indiana University Press.

Shelah, Ofer, & Limor, Yoav (2007). *Prisoners in Lebanon*. Tel Aviv: Miskal (in Hebrew).

Shenhav, Shaul R. (2004). Once Upon a Time There was a Nation: Narrative Conceptualization Analysis. The Concept of "Nation" in the Discourse of Israeli Likud Party Leaders. *Discourse & Society, 15* (1), 81–104.

Shenhav, Shaul R. (2005a). Concise Narratives: A Structural Analysis of Political Discourse. *Discourse Studies, 7 (3)*, 313–35.

Shenhav, Shaul R. (2005b). Thin and Thick Narrative Analysis: On the Question of Defining and Analyzing Political Narratives. *Narrative Inquiry, 15* (1), 75–99.

Shenhav, Shaul R. (2006). Political Narratives and Political Reality. *International Political Science Review, 27* (3), 245–62.

Shimko, Keith L. (2004). The Power of Metaphors and the Metaphors of Power: The United States in the Cold War and After. In Francis A. Beer & Christ'l De Landtsheer (Eds.), *Metaphorical World Politics* (pp. 199–216). East Lansing: Michigan State University Press.

Shi-xu (2005). *A Cultural Approach to Discourse*. New York: Palgrave Macmillan.

Shi-xu (2007). Discourse Studies and Cultural Politics: An Introduction. In Shi-xu (Ed.), *Discourse as Culture Struggle* (3–16). Hong Kong: Hong Kong Universtiy Press.

Shlonsky, Avraham (Ed. & Trans.) (1932). *Thou Shalt Not Kill!: A Small Compilation of Poems Against the War*. Tel Aviv: Yachdav (in Hebrew).

Smith, Ruth L. (1990). Order and Disorder: The Naturalization of Poverty. *Cultural Critique, 14*, 209–29.

Soffer, Michal, Rimmerman, Arie, Blancka, Peter & Hill, Eve (2010). Media and the Israeli Disability Rights Legislation: Progress or Mixed and Contradictory Images? *Disability and Society, 25* (6), 687–99.

Sontag, Susan (1989). *Illness as Metaphor: AIDS and Its Metaphors*. New York: Picador/ Farrar, Straus & Giroux.

Sontag, Susan (2004). *Regarding the Pain of Others*. New York: Farrar, Straus & Giroux.

Sovran, Tamar (2000). *Investigations in Conceptual Semantics—Semantic Fields and the Anatomy of Abstract Concepts*. Jerusalem: The Hebrew University Magnes Press (in Hebrew).

Sperber, Dan, & Wilson, Deirdre (1981). Irony and the Use-Mention Distinction. In Peter Cole (Ed.), *Radical Pragmatics* (pp. 295–318). New York: Academic Press.

Steinhart, Eric, & Kittay, Eva (1994). A Formal Interpretation of the Semantic Field Theory of Metaphor. In Jaakko Hintikka (Ed.), *Aspects of Metaphors* (pp. 41–94). Dordrecht: Kluwer Academic Publishers.

Stenvall, Maija (2007). "Fear of Terror Attack Persists": Constructing Fear in Reports on Terrorism by International News Agencies. In Adam Hodges & Chad Nilep (Eds.), *Discourse, War and Terrorism* (pp. 205–22). Amsterdam/Philadelphia: John Benjamins.

Steuter, Erin & Wills, Deborah (2008). *At War with Metaphor: Media, Propaganda, and Racism in The War on Terror*. Lanham: Lexington Books.

Sullivan, Mary W. (1998). How Brand Names Affect the Demand for Twin Automobiles. *Journal of Marketing Research, 35* (2), 154–65.

Swidler, Ann (1986). Culture in Action: Symbols and Strategies. *American Sociological Review, 51* (2), 273–86.

Sylvester, Judith, & Huffman, Suzanne (2005). *Reporting from the Front: The Media and the Military*. Lanham, MD: Rowman & Littlefield.

Tannen, Deborah (1993). What's in a Frame? Surface Evidence for Underlying Expectations. In Deborah Tannen (Ed.), *Framing and Discourse*, (pp. 14–56). New York: Oxford University Press.

Thiesmeyer, Lynn (Ed.) (1990). *Discourse and Silencing*. Amsterdam: John Benjamins.

Thompson, John B. (1990). *Ideology and Modern Culture*. Stanford: Stanford University Press.

Thornborrow, Joanna. (1993). Metaphors of Security: A Comparison of Representation in the Defence Discourse in Post Cold-War France and Britain. *Discourse and Society, 4 (1)*, 99–119.

Threadgold (Cardiff), Terry (2003). Cultural Studies, Critical Theory and Critical Discourse Analysis: Histories, Remembering and Futures. *Linguistik Online 14 (2)*.

Titscher, Stefan, Meyer, Michael, Wodak, Ruth, & Vetter, Eva (Eds.) (2000). *Methods of Text and Discourse Analysis*. London: Sage Publications.

Tuchman, Gaye (1978a). Introduction. In Gaye Tuchman, Arlene Kaplan Daniels & James Benet (Eds.), *Hearth and Home: Images of Women in the Mass Media*, (pp. 3–38). New York: Oxford University Press.

Tuchman, Gaye (1978b). *Making News: A Study in the Construction of Reality*. New York: The Free Press.

Turner, Victor W. (1970) *The Forest of Symbols: Aspects of Ndembu Ritual*. Ithaca: Cornell University Press.

Turner, Victor W. (1974). *Drama, Fields, and Metaphors: Symbolic Action in Human Society*. Ithaca: Cornell University Press.

Tzur, Nadir (2004). *Political Rhetoric: Israeli Leaders in Stressful Situations*. Tel Aviv: Hakibbutz Hameuchad (in Hebrew).

Van Dijk, Teun A. (1988). *News as Discourse*. Hillsdale: Lawrence Erlbaum.

Van Dijk, Teun A. (1995). Discourse Analysis as Ideology Analysis. In Christina Schäffner & Anita L. Wenden (Eds.), *Language and Peace* (pp. 17–33). Dartmouth: Aldershot.

Van Dijk, Teun A. (1998). *Ideology: A Multidisciplinary Approach*. London: Sage.

Van Dijk, Teun A. (2001). Critical Discourse Analysis. In Deborah Tannen, Deborah Schiffrin & Heidi Ehernberger Hamilton (Eds.), *Handbook of Discourse Analysis* (pp. 352–71). Oxford: Blackwell.

Van Dijk, Teun A. (2005). Contextual Knowledge Management in Discourse Production: A CDA Perspective. In Ruth Wodak & Paul Chilton (Eds.), *A New Agenda in (Critical) Discourse Analysis* (pp. 71–100). Amsterdam, Philadelphia: John Benjamins.

Van Dijk, Teun A. (2006). Discourse and Manipulation. *Discourse and Society, 17* (3), 359–83.

Van Dijk, Teun A. (2007). War Rhetoric of a Little Ally: Political Implicatures and Aznar's Legitimatization of the War in Iraq. In Lilie Chouliaraki (Ed.), *The Soft Power of War* (pp. 61–84). Amsterdam: John Benjamins.

Van Dijk, Teun A. (2008). *Discourse and Power*. Houndsmills: Palgrave.

Van Dijk, Teun A. (Ed.) (1993). Critical Discourse Analysis, Special Issue. *Discourse and Society, 4* (2).

Van Leeuwen, Theo (2000). Visual Racism. In Martin Reisigl & Ruth Wodak (Eds.), *The Semiotics of Racism—Approaches in Critical Discourse Analysis* (pp. 333–50). Vienna: Passagen Verlag.

Van Leeuwen, Theo (2007). Legitimization in Discourse and Communication. *Discourse and Communication, 1* (1), 91–112.

Van Leeuwen, Theo, & Wodak, Ruth (1999). Legitimizing Immigration Control: A Discourse Historical Analysis. *Discourse Studies, 1* (1), 83–118.

Vliegenthart, Rens, & Roggeband, Conny (2007). Framing Immigration and Integration: Relationships between Press and Parliament in the Netherlands. *International Communication Gazette, 69* (3), 295–319.

Walton, John (2001). *Storied Land: Community and Memory in Monterey*. Berkeley: University of California Press.

Weimann, Gabriel (2007/2008). *Public Criticism of the Media During the 2006 War in* Lebanon. The Media in the Lebanon War Series. Tel Aviv: The Rothschild-Caesarea School of Communication, Tel Aviv University (in Hebrew).

Weiss, Avi (1998). *A Prisoner of Egypt on the Yom Kippur War*. Tel Aviv: The Ministry of Defense (in Hebrew).

Wenden, Anita L. (2003). Achieving a Comprehensive Peace: The Linguistic Factor. *Peace and Change, 28* (2), 169–201.

Wenden, Anita. L. (2008). Planning Language Change: A Strategy for Promoting Human and Ecological Security. *Current Issues in Language Planning, 9* (2), 193–206.

Wen-Yu, Chiang, & Ren-Feng, Duann (2007). Conceptual Metaphors for SARS: "War" between Whom? *Discourse and Society, 18*, 579–602.

White, Hayden (1980). The Value of Moralitivity in Representation of Reality. *Critical Inquiry, 7* (1), 5–29.

Williams Camus, Julia T. (2009). Metaphors of Cancer in Scientific Popularization Articles in the British Press. *Discourse Studies 11*, 465–95.

Witztum, David (2006). *Television Broadcasts during Times of Trouble*. Jerusalem: Keter (in Hebrew).

Wodak, Ruth (1996). *Disorders of Discourse*. London: Longman.

Wodak, Ruth, & Meyer, Michael (2001). *Methods of Critical Discourse Analysis*. London: Sage.

Wodak, Ruth, & Chilton, Paul (Eds.) (2005). *A New Agenda in (Critical) Discourse Analysis*. Amsterdam: Benjamins.

Wodak, Ruth, & Matouschek, Bernd (1993). We Are Dealing with People Whose Origins One Can Clearly Tell Just By Looking: Critical Discourse Analysis and the Study of Neo-Racism in Contemporary Austria. *Discourse and Society, 4*, 225–48.

Wodak, Ruth, & Meyer, Michael (1999). Critical Discourse Analysis: History, Agenda, Theory and Methodology. In Ruth Wodak and Michael Meyer (Eds.), *Methods of Critical Discourse Analysis* (pp. 1–33). London: Sage.

Wodak, Ruth, & Van Leeuwen, Theo (2002). Discourses of Un/Employment in Europe: The Austrian Case. *Text, 22* (3), 345–67.

Wodak, Ruth, & Weiss, Gilbert (2005). Analyzing European Union Discourses: Theories and Applications. In Ruth Wodak & Paul Chilton (Eds.), *A New Agenda in (Critical) Discourse Analysis* (pp. 121–35). Amsterdam: John Benjamins.

Wodak, Ruth, de-Cillia, Rudolf, Reisigl, Martin, & Liebhart, Karin (1999/2009). *The Discursive Construction of National Identity*. Edinburgh: Edinburgh University Press (2nd edition).

Wolfsfeld, Gadi (1997). *Media and Political Conflict: News from the Middle East*. Cambridge: Cambridge University Press.

Wolfsfeld, Gadi (2004). *Media and the Path to Peace*. Cambridge: Cambridge University Press.

Wolfsfeld, Gadi, Frosh, Paul, & Awabdy, Maurice T. (2008). Covering Death in Conflicts: Coverage of the Second Intifada on Israeli and Palestinian Television. *Journal of Peace Research, 45* (3), 401–17.

Yaguri, Assaf (1979). *Living with Them, They Are All Mine*. Jerusalem: Idanim (in Hebrew).

Yang, Jin (2003). Framing the NATO Air Strikes on Kosovo across Countries: Comparison of Chinese and U.S. Newspaper Coverage. *Gazette, 65*, 234–40.

Yariv, Aharon (Ed.) (1985). *A Choice War*. Tel Aviv: Tel Aviv University (in Hebrew).

Yehoshua, A. B. (1972). *Early in the Summer of 1970*. Tel Aviv & Jerusalem: Shocken (in Hebrew).

Yehoshua, A. B. (1975). *Until the Winter of 1974: Collection*. Tel Aviv: Hakibutz Hameuchad (in Hebrew).

Yosef, Raz (2001). The Military Body: Male Masochism and Attitudes toward Homosexuality in Israeli Film. *Te'oria U'vikoret, 18*, 11–46 (in Hebrew).

Yule, G. (1996). *Pragmatics*. Oxford: Oxford University Press.

Zandberg, Eyal & Neiger, Motti (2005). Between the Nation and the Profession: Journalists as Members of Contradicting Communities. *Media, Culture & Society, 27* (1), 131–41.

Zanger, Anat (1999). Filming National Identity: War and Woman in Israeli Cinema. In Edna Lomsky-Feder & Eyal Ben Ari (1999), *The Military and Militarism in Israeli Society* (pp. 261–79). New York: State University of New York Press.

Zelizer, Barbie (2003). *Journalism after September 11*. London: Routledge.

Zerubavel, Eviatar (2006). *The Elephant in the Room: Silence and Denial in Everyday Life*. New York: Oxford University Press.

Zerubavel, Yael (1995). *Recovered Roots*. Chicago: University of Chicago Press.

Zisser, Eyal (2009). *Lebanon: Blood in the Cesar's: From the Civil War to the Second Lebanon War*. Tel Aviv: Hakibbutz Hameuchad (in Hebrew).

Zoch, Lynn M., & VanSlyke Turk, Judy (1998). Women Making News: Gender as a Variable in Source Selection and Use. *Journalism and Mass Communication Quarterly, 75* (4), 762–75.

Index

About the Author

Dalia Gavriely-Nuri, PhD, is a senior lecturer in the Department of Politics and Communication, at Hadassah Academic College, Jerusalem, and a research fellow at the Truman Institute for Peace Research, the Hebrew University of Jerusalem. Her research focuses on the cultural and discursive aspects of peace and war, national security, and the Israeli-Arab conflict.

www.ingramcontent.com/pod-product-compliance
Lightning Source LLC
Chambersburg PA
CBHW030650110726
47901CB00002B/654